BECOMING BROWNSON

BECOMING BROWNSON

The Early Life of Orestes A. Brownson 1803-1829

Lynn Gordon Hughes

Blackstone Editions

Blackstone Editions
Providence, Rhode Island & Toronto, Ontario, Canada
www.BlackstoneEditions.com

© 2016 by Lynn Gordon Hughes. All rights reserved

Printed in the United States of America

ISBN: 978-0-9816402-5-9

A version of Chapter 8 was previously published as "Orestes A. Brownson's This-Worldly Universalism" in the *Journal of Unitarian Universalist History* (2008). A version of Chapters 9-10 was previously published as "Orestes A. Brownson, Universalist Infidel?" in the *Journal of Unitarian Universalist History* (2009-2010).

Contents

	Illustrations	vii
	Acknowledgments	ix
	Introduction	1
1	Childhood	10
2	Apprenticeship	25
3	Universalism and Skepticism	38
4	Presbyterianism and Despair	48
5	Journey to the West	64
6	Return to Universalism	75
7	Universalist Ministry	95
8	Changing Beliefs	112
9	Accusations of Infidelity	127
10	Expulsion	147
	Afterword: Brownson's Infidelity	164
	Notes	169
	Index	201

Illustrations

Portrait of Orestes A. Brownson   *frontispiece*
    Engraving by A. L. Dick for *U.S. Magazine & Democratic Review*, c. 1843; based on a daguerreotype miniature by Augustus Morand, Jr. (Library of Congress)

Map of Windsor County, Vermont, 1810   14
    Detail of James Whitelaw's map of the state of Vermont, 1810. Image courtesy of Dave Allen, www.old-maps.com.

Ballston Spa in 1815   26
    From Edward F. Grose, *Centennial History of the Village of Ballston Spa 1763-1907* (1907).

The Sans Souci Hotel, Ballston Spa   28
    Illustration from an 1823 advertising circular. From Edward F. Grose, *Centennial History of the Village of Ballston Spa 1763-1907* (1907).

Elhanan Winchester   41
    Frontispiece of Edwin M. Stone, *Biography of Rev. Elhanan Winchester* (1836).

Hosea Ballou   41
    Engraving, c. 1853; based on a painting by H. C. Pratt, 1847. Frontispiece of Thomas Whittemore, *Life of Rev. Hosea Ballou*, vol. 1 (1854).

John W. Taylor   51
    From Edward F. Grose, *Centennial History of the Village of Ballston Spa 1763-1907* (1907).

ILLUSTRATIONS

A view of Detroit in 1826   68
A sketch of the city of Detroit from the Detroit River by General Alexander Macomb, 1826. From Clarence M. Burton, *The City of Detroit, Michigan, 1701-1922* (1922).

Ste. Anne's Church, Detroit, in 1818   69
From Silas Farmer, *History of Detroit and Wayne County and Early Michigan* (1890).

Gabriel Richard   70
Photograph of a painting by James O. Lewis. (Gabriel Richard Photographs HS 12907, Bentley Historical Library, University of Michigan)

Front page of the *Evangelical Repertory*, April 15, 1824   78
Universalist newspaper edited and published by Rev. Edward Turner, Charlestown, Massachusetts.

Map of central New York State, 1827   96
Detail of William Williams, *The Tourist's Map of the State of New York*, 1827. Image courtesy of David Rumsey Map Collection, www.davidrumsey.com.

Abner Kneeland   136
Engraving by Bass Otis, c.1818. Frontispiece of Abner Kneeland, *A Series of Lectures On the Doctrine of Universal Benevolence* (1818).

Frances Wright   138
Engraving by J. C. Buttre, based on a portrait by J. Gorbitz. Frontispiece of Elizabeth Cady Stanton, *History of Woman Suffrage* (1881).

Dolphus Skinner   155
Portrait by an unknown artist, c. 1850. Image courtesy of Oneida County Historical Society, Utica, New York.

A page from the *Gospel Advocate*, November 14, 1829   158
Universalist newspaper edited by O. A. Brownson. Published by U. F. Doubleday, Auburn, New York.

Acknowledgments

This book got its start as my master's thesis. I am grateful to the faculty, staff, and students of the Brown University History Department for supporting my unconventional approach to graduate studies. In a department where nearly everyone is a full-time Ph.D. candidate, I chose to do a stand-alone master's degree including the optional master's thesis, which no one in living memory had ever done, and I did it part-time over a period of ten years, while working full-time for Brown's department of Computing and Information Systems. I am grateful to my friends and colleagues in CIS and in the Registrar's Office for their support and encouragement. In particular, I would like to thank my advisor, Michael Vorenberg, for continuing to believe in the project during the six years it took me to complete it.

I would like to acknowledge the generous assistance of scholars of Brownson and of American Universalism. Dean Grodzins, Peter Hughes, and David Voelker read my work in progress and made numerous helpful suggestions. I am particularly grateful to today's foremost Brownson scholar, Patrick W. Carey, whose work in transcribing Brownson's diaries, editing his early writings, and disentangling the chronology of his early life has laid the groundwork for this study. I thank him for answering my email queries and for giving me access to his unpublished transcription of Brownson's "Diary #2."

The research for this project was done with the assistance of the Brown University Libraries; the Houghton Library and Andover-Harvard Theological Library at Harvard University; the Rhode Island Historical Society; and the numerous amateur historians who have made their town, county, church, and family histories available via the Internet. I would particularly like to acknowledge the assistance of the late Frances O'Donnell, curator of the Unitarian Universalist Collection at Andover-Harvard Theological Library.

Not all information comes out of books and libraries. The Brookside Museum in Ballston Spa, New York, gave me a glimpse into a corner of Brownson's world. The congregation of the First Universalist Church in Woonsocket, Rhode Island, taught me first-hand what it means to be an American Universalist.

Heartfelt thanks to Laurie Stearns for her careful and sensitive editing, unwavering encouragement, and decades of devoted friendship.

In this project, as in all else in life, my deepest gratitude is to my husband, Peter Hughes: minister, historian, devoted friend, and generous colleague.

Introduction

For fifty years, from the time Orestes Brownson wrote his first newspaper article in 1826 until his death in 1876, there was hardly a time when he was not an editor, publisher, or primary contributor to a newspaper or magazine. His writing forms a running commentary on the religious, social, political, and intellectual concerns of nineteenth-century America. He began his journalistic career as editor of a Universalist newspaper, where his outspoken views on religion and science, church and state, ethics and social justice scandalized the denomination and earned him a reputation as an "infidel." He went on to edit the *Boston Quarterly Review*, which included contributions by leading Transcendentalists such as Ralph Waldo Emerson, Bronson Alcott, and Theodore Parker, as well as his own observations of the Transcendentalist movement and his incendiary essay *The Laboring Classes*. A perceptive observer and theorist of politics and economics, he had a prescient understanding of the nature of industrial capitalism that has earned him the reputation of being a "Marxist before Marx." He was one of the first to analyze the transformation in American politics brought about by the rise of special interests and mass media. After converting to Catholicism, he became a leading American Catholic journalist and essayist, introducing Catholicism to Americans and encouraging the largely immigrant population of American Catholics to adopt American values, integrate themselves into American institutions, and claim their rightful place in American society.

Orestes Augustus Brownson was born in 1803 to a Presbyterian father and a Universalist mother. Before he was two years old, his father died, leaving the family destitute. Between the ages of six and fourteen he lived with Congregationalist foster parents, who taught him the rudiments of the Reformed faith but left him free to explore the other religious options that their rural Vermont town had to offer. At thirteen he was "born again" under the influence of a heterodox evangelical sect called the Christian Connection. The following year he returned to his family and to Universalism. During his teens, as an apprentice printer in the resort town of Ballston Spa, New York, he absorbed the prevailing attitude of worldliness and cynicism about religion. For nine unhappy months when he was nineteen, he belonged to a Presbyterian church and tried hard to adopt orthodox Calvinist beliefs. After a brief stint as a schoolteacher on the outskirts of Detroit – then a frontier settlement populated largely by French-speaking Catholics – he declared himself a Universalist once more and began studying for the Universalist ministry. He was ordained in 1826 and served a succession of small Universalist societies in New York State from 1826 to 1829. By the time he was twenty-six, he had been a Universalist minister and editor, made new and creative contributions to Universalist theology, participated in some of the most significant controversies in the denomination's history, and been driven from his pulpit, amid a blaze of notoriety, by fellow Universalists who considered him an "infidel" and a danger to the denomination. He left the ministry and turned instead to political journalism on behalf of the Workingmen's Party.

Even when he was outside of any denomination, religion remained Brownson's central concern. After a few months as an "independent preacher," in 1831 he declared himself a Unitarian. As a Unitarian minister he served churches in Walpole, New Hampshire, and Canton, Massachusetts. In 1836, with the assistance of George Ripley and other members of the Transcendentalist movement, he founded a new religious institution, the Society for Christian Union and Progress in Boston. Its mission was to develop a form of liberal Christianity that would be meaningful to the urban poor and working classes, who were often excluded by the socially elite Unitarians.

By 1840, Brownson had become dissatisfied with what he perceived to be the options available within Unitarianism: either a vague and misty Transcendentalism, or a futile attempt to retain traditional doctrines while rejecting the theological and philosophical foundations on which they were based. With the aid of ideas borrowed from the French socialist philosopher Pierre Leroux, he set out to develop his own synthesis of reason, religion, and social theory. Somewhat to his surprise, he found himself affirming such traditional Christian beliefs as original sin and the divinity of Christ. Reflecting on the failure of his previous attempts to reform society, he came to believe that "the solution of every problem, theological, political, social, or ethical," lay in the true Gospel, which was to be found in the keeping of the true Church, "the authoritative representative of the will of God on earth."[1] These ideas placed Brownson not only outside Unitarianism, but outside any form of Protestantism. In 1844 he joined the Roman Catholic Church.

In this book I tell the story of Brownson's early life, from his birth in 1803 to the end of his Universalist ministry in 1829. The story is shaped in part by the times and places in which it unfolded: rural Vermont, at a time when it still retained some of the character of the northern frontier; Ballston Spa during its heyday as a fashionable resort; the "burned-over district" of western New York State; and the French Catholic enclave of Detroit. Each of these places had its own particular ethos, its own set of religious and cultural institutions, its own forms of social interaction. Each presented a different set of challenges and opportunities for a young man bent on educating himself and making a place for himself in the world.

In particular, I examine Brownson's relationship with Universalism. Before he was a Unitarian, a Transcendentalist, or a Catholic, Brownson was a Universalist. The child of a Universalist family, by the time he was fifteen he had read deeply in the classics of Universalist literature. A work of Universalist theology touched off the first of many religious crises that would shape his life. Between the ages of seventeen and twenty-two, even as he was struggling to make a living, courting his future wife, journeying to the west and returning, his mind was occupied with the question of whether he believed that all souls would ultimately be saved.

In his 1857 autobiography, *The Convert*, Brownson said practically nothing about his three and a half years as a Universalist minister and journalist. By the time he wrote *The Convert*, he understood his conversion to Catholicism as the central drama of his life. The details of his Universalist ministry must have seemed irrelevant in a spiritual autobiography tracing his path "from the abyss of doubt and infidelity to the light and truth of [God's] Gospel, in the bosom of his Church."[2] Yet even here, he described his decision to embrace Universalism as the commencement of his intellectual life.[3]

Brownson devoted little more than a page of *The Convert* to the period between his ordination and his resignation from Universalist fellowship, and most of his biographers have followed his lead in this regard.[4] I have attempted to fill this gap, piecing together the story of his Universalist ministry from the minutes of the New York State Convention of Universalists and the New England Universalist General Convention, the fragments of church history left by some of the churches he served, and the Universalist press: not just Brownson's own *Gospel Advocate*, but also the *Gospel Herald*, *Evangelical Magazine*, *Christian Intelligencer*, *Trumpet and Universalist Magazine*, and other papers that made up the denominational communication network.

The one aspect of his Universalist career that Brownson did discuss at length was his decision to leave it. He explained in *The Convert*, with much corroborative detail and closely reasoned argumentation, that he resigned from the ministry because "Universalism made me, so far as logic could go, not only a non-Christian, but an anti-Christian."[5] His Universalist colleagues agreed, and removed him from fellowship with the Universalist General Convention in 1830 on the grounds that he had "renounced [his] faith in the Christian Religion."[6] To the extent that he is remembered in Universalist history, it is as an example of "infidelity."[7] At first glance, this seems straightforward enough. If Brownson had lost his Christian faith, it is not surprising that he should leave Universalism, whether by choice (as he indicated in *The Convert*), or by expulsion (as the records of the Universalist General Convention show), or by a mutual parting of the ways (as Patrick W. Carey has it in his recent biography of Brownson).[8]

There is, however, a problem with this seemingly well-attested story. On looking into Brownson's writings from his last year as a Universalist, I can find no trace of his supposed infidelity. On the contrary, I have found abundant evidence that he held strongly to Universalism in the period before, and for some time after, the end of his ministry. In 1829 he vehemently denied that he was an infidel, unbeliever, or deist. He asserted over and over that he was a believing Christian and a good Universalist. In response to the accusations of infidelity that were circulating in the Universalist press, he protested, "I do not essentially differ from any intelligent Universalist, with whom I am acquainted."[9] Among the last items he wrote for the *Gospel Advocate* was this short piece entitled "Reasons for Loving God":

> He is our Creator and Preserver; He is the Author of every blessing which we enjoy, and he renders all our afflictions and disappointments the means of promoting our best interests. Our Creator knows all our infirmities, our proneness to err, and our appetites for injurious indulgences, and is merciful to all our faults. He punishes our sins in mercy – never from a disposition of revenge; but that we may be partakers of His holiness. Through the mediation of the Redeemer, He has given us the knowledge and hope of a glorious and immortal life, and the interminable continuance of his fatherly kindness.[10]

These do not sound like the words of someone who was "not only a non-Christian, but an anti-Christian."

Even if we accept Brownson's explanation that, while serving as a Universalist minister, he developed theological views that the majority of his colleagues found unacceptable, this does not explain the suddenness of his departure. By his own account, he held "anti-Christian" views for the last two years of his Universalist ministry.[11] Why, then, did the colleagues who had welcomed him as editor of the *Gospel Advocate* in January 1829 denounce him as an infidel two months later?

To make sense of these events, we must consider the interactions between Brownson and his colleagues in the context of the situation of liberal religion in 1829. Thus, in addition to being a biographical study of Brownson, this is a work of Universalist history. By examining the internal and external stresses on Universalism during the 1820s, I hope to provide a more nuanced understanding of why the usually latitudinarian Universalist denomination felt compelled, at this point in its history, to enforce a degree of theological conformity.

Though this study focuses on Brownson's early years, I hope it will also shed some light on the larger questions that puzzled Brownson's contemporaries and have fascinated and frustrated biographers ever since.

Brownson's much-publicized shifts of belief and affiliation – and the vehemence with which he argued each view while he held it – led many of his contemporaries to question his judgment, his stability, and his integrity. James Freeman Clarke, once a friend and colleague of Brownson's in the Unitarian ministry, explained why he could not take seriously Brownson's conversion to Catholicism:

> No man has ever equaled Mr. Brownson in the ability with which he has refuted his own arguments. He has shown that no man can possibly be a Christian, except he is a transcendentalist; and he has also proved that every transcendentalist, whether he knows it or not, is necessarily an infidel. He has satisfactorily shown the truth of socialism ... [and] demonstrated that the whole system of socialism is from the pit, and can lead to nothing but anarchy and ruin ... He labors now with great ingenuity and extraordinary subtilty to show that there must be an infallible church with its infallible ministry, and that out of this church there can be no salvation. But formerly he labored with equal earnestness to show that there could be no such thing as a church at all, no outward priesthood or ministry.

> His former arguments, then, for aught that we can see, were just as acute, plausible, and effective as his present ones.[12]

James Russell Lowell, in his satiric poem "A Fable for Critics," came up with the enduring image of Brownson as a "weathercock" whose opinions shift with every change of the wind:

> He shifts quite around, then proceeds to expound
> That 'tis merely the earth, not himself, that turns round,
> And wishes it clearly impressed on your mind
> That the weathercock rules and not follows the wind;
> Proving first, then as deftly confuting each side,
> With no doctrine pleased that's not somewhere denied.[13]

Though he remained a Catholic until his death, over thirty years after his conversion, Brownson never quite lived down his reputation as a wildly swinging weathercock – erratic, impulsive, shallow in his attachments, and lacking in firm convictions. As James Freeman Clarke put it, "There must be something fixed, and fixed for ever; some permanent convictions, some central truths, which are the foundations on which everything else is built. The misfortune of Mr. Brownson, as it seems to us ... is simply this: that he has had no such central truths, no primal convictions."[14]

Clarke's criticism defined what is perhaps the most important question in any study of Brownson's life: What were his central truths, his primal convictions? Generations of sympathetic biographers have sought the golden thread that might lead them through the labyrinth of Brownson's life – the underlying consistency which makes sense of the twists and turns of his extraordinary life story.

Brownson himself insisted that he had, throughout his life, faithfully pursued the path of truth, wherever it might lead. He knew that he was regarded as lacking in wisdom and prudence, but he dismissed what the world called wisdom and prudence as mere timidity, hypocrisy, or "policy." If his fellows did not understand his quest, he said, it was because "we live in an age and country where honesty and candor, fidelity to one's honest convictions, and moral courage in avowing them" are not sufficiently valued. He was, he said,

> ready to follow the truth under whatever guise it may come, to whatever it may lead, to the loss of reputation, to poverty, to beggary, to the dungeon or the scaffold, to the stake or exile. I have had my faults, great and grievous faults, as well as others, but I have never had that of disloyalty to principle, or of fearing to own my honest convictions, however unpopular they might be, or however absurd or dangerous the public might regard them.[15]

The notion of Brownson's life as a pilgrimage in search of truth has been particularly congenial to those studying his life from within the Catholic tradition. In *Orestes Brownson: Yankee, Radical, Catholic* (1943), Theodore Maynard wrote, "The vagaries of his early life had an underlying consistency which was all the time bringing him nearer to his Catholic goal."[16] Thomas R. Ryan's massively detailed but uncritical *Orestes A. Brownson: A Definitive Biography* (1976) concludes, "He had canvassed all social theories, had probed deeply into all forms of religion, had tried everything outside the Catholic Church ... But when he became a Catholic, all this roaming and changing came to an end."[17]

In his influential biography of Brownson, *A Pilgrim's Progress* (1939), Arthur M. Schlesinger, Jr., endorsed the view of Brownson's life as a pilgrimage, but saw his quest as more tragic than heroic: "The lonely pursuit of truth, with its worship of unflinching honesty and rigorous logic, was the secret of his failure ... Set apart by his love for truth, too proud to abandon his desolate quest, he could shout only to the wind and the waves."[18] Schlesinger emphasized the sad irony of a life which, though dedicated first to "the religion of humanity" and later to "life by communion," was nevertheless lived largely in isolation from ordinary human warmth and social interaction.

Some have sought psychological motives for Brownson's wanderings. One often-proposed explanation focuses on the death of Brownson's father and consequent breakup of the family.[19] Patrick W. Carey wrote that "The experience of death and fatherlessness ... became one of the controlling interests in Orestes Brownson's later life."[20] Carey suggested that Brownson's lonely childhood, spent largely among people with whom he had no strong emotional ties, created in him both a habit of self-sufficiency and a never-satisfied longing for friendship and community.[21]

Other biographers have tried to make sense of Brownson's life by proposing, as the main driving forces behind his wanderings, not a single principle but a pair of opposed principles, such as reason and revelation, individual and community, or freedom and authority. According to this view, Brownson's dramatic changes and reversals are the result of the alternating push and pull of opposed qualities which he sought to integrate and harmonize. In his 1971 dissertation, *Orestes Brownson and New England Religious Culture*, William Gilmore blamed the conflicting religious messages to which Brownson was subjected in his youth for creating a "stunting psychological dualism" that left him oscillating between extremes of libertarian and authoritarian religion.[22]

Carey likewise sees Brownson's life as "a restless search for a balance ... in his relations with God, nature, and the human community."[23] Where Gilmore saw Brownson as crippled and tormented by the struggle between conflicting forces, however, Carey's view is more positive. In *Orestes A Brownson: American Religious Weathervane* (2004), he tried to rehabilitate Brownson's "weathervane" reputation by exploring the flexibility, openness, and sensitivity implicit in this image. "The weathervane image captures something of the truth," he wrote. "Brownson experienced the tumultuous religious, intellectual, political and cultural ferment of the times in which he lived, and he changed with the times."[24]

Brownson's biographers have done a great deal to challenge (or, in Carey's case, to redeem) the facile "weathervane" image. Taken together, their insights provide a convincing refutation of James Freeman Clarke's view of Brownson as "a man [who], with every change of opinion, throws away his whole past belief."[25] Those who have carefully studied Brownson's life and work agree that he did have a stable core of values and concerns. Furthermore, this stable core appears to have been well established by the time he was in his mid-twenties. Carey noted:

> The Universalist years helped him formulate religious and political questions that would remain with him for the remainder of his life. The origin of the idea of God, the relation of divine sovereignty to human freedom, the correspondence of divine justice and goodness, the meaning of salvation, the interdependence of Christianity and the social order, the relationship between church and state, the nature of the state, the link between doctrine and free inquiry, the interrelatedness of reason, intuition, and revelation – these were some of the issues that arose during these years.[26]

Here, then, is a reason to look carefully at Brownson's early life. A detailed examination of his formative years helps to make sense of his whole life.

If you are interested in Brownson's proto-Marxist critique of industrial capitalism or his analysis of American politics and democracy, you will find in his early life the roots of his sympathy with the laboring classes, his resentment of pampered idleness, and his distrust of organized religion that seeks only to preserve the status quo. You will witness the shock of his first encounter with social inequality, and how this affected his ideas on race and class, chattel slavery and wage slavery. You will see how he came of age as an apprentice journalist in the midst of controversy over democratic reforms, the extension of the franchise, the sovereignty of the people, and the role of money and influence in politics.

If you are interested in Brownson as a Transcendentalist, you will find here the dawning of his conviction that religion transcends reason; that the spirit can perceive realities unknown to the senses; and that spiritual truths such as the nature and existence of God cannot be deduced from nature or proved by "evidences of Christianity." You will also find the beginning of his understanding of sin and salvation as collective rather than individual states, which links him with communitarian Transcendentalists such as George Ripley.

If you are interested in him as a Catholic convert, you will discover how he was unlike the typical Protestant of his day, even before he ever encountered Catholics or Catholicism. You will witness his first encounter with a Catholic church, and discover how he was changed by his sojourn in a Catholic community in Michigan.

It is my hope that this examination of Brownson's first twenty-six years will help to make sense of the complex, brilliant, difficult man he became: Orestes A. Brownson, American religious weathervane, radical, conservative, Protestant minister, Catholic convert, and passionate pilgrim in search of truth.

CHAPTER 1

Childhood

> *We must be pardoned a little patriotic pride in speaking of Vermont. We feel towards that State, though it has not been our home for many a year, all the affection of a son for his mother.*
>
> – Orestes Brownson, "Thompson's History of Vermont"

Evangelicalism and Universalism on the Northern Frontier

In the winter of 1802, Sylvester Augustus Brownson and his wife, Relief Metcalf Brownson, settled in the township of Stockbridge, Vermont, and set about making a home for themselves and their growing family. Stockbridge, in the hills overlooking the White River on the western edge of Windsor County, had been settled for less than twenty years, and still retained some of the character of the frontier. The steep, rocky land was ill suited to farming but provided good pasturage for sheep.[1]

The Brownsons were part of a migration, which had begun in the 1760s, from southern New England to the Connecticut Valley. In 1800 the adult population of Windsor County consisted almost entirely of migrants from southern New England. They came in search of freedom and opportunity: economic opportunity certainly, but also freedom from the social hierarchy and religious establishment that characterized the long-settled parts of New England.

About two-thirds of the original settlers in the Connecticut Valley region of Vermont belonged to the "New Light," or evangelical, wing of New England Calvinism. Evangelicals placed great emphasis on the conversion experience, and restricted full church membership to those who could give evidence of having experienced God's saving grace. Many considered the established churches cold and formal in their worship, lukewarm in their piety, more impressed by worldly status and education than by evidence of God's favor. They hoped to establish a new commonwealth in the wilderness, in accordance with their vision of the covenanted community.[2]

The New Lights' dream of an orderly, harmonious, and God-fearing community proved elusive, for the northern frontier also attracted large numbers of dissenters who rejected the Calvinist formulation in whole or in part. Arminians, such as Methodists and Freewill Baptists, rejected the doctrine of predestination and taught that God offers salvation to all, but leaves individuals free to accept or reject the offer. Religious liberals questioned the doctrine that the unregenerate human soul was totally corrupt and depraved. Universalists argued that an infinitely good Deity would never consign any creature to eternal damnation. Finally, there was a sprinkling of freethinkers and deists, followers of Thomas Paine or of Vermont's own Ethan Allan.[3]

Universalism in particular flourished in the Connecticut Valley, as it did wherever the evangelical form of Calvinism was strong. As Edward Turner, a Universalist minister in central Massachusetts in the early years of the nineteenth century, wrote, "Those representations of God, which show him to the terrified mind as a partial, vindictive, inexorable tyrant, furnish the proper materials of a hot-bed, adapted to the speedy growth and wide extension of directly adverse opinions."[4] The core geographic area for Universalism in the late eighteenth century was the same as that dominated by the New Lights: central Massachusetts and the Connecticut Valley. Between 1795 and 1815, twenty-three Universalist churches were organized in the Connecticut Valley area of Vermont.[5] In the early nineteenth century, Universalism spread through the "burned-over district" of central New York in the wake of the revivals.[6]

The combination of the evangelical emphasis on conversion with the determinism of Calvinist theology could put people into an intolerable position. Caleb Rich, the great frontier evangelist of Universalism, recalled being taught as a child "that Christ would have but few, yea but very few as trophies of his Mission into the world, while his antagonist would have his countless millions to play the tyrant over." Rich described his despair:

> I was not more than 9 or 10 years old before I had the most serious and shocking reflections on my hard fortune, to be born of Adam's vice. My situation appeared more precarious than a ticket in a lottery, where there was an hundred blanks to one prize. I often looked upon insects and poison reptiles, thinking how much better their lot was in this world than mine.[7]

A prominent feature of evangelical preaching was its vivid evocation of hell and damnation. In keeping with the new emphasis on conversion, such preaching was intended to rouse listeners to an awareness of their sinfulness and unworthiness, the essential first step of the conversion process. This was something new in New England; traditional Calvinist preaching did not dwell on the torments of hell. Calvin himself did not even believe in a literal hell, but explained the references in the Bible to weeping, gnashing of teeth, fire and brimstone, and so on as metaphors for "how wretched it is to be cut off from all fellowship with God."[8] The notion that only some were elected to salvation seemed more acceptable when salvation was understood as the gift of fellowship with God, and damnation as the absence of this gift. Once damnation began to be depicted as a state of positive torment, predestination began to seem like the act of a cruel and arbitrary tyrant rather than of a beneficent sovereign.

Belief in universal salvation was one way out of this impasse. Universalism attracted people who were frightened, offended, or revolted by the revivalists' evocations of the torments of the damned, but who were not prepared to give up belief in the absolute sovereignty of God. Since God is infinitely good, they argued, he wills the best for each of his creatures; since he is infinitely powerful, his will cannot be thwarted. Therefore, all souls will eventually be saved.

The Brownsons in Stockbridge

The Brownsons were part of Windsor County's tradition of non-Calvinist dissent. Sylvester was a nominal Presbyterian, but the family's naming practices suggest an interest in pagan mythology, more typical of Enlightenment rationalism than of Puritan piety. The first two children, Daniel and Oren, had conventional Old Testament names, but the third, Thorina, was named for a Norse god, and the twins, Orestes and Daphne, for characters from Greek mythology. Relief Brownson was a Universalist. She and at least one of her sisters had converted to Universalism in their native town of Keene, New Hampshire, possibly after hearing Elhanan Winchester preach in 1794.[9] Winchester, a successful Baptist revivalist prior to his conversion to Universalism, became a notable evangelist for his new faith. He founded the first Universalist church in Philadelphia and made many converts in England and New England.[10]

By the time the twins were born, on September 16, 1803, the Brownsons had been settled in Stockbridge for nearly two years. They could look forward, not perhaps to great prosperity, but to a modest independence. That changed when Sylvester died of pneumonia in 1805, leaving Relief, at twenty-eight, a widow with five children. The oldest was eight or nine; the twins were not yet two. The extended family could provide little help.

Sylvester's relatives had never had more than a bare subsistence, and Relief's father had recently suffered severe financial losses.[11] The family fell into desperate poverty. At one point Relief and her children were "warned out" of Windsor County as persons likely to become public charges.[12] One by one, the children were sent to live with families that could afford to care for them. Only the oldest, Daniel, stayed with his mother.[13]

Though her family was unable to help, Relief Brownson was not without resources. Chief among them was her church community. Relief had not attended Universalist meetings while her husband was alive, but some two years after his death she began attending Universalist services in the neighboring town of Barnard, just east of Stockbridge.[14] The Barnard church was one of five Universalist societies served by Hosea Ballou, the most influential Universalist preacher and theologian of his generation.

As she struggled to raise her children, Relief did her best to pass on to them her sense of God's benevolence and mercy. When he was twenty, Orestes wrote to a friend of his fond recollection of the religious instruction he had received from his mother:

> In the early age of childhood when the mind is tender and readily receives instruction, I was privileged with the pious guardianship of maternal tenderness. A mother whose ardent affection for her children manifested itself in precepts more precious than [...] gems, was my earliest and best earthly friend. Often did she inculcate the important lesson of duties owed to God [and the] gift of a Saviour's love to sinners.[15]

When it became necessary to place her children in foster homes, Relief looked first to friends in the church. Oren went to live with Benoni and Bridget Wight, fellow parishioners of Relief's own generation. Thorina went to the home of Seth Dean, who had recently married an aunt of Benoni Wight, and whose son Paul was a Universalist minister in Montpelier. Thorina appears to have been not only sheltered but adopted by the Deans; to the end of her life, she signed her name "Thorina Dean."[16] The twins were the last to be sent away. They stayed with their mother until 1809 or 1810, when they were six. Daphne is said to have been placed with "friends," but their names are not recorded.[17] Orestes was placed in the household of William and Lydia (Wheeler) Hunting and their son Luther in Royalton, Vermont. William and Lydia were a generation older than Relief Brownson; Luther was a young man of about her own age.[18] The Huntings were not Universalists, but they had Universalist relatives, and young Orestes often heard them speak of Hosea Ballou.[19]

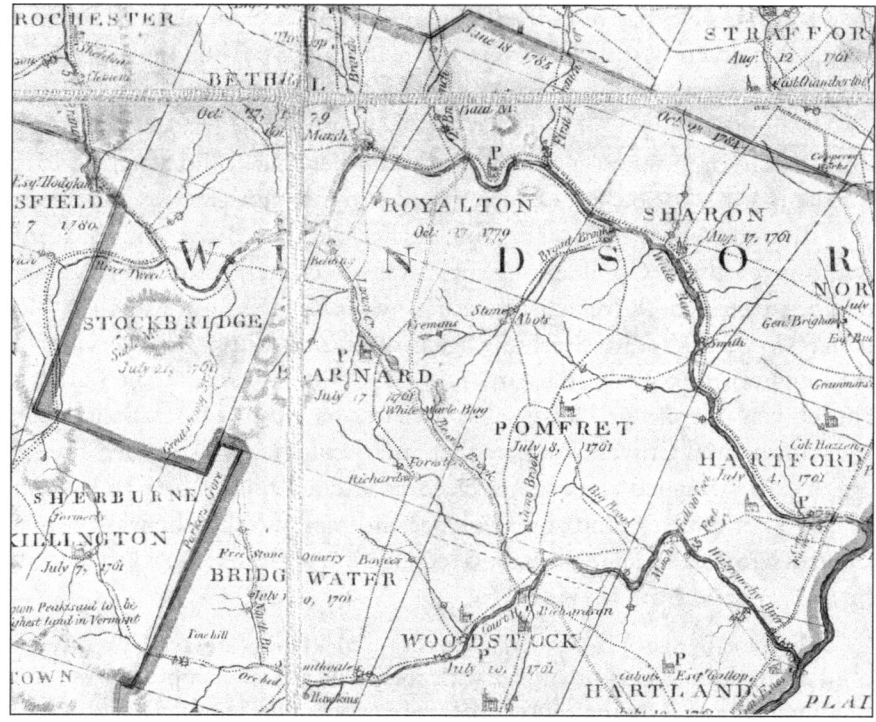

The world of Brownson's childhood. This detail from an 1810 map of Vermont shows Stockbridge, where Brownson was born; Royalton, where he lived between the ages of six and fourteen; and Barnard, where Relief Brownson attended Hosea Ballou's Universalist church.

The breakup of the Brownson family left an enduring and painful mark on the children. Eighty years later, Daphne told her nephew that she looked on the separation from her twin brother as "one of the great griefs of her life."[20] For years, she regularly wrote to Orestes on their shared birthday. In painstakingly penned, poorly spelled letters, she wrote of her sorrow at being separated from him. On their forty-first birthday she wrote, "you no how we were parted when little children that was wrong then in our youth that was wrong now we are parted is not this wrong."[21]

Orestes, though a far more accomplished writer than his sister, was less able to express his feelings about the disaster that befell his family. When, some fifty years later, he wrote his autobiography, he began, "I was born in the town of Stockbridge, Windsor County, Vermont, September 16, 1803. My father was a native of Hartford County, Connecticut; my mother of the beautiful village of Keene, New Hampshire." That is the last mention of his parents in the entire book. He did not mention the death of his father, the years of poverty, the parting with his mother and siblings, or the fact that the family was later reunited. His family simply disappeared from the book, as they had from the child's life.

Religion in Royalton

In an autobiographical letter to his Universalist friend and mentor Edward Turner, Brownson described his foster father, William Hunting, as "an old fashioned Congregationalist, who said his prayers for himself."[22] The Huntings, in other words, were Congregationalists, but not churchgoers. This was partly because the meetinghouse in Royalton was several miles from their farm, but also because they were Old Lights, traditional Calvinists who were uncomfortable with the evangelical form of Calvinism that dominated Windsor County. The Congregational church in Royalton had experienced a series of "awakenings," or revivals of religion, in the first decade of the nineteenth century. A "rich harvest" in 1810 had been followed by what the town's historian described as "unfortunate dissensions," which split the church and left it without a settled minister from 1813 to 1818.[23] William Hunting and his family seem to have been among those who left the church in the wake of the revivals.

Though lax in the matter of church-going, the Huntings were careful to instruct their charge in the basic documents of the Reformed faith: the Apostles' Creed and the Shorter Catechism.[24] The Catechism taught that "all mankind by their fall lost communion with God, are under his wrath and curse, and so made liable to all the miseries of this life, to death itself, and to the pains of hell forever"; that "no mere man, since the fall, is able … to keep the commandments of God"; and that "every sin deserveth God's wrath and curse, both in this life, and that which is to come." The only hope for escape from these grim prospects lay in "God, having out of his mere good pleasure, from all eternity, elected some to everlasting life."

It is unclear to what extent young Brownson was taught to believe these doctrines. In his study of Brownson's formative years, William Gilmore wrote of Brownson's "rigorous and dismal experience" with his foster family's "hard shelled Calvinism." Gilmore interpreted Brownson's description of his foster parents as "old fashioned Calvinists" to mean that they were "seventeenth century 'Old Calvinists' on theological matters … the most theologically conservative species" of New England religion.[25] He ascribed to Brownson the childhood experiences described in Brownson's 1831 story "Patrick O'Hara," which describes the feelings of a child of eight on becoming acquainted with the harsh doctrines of orthodox Calvinism. "I was soon informed that ... I was born with a nature wholly corrupt; that I was infinitely hateful in the sight of my God; that I was not only born to die, but I was in danger of going to hell where I should be endlessly miserable." In the story, the child responded to these ideas with a mixture of dismay and disbelief. Gazing with delight and adoration on the beauty of his mountain home, he reminded himself that "all this delight, all this pleasure, all this awe and devotion, proceeded from a corrupt heart, and could only be abomination to God ... I cursed my maker for the wretched, the thankless existence he had given me." As to the doctrine of election and reprobation, he could not bring himself to believe it. "The Bible had given me to understand that God was good to all, better than an earthly parent, and I could not believe that earthly parent very good, who would give all his good things to a small part of his children and starve the rest to death." Nor could he easily accept the doctrine of endless misery. "All my notions of justice, love and mercy seemed to forbid it."[26]

Brownson wrote this story when he was a Unitarian, for publication in a Unitarian newspaper, in order to illustrate the pernicious effects of a Calvinist upbringing. Though written in the form of a memoir, it is not autobiography, but didactic fiction. Brownson drew on his own memories of childhood in writing it, but Patrick O'Hara is not Orestes Brownson. In the absence of corroborating evidence, the story cannot be taken as an accurate depiction of Brownson's early religious education. In *The Convert*, Brownson wrote that his foster parents "were honest, upright, strictly moral ... but had no particular religion." They taught him the Shorter Catechism, "but I was not taught it as something I must believe; and I soon learned that they who taught it to me did not themselves believe it."[27] It is more likely that the Huntings were at the liberal or "Arminian" end of the Congregational spectrum than that they were strict Calvinists. Liberals believed, above all, in the benevolence of the Deity. Their God was not an arbitrary tyrant, but a just and wise father whose purpose in creation was the happiness of his creatures. Though most did not go so far as belief in universal salvation, the logic of their position tended in that direction. If the Huntings were liberal Congregationalists, Brownson would not have noticed a dramatic difference between their beliefs and those of his Universalist mother.

Whatever the Huntings' personal beliefs, they evidently did not think it was their place to tell their young charge what he must believe. Brownson wrote that they "left me to stay at home or to go to meeting, and to any meeting I chose."²⁸ With little guidance from any adults, he set out to explore the religious options Royalton had to offer.

Organized religion in Royalton was almost exclusively of the evangelical variety. Evangelical Calvinism was represented by the Congregational church and by a small Baptist society. Brownson had little contact with either of these groups. He was more attracted to the Methodists and the Christian Connection, non-Calvinist evangelicals who proclaimed that all might be saved if they would accept God's proffered grace. In *The Convert*, he mentioned that there were Universalists in town, but he does not seem to have come into contact with them. There was no organized Universalist society in Royalton until the 1820s.²⁹ With this possible exception, what Brownson encountered was a choice of evangelical sects. However else they might differ, all agreed on the centrality of the conversion experience. Brownson became familiar with the language of evangelicalism, but the spirit of it eluded him. "I was told ... that I must 'get religion,' 'experience religion,' have 'a change of heart,' 'be born again;' but how this was to be brought about, I could not understand." But though he did not fully understand what was required of him, he had a clear understanding of the price of failure. The Methodists, whose meetings he sometimes attended, "gave the most vivid pictures of hell-fire, and the tortures of the damned ... Love gave place to terror; and I became constantly afraid that the devil would come and carry me off bodily."³⁰

Though he joined no church and did not think of himself as having "experienced religion," Brownson had a private, intensely felt religious life. In *The Convert* he recalled, "My young heart often burned with love to our Blessed Lord, who had been so good as to come into the world, and to submit to the most cruel death of the cross that he might save us from our wicked dispositions, and make us happy forever in heaven. I wanted to know everything about him, and I used to think of him frequently in the day and the night." He held "long familiar conversations" with Jesus, the Virgin Mary, and the angels. He did not question these visions, but accepted them for the comfort they gave him. "It all seemed real to me, and I enjoyed often an inexpressible happiness ... I was rarely less alone than when alone."³¹ Twenty-five years earlier, writing for a Unitarian audience, he had described his childhood religion in similar terms (though without mentioning Mary or the angels): "In the early dawn of youth, there was nothing I so much dreaded as that which should divert my thoughts from the Deity, and interrupt my silent, but blissful intercourse of soul with the

'Father of our spirits.' I loved the night, for it seemed to shadow him forth and give him a local habitation ... I was never alone."³²

In earthly terms, he was very much alone. The Huntings were conscientious caretakers, but Brownson does not seem to have formed an affectionate bond with anyone in the household. He had no friends of his own age. "Properly speaking I had no childhood," he wrote in *The Convert*. "Brought up with old people, and debarred from all the sports, plays, and amusements of children, I had the manners, the tone, and tastes of an old man before I was a boy." Emotionally sustaining religious experiences comforted him in his loneliness and supplied the place of human affection. Religious images filled his imagination. The sermons of Jonathan Edwards, the poems of Isaac Watts, and above all the Bible fed his developing intellect. Not surprisingly, he thought of himself "as one called and set apart to the service of religion." He dreamed of becoming a minister, and bringing people to the knowledge and love of God. In a famous anecdote, he told of having gone to see a militia muster at the age of nine:

> On returning home, I was asked what I had seen to interest me. I answered that it was two old men talking on religion. In fact, I was so much interested in their discussion that I quite forgot the soldiers ... and almost forgot to eat my card of gingerbread. The discussion, I remember, was on free-will and election, and I actually took part in it, stoutly maintaining free-will against [Jonathan] Edwards.³³

Conversion

Brownson grew to be an adolescent with an "active" conscience, a tender heart, a thorough knowledge of the Bible, and a well-stocked religious imagination. However, he still had not "experienced religion," and was not attached to any church. He wished to be born again, and flirted with the idea of joining the Methodists, but something always stopped him. In a much-quoted passage in *The Convert*, he described a conversation with an elderly neighbor, whom he consulted about whether to submit to the Methodist conversion process. Her words, he said, "prevented me from ever being a genuine, hearty Protestant." (She herself was a Congregationalist, "but her argument is one which ... none save a Catholic can consistently urge.") As Brownson described it:

> "My poor boy," she replied, "God has been good to you, and has no doubt gracious designs towards you ... But go not with the Methodists or with any of the sects. They are New Lights, and not to be trusted. The Christian religion is not new, and Christians have existed from the time of Christ.

Those New Lights are of yesterday ... When you join any body calling itself a Christian body, find out and join one that began with Christ and his apostles, and has continued to subsist the same without change of doctrine or worship down to our own times. You will find the true religion with that body, and nowhere else. Join it, obey it, and you will find rest and salvation. But beware of sects and New Lights: they will make you fair promises, but in the end will deceive you to your own destruction."[34]

Brownson did not join the Methodists. But, though he did not mention it in *The Convert*, he did have a conversion experience in early adolescence, under the auspices of the Christian Connection. In his letter to Turner, Brownson recalled how that he had "experienced religion as it was called at the age of thirteen under the preaching of a Christian, and henceforth became very serious."[35] The "Christians,"* like the Methodists, believed that a spirit-filled conversion was necessary for salvation, but they did not believe in eternal torment or dwell in their preaching on the pains of hell as the Methodists did. They were "destructionists," teaching that the wages of sin was death – absolute non-existence – and not hell.

The Christian Connection of New England was one of several similar, though independent, religious movements that arose simultaneously in different regions of the United States during the early years of the nineteenth century. Their rallying cry was, "No master but Christ, no creed but the Bible, no other name than that of Christian." They opposed creeds on principle and viewed theology with deep suspicion, believing that "man-made" and "unscriptural" doctrines, such as the Trinity, original sin, and the immortality of the soul, were responsible for sectarian strife. They insisted that ordinary people could read and understand the Bible and judge for themselves what was truth.[36]

This belief was less liberal than it sounds, for the "Christians" assumed that all who approached the Bible with an unbiased mind would come to the same conclusions. "The Bible is a magnet," wrote one of their leaders. "It will draw all men to the same point, if they will but yield to its attractive influence."[37] The unwritten creed of the Christian Connection was recorded by Adin Ballou (a distant cousin of Brownson's mother's minister, Hosea Ballou), who later became a colleague of Brownson's in the Universalist ministry. Adin Ballou, like Brownson, "experienced religion" as an adolescent as a result of a Christian Connection revival. At the age of fifteen

---

* To avoid confusion with the generic term *Christians*, comprising all denominations and sects, I will use the term "*Christians*," in quotation marks, when referring to the members of the Christian Connection.

he formulated a twelve-point theology deduced from the preaching and writings of the "Christian" leaders, who "though constantly denouncing creeds, had one, as a matter of fact, of pretty sharp points."[38]

The "Christians" had much in common with the Universalists, from whom they differed chiefly in putting more emphasis on free will. Although they taught that God was willing that every soul should be saved, for the most part they did not believe in universal salvation since they believed that the soul must consent to its own salvation. However, Elias Smith, one of the founders of the movement, never fully made up his mind about the issue, and actually spent several years as a Universalist minister. This did not prevent the "Christians" from expelling members whom they suspected of universalist tendencies. Adin Ballou was dismissed from the Christian Connection ministry for professing a belief in universal salvation, as was Elias Smith himself.[39]

Brownson, too, may have run up against the "sharp points" of the Christians' creedless creed. In his late twenties, as a Universalist minister in New York State, he wrote quite bitterly about advocates of "Christian union" who condemn sectarianism but "are, so far as the writer of this knows any thing about them, as violent sectarians as there are in ... [any] country in Christendom."

> They have no creed, forsooth; but if every one does not understand the bible according to their construction they brand him "sectarian," and heap upon his back all the epithets of reproach, found in the Jewish or Christian scriptures ... "They are liberal," it is said. No doubt of that: we never saw a bigot but what was liberal enough to let one believe just like himself.[40]

Brownson's story "Patrick O'Hara" contains a satirical account of an adolescent conversion experience, which is often taken to be autobiographical.[41] The most interesting part of the story is the description of the boy's efforts to work himself into the requisite state of "conviction of sin":

> It was a long and weary time I had. Long, long did I weep over my sins, without being able to recall one thing I had done for which conscience condemned me. I prayed and prayed, but all to no avail. They told me to give myself up to God. I strove to do it; I was anxious to do it; I wished the assistance of his holy spirit; sought it with tears, but all in vain.

Eventually, by dwelling on the torments of hell and imagining himself consigned to the outer darkness by a callous God "seated upon his great white throne, laughing, *tête à tête* with his Son and the Holy Ghost,"

Patrick manages to make himself sufficiently miserable to earn his glimpse of heaven.[42]

The fact that Brownson joined the "Christians" is somewhat at odds with the explanation he gave in *The Convert* for not joining the Methodists. If the Methodists were "New Lights," what were the "Christians"? After all, the Christian Connection had been founded right in his home state of Vermont, some fifteen years earlier; as his neighbor had reminded him, "You yourself know the founder of the *Christian* sect."[43] Thus, his decision not to join the Methodists was probably because he did not like their beliefs about hell, and his claim that the conversation with his neighbor prevented him from ever becoming a thoroughgoing Protestant was a later reinterpretation of his experience in the light of his Catholic faith.[44] Until the 1840s, he accepted the legitimacy of Protestantism without question. The important question of Brownson's youth was which sect or denomination of Protestants came closest to the truth as he understood it. Like his fictional character Patrick O'Hara, he could not bring himself to believe in total human depravity, predestination, and eternal punishment. Of the options available to him in Royalton, the "Christians," with their mild, unthreatening evangelicalism, seemed to be the best choice.

The Rural Intelligentsia

Brownson's son Henry once quoted his father as saying "I had no schooling," but this statement should not be taken literally.[45] In fact, Brownson had the usual education for one of his class: a few terms at the local district school followed by a few months at an academy. Royalton in Brownson's day was considered to have an excellent district school system; well over eighty percent of its children attended school. In 1808 there were thirteen district schools in Royalton, including one located on Broad Brook, not far from the Huntings' farm.[46]

Schools could be places of brutality as well as of learning. Brownson never referred directly to his early school experiences, but, from a fragment written when he was nineteen, we can surmise that he encountered his share of misery. In his diary, which also served as a composition book for practicing various forms of writing, he began a descriptive piece entitled "A Winter Reflection." From a depiction of frozen lakes and snow-covered hills, he passed on to a catalogue of the human figures in the landscape: the shepherd tending his flock, the traveler harnessing his sled, and so on. The figure of a boy heading to school brought the piece to an abrupt end in a barely coherent outburst: "And now to school the boy trudging with satchel on his back screaming hate to teacher longs for night that he may be delivered from his cruel tyrant and blistered hand and the school room his pent up dungeon – now enraged the parents anathematize the teacher and keep their boy at home."[47]

As an adult Brownson was critical of the education offered by the nation's common schools, though he thought them "incomparably better than our high schools or colleges." He complained that schools do not teach children to think for themselves, or to understand "the nature or reason of things." Instead,

> they put into his hand a book he does not understand, and compel him, through fear or flattery, to wade through it and commit it perhaps [to memory], without exercising a single faculty of mind, except the memory; and after wasting eight or ten years of his time, they send him out into the world, learned perhaps, but nearly as ignorant of every thing, as he commenced, with the exception of a few words and sentences, he may have committed to memory, without once thinking of their import.[48]

Young Brownson's great passion was reading. At first he read indiscriminately whatever books came to hand, whether or not he could understand them, as an escape from loneliness and deprivation. "I felt neither hunger nor thirst, and no want of sleep, my book was meat and drink, home and raiment, friend and guardian, father and mother." As he grew in understanding of the books he read and of the ways of the world, he discovered that his ability to master hard texts was unusual, and he began to pride himself on his intellectual accomplishments. Years later, he gave thanks that in his youth he had read no children's books, but only works that taxed his intellect and strengthened it by constant exercise. "The harder [children] are obliged to struggle to find some meaning in what they read the better it is for them ... I think it was a great advantage to me that I read books beyond my age, and could think, reason, reflect before I had a beard on my upper lip."[49]

Brownson belonged to what is sometimes called the "rural intelligentsia" – persons of intellectual temperament whose access to formal education was limited by geography, class, culture, or gender.[50] His formal education may have been scant and unhappy, but his reading formed a bond between himself and other rural intellectuals. He would always defend Vermont against any suggestion of rural backwardness, insisting that "no state in the Union has ... a population, taken generally, so well educated, and so remarkable for intellectual power and general intelligence."[51] He recalled:

> It is astonishing how many valuable and standard works there can be picked up, one here and one there in almost any neighborhood in our country. I found with one gentleman the English classics of Queen Anne's reign, with another some 50 volumes of the English poets, with another a work on universal history, Locke's Essay on the Human Understanding, and Pope's Homer, with still another various monographs of American history, the planting of the colonies, wars with the Indians, Robinson Crusoe, Philip Quarles, and the Arabian nights.[52]

Through these works, and the intellectual mentors who supplied them, Brownson was brought into contact with the world beyond Royalton. He was also laying the foundation for his intellectual development. When, in the years to come, he found himself at a loss as to what he could believe, works such as Locke's *Essay Concerning Human Understanding* supplied a method of philosophical investigation. Though his religion was the product of the American frontier, his intellectual culture was that of the European Enlightenment.

Brownson's reading was important to his social and emotional well-being as well as to his intellectual development. He may not have been popular with companions of his own age, but his efforts to educate himself brought him to the attention of sympathetic older people who encouraged his ambitions, lent him books, and talked to him of history and poetry and religion. Though he lacked family and close friends in Royalton, he had a comforting sense of belonging to the village itself. "In any part of New England," he later wrote, inaccurately but tellingly, "we have an old permanent population, born where they live, and not a miscellaneous population, made up of strangers and adventurers."[53] Though his native part of Vermont had been wilderness a mere twenty-five years before he was born, to him it was the ideal type of the stable, traditional New England town.

Brownson had fond memories of growing up in Royalton. In *The Convert* he described his childhood as "blameless" and "happy."[54] His son Henry claimed – on what authority he did not say – that "the boy verging on manhood was serene and contented."[55] It may well have been so. Certainly in later years Brownson expressed himself proud and happy to have been *brought up* ("In New England they *raise* stock, rye, corn, potatoes, etc., but they *bring up* children") in Vermont.[56] Reviewing a history of Vermont in 1844, he wrote, "To Vermont we owe our hardy constitution, our fearless love of freedom, and our indomitable spirit of independence."[57]

By his early teens Brownson had begun to take his place among the citizens of Royalton. He was tall and strong, and took pride in his ability to earn money by his labor.[58] He may have begun to take an interest in public affairs; at least, he later wrote that New Englanders were "trained from boyhood" in the arts of government in the town meeting.[59] He had come through the crisis of conversion and resolved, for the moment, his religious doubts and perplexities. Despite the losses and separations of his early years, he seemed to have found a home.

CHAPTER 2

Apprenticeship

> *The worldly, fashionable, dashing, good-for-nothing people of every state ... flock to the Springs – not to enjoy the pleasures of society, or benefit by the qualities of the waters, but to exhibit their equipages and wardrobes, and to excite the admiration, or what is much more satisfactory, the envy of their fashionable competitors.*
>
> – Washington Irving, "Style at Ballston"

The Brownsons in Ballston

When Brownson was fourteen years old, his world was turned upside down once again. As he described it in *The Convert*, "I left the kind old people, who had so far brought me up, and went forth into the world alone, to make my way as best I could."[1] This statement, like many of Brownson's recollections, tells more about his inner experience than about the external facts. What actually happened was that his mother, whom he had not seen for seven years, collected her scattered family and moved with her children to Ballston, New York, where her sister Asenath Delano and her family lived.[2] Going "into the world alone, to make my way as best I could" meant settling with his mother, brothers, sisters, aunt, uncle, and cousins, in a place where he would attend school and learn a trade.

Still, we should take seriously Brownson's memory of having been "thrown upon a new world, into the midst of new and strange scenes, and exposed to new and corrupting influences."[3] The move to Ballston meant the loss of the only home Brownson could remember, the place he was making for himself in Royalton, and the adult identity he was beginning to form. It took him to a place utterly unlike sober, hardworking Royalton. Ballston was a fashionable resort, built around a complex of hotels and mineral springs, in imitation of such European models as Bath in England and Spa in Belgium. Though it would later be eclipsed by Saratoga Springs, six miles to the north, in 1817 Ballston Spa was the premier resort in the region, if not in the country.

The springs at Ballston had been frequented by travelers seeking health and recreation since the 1780s. At that time, in the words of a town historian, "it was a simple forest spring, and not a Vanity Fair." The first accommodation for visitors was a log tavern, built in 1787 by the father and grandfather of the future presidential candidate, Stephen A. Douglas. Progressively grander hotels followed, culminating in the opening of the Sans Souci, the largest resort in the United States, in 1804. At the Sans Souci a hundred guests congregated "in pursuit of health or pleasure, of matrimony or of vice." Daniel Webster, Henry Clay, John C. Calhoun, Andrew Jackson, Martin Van Buren, James Fenimore Cooper, and Washington Irving all visited the Sans Souci. The former king of Spain, Joseph Bonaparte, was staying there in 1821 when he received the news of the death of his brother, Napoleon.[4]

Outside of the village of Ballston Spa, the town of Ballston was principally agricultural, like the surrounding region. The Brownsons and Delanos belonged to this agricultural hinterland, and probably had little contact with the resort. There is no direct evidence as to the Brownsons' occupations in the early years in Ballston, but family letters attest to the fact that Relief Brownson was a small-scale farmer and weaver in later years. In a letter of 1845, for example, she wrote that she had bought hay for her cow and heifer, butchered a hog and a yearling cow, and "worked some in the loom."[5] Orestes, however, was well positioned to observe the manners and mores of Vanity Fair. The family having settled on printing as a suitable

Ballston Spa in 1815. The original spring is in the fenced enclosure at the lower right.

career for the bookish youth, he was apprenticed to the publisher, editor, and printer, James Comstock.[6]

The Independent American

James Comstock had come to Ballston Spa in 1803 to work on Saratoga County's first newspaper, the *Saratoga Register or Farmer's Journal*. In 1811 he became the proprietor of the paper, which he renamed the *Independent American*. He was also a book printer and publisher, specializing in books on evangelical religion, temperance, and peace. In partnership with his brother-in-law, the Presbyterian minister Reuben Sears, he owned a bookstore, a circulating library (for "Gentlemen and Ladies, Visitants at Ballston Spa") and a reading room (for gentlemen only).[7] Brownson thus served his apprenticeship at one of Ballston's central clearinghouses for news, gossip, religious discussion and political debate.

Brownson took readily to the newspaper business, advancing rapidly from apprentice to journeyman. Typically, an apprenticeship in the printing trade in early nineteenth-century New York began at age fourteen to sixteen and ran for five to seven years, or until age twenty-one.[8] Shorter periods were by no means unknown, but Brownson's apprenticeship seems to have been particularly brief – just over two years.[9] He left Comstock's employ in 1822, when he was nineteen. By that time, he had been working as a journeyman printer for long enough to save the money needed to continue his education at Ballston Academy.[10]

While it lasted, the paternal relationship between master and apprentice seemed to suit the fatherless boy. Comstock became one of a line of respected older men – including the rural intellectuals of Royalton, the Presbyterian minister Reuben Smith, the Universalist ministers Edward Turner and Linus Smith Everett, the Unitarian minister William Ellery Channing, and the Catholic priest John Bernard Fitzpatrick – whom Brownson treated as surrogate fathers and whose views, at least for a time, he adopted.

Vanity Fair

In discussing Brownson's move from Royalton to Ballston, William Gilmore emphasized the "cultural stimulation" of life in Ballston, a "thoroughly cosmopolitan" environment "bursting with possibility."[11] Brownson certainly found Ballston a more stimulating setting than Royalton, but he also found much there to disturb, distress, and shock him.

In Ballston Brownson encountered a class system such as he had never known. He was, of course, familiar with poverty, but the poverty he had known in childhood had been tempered by relative equality and by that fabled spirit of independence which he always associated with Vermont.[12] He remembered it as something wholesome and bracing: "We are very wrong when we class the very poor generally with the criminal or dangerous classes, I have seen with the poor a self-denial, a strict sense of justice, a resistance to temptation, an heroic virtue, which I have never found in the more prosperous classes."[13] The spa culture of Ballston was at odds with these austere virtues, and with the ideals of republican simplicity and equality. An economy based on tourism is an economy of privilege and deference. It magnifies, rather than minimizes, differences of wealth and social status.

The population of Ballston Spa was far more diverse than any Brownson had seen before, and was organized into a highly stratified social hierarchy. At the top was the landlord, Nicholas Low. He owned most of the land in the village, the mineral springs, the Sans Souci, and numerous other local enterprises including billiard rooms, stables, a reservoir, a sheep farm, and a textile mill. Next came the guests who patronized the resort (of whom Low may be counted as one, as he lived in New York City and stayed at the Sans Souci during his thrice-yearly visits to Ballston). The guests were persons of wealth, elegance, and social standing – or at least were treated as if they were. In his study of early American resorts, Theodore Corbett suggested that one reason Ballston Spa was eclipsed by Saratoga Springs was that, whereas Saratoga provided accommodations suitable for a variety of tastes and price ranges, the developers of Ballston Spa were committed to maintaining an elite society.[14]

This 1823 advertising circular shows Ballston Spa's most elegant hotel, the Sans Souci.

Believing that the resort's chief asset was neither its mineral springs nor its grand hotels, but "the fame of its stylish company," its promoters were prepared to pamper, indulge, and flatter their exclusive clientele. This was the task of the resort's workforce. In addition to accommodating the guests' own servants and slaves, the resort employed an army of cooks, waiters, maids, and launderers to wait upon the guests; musicians and entertainers to amuse them; and builders, gardeners, and laborers to maintain the buildings and grounds. The auxiliary businesses that surrounded the spa – dressmakers, tailors, jewelers, livery stables – had their own hierarchy of proprietor, employees, apprentices and servants. The lower ranks of these workers were recruited locally, but the more specialized, including those with most direct contact with the guests, were often outsiders brought in for the season. The waiters at the Sans Souci, for example, were African American men from New York City; only these, in Low's opinion, combined the necessary skills and experience with the requisite habit of deference.[15]

This first contact with people of color, both free and enslaved, gave Brownson a set of ideas about race and slavery that proved surprisingly resistant to time and changing circumstances. He accepted that all races were equal in the sight of God, but thought black people were less "developed" than white, and thus unfit for full civil and political equality. His most vivid impression was of the virulence of racial prejudice, which, he believed, would make it impossible for the races ever to live together in peace. As late as 1862 he advocated emancipation followed by emigration of the black population.[16] He believed that slavery was wrong, but not fundamentally different from other kinds of subsistence labor. He saw the abolition of slavery as but a small part of the emancipation of the proletariat. "We would see the slave a man, but a free man, not a mere operative at wages," he wrote in 1840. "Could the abolitionists effect all they propose ... still it would do the slave no good. He would be a slave still, though with the title and cares of a freeman."[17]

Observing Ballston society from his position near its lower end, Brownson was outraged by the deference paid to those with money to spend, regardless of their real merit. He expressed his indignation in a piece of quite precise, if caustic, social observation:

> [In America] titles are not run after indeed, but wealth, more frequently the veriest shadow of wealth, no matter how got or how used, is the real god, the omnipotent Jove, of modern idolatry. The man is nothing without his trappings. Humble virtue is commended in words, for are we not

> Christians? – but disdained, despised, and cast out to die of cold, hunger, and nakedness. Get money, the spirit saith, get rich, no matter how, by gambling in stocks, by false pretenses, by extortion, by swindling, cheating, feeing lawyers, buying up legislators, corrupting incorruptible courts of justice, and you will be great, honored and followed. Add to this that out of some portion of the money you have contrived to transfer from the pockets of others to your own, you ... take care, with sounding of trumpets, beating of drums, fanfaronade and bluster, to dispose of your wealth to the poor, but so that the real poor and needy will receive no benefit from it, and count with certainty on your apotheosis ... Thy gods ... are mammon and cant – cant pious, cant liberal, cant philanthropic.

"I am nobody," he wrote bitterly, "and if I venture to say anything, the only answer is, he is a poor devil, has not a red cent in his pocket, – heed not his sayings."[18]

Brownson never ceased to be infuriated by claims of personal superiority based on the mere accumulation of wealth. Thirty-five years after he left Ballston, he still seemed to be describing its society when he complained in *The Convert* that "moral worth and intellectual superiority count for nothing" with "the upstart, the *novus homo* ... [who] has nothing to sustain him but his money."

> He enters on a career of lavish expenditure, and aids to introduce an expensive and luxurious style of living, destructive of genuine simplicity of manners, and of private and social morals ... The man of moderate income cannot live within his means ... All are striving to be, or to appear, what they are not, to work their way up to a higher social stratum, and hence society becomes hollow, a sham, a lie.[19]

Brownson responded to the sham and dishonesty of spa society by developing his own social hierarchy, in which simplicity, sincerity, and kindness counted for more than wealth or elegance. In his youth, he later told his son, he was "bashful, awkward, blundering, ill-at-ease if I found myself even in humble employment among people who were my social superiors." However, "with really high-bred people I could get along passably well, for their manners were simple and unaffected, and they knew the art without displaying it of putting me at my ease."[20] He was not the only person to draw such a distinction. Spa society was marked by what has been called the "cult of sensibility": the belief that the worth of new acquaintances, whose character, motives, and antecedents were unknown, could be judged by the evidence they gave of "true feeling, sincerity, emotion, and proper manners." Such inner qualities, it was hoped, were less easy to counterfeit than the outward trappings of wealth and social status.[21]

The People's Party

Brownson's work on the newspaper in Ballston was the beginning of his political education. His apprenticeship took place during a time of intense political excitement in Saratoga County. Nationally, it was a time of relative political calm, the decline of the Federalist party having left the Republicans in a position of undisputed dominance. In Saratoga County, however, factions known as the Oldline and the Newline, each claiming to be the legitimate branch of the Republican party, fought bitterly contested elections and abused each other roundly in newspapers and pamphlets. When, in 1818, representatives of the Oldline and Newline arranged a compromise whereby the Oldline would support the Newline candidate for Congress in return for three of the county's four seats in the state legislature, a self-proclaimed "People's Party" arose to denounce the compromise as "a *bargain* and *sale* of the VOTES of the free and independent ELECTORS of this county" and the nominating caucus as an "aristocratic" or "court party" bent on opposing its will to that of the people.[22]

The development of the "court" and "people's" parties brought substantive political and even moral issues into what had initially been straightforward intra-party competition for influence and offices. In addition to rejecting the compromise ticket, the People's Party challenged the legitimacy of the traditional party caucus, calling instead for a non-partisan nominating convention. They ultimately rejected the convention as well, nominating "a ticket to suit themselves the sovereign people" at an irregular meeting "composed of the people themselves, without reference to towns, sections, delegates or parties."[23] In effect, Saratoga County was rehearsing the debates that would dominate the New York State constitutional convention three years later. After triumphing in the 1818 election, the People's Party went on to advocate "constitutional reform in regard to the elective franchise and the power of appointing to office."[24] A statewide People's Party was formed after the convention to represent those who felt the reforms had not gone far enough.[25]

James Comstock was a fierce partisan of the People's Party and its candidate for Congress, John W. Taylor of Ballston. Taylor, a well-respected lawyer with a reputation for scrupulous honesty, had served in Congress since 1813, and would continue to be re-elected until 1833. When he was passed over for the Republican nomination in 1818, public opinion was outraged that a popular incumbent could be unseated by machinations within the party caucus, without regard to the wishes of the electors. The pages of the *Independent American* were filled with editorials, resolutions, notices of meetings, and letters to the editor, all crying out against the "small number of assuming dictators," the "knot of cormorants" represented by lawyers, bankers, and moneylenders, who presumed to "[bargain] between themselves for all the emoluments and honors, which it is the province of the people to bestow."[26]

Fueling the outrage was anxiety about the role of money and privilege in public affairs. There was a widespread belief, implicit in the People's Party rhetoric though not substantiated by specific charges, that the nomination had been not only bargained away, but sold. As one correspondent of the *Independent American* put it,

> I *have seen* ... the simplicity of our forefathers fast descending to the tomb of extravagance ... The *monied Aristocracy* which is so fast rising, if not checked, will soon draw THE LINE OF DISTINCTION BETWEEN THE RICH AND POOR ... RICHES [will be] the scale and standard by which a man will be estimated both for office and respectability.[27]

This concern cut across party lines. The *Independent American*, originally a Federalist paper, had up to this time remained neutral in the squabbles between the Oldline and Newline Republicans. But in the face of the threat posed by money and privilege, Comstock wrote, "honest men of all parties are disposed calmly and seriously to look to the true interests of their country. Is it not time for the people to awake, when their liberties are in jeopardy?"[28]

The People's Party triumphed in the 1818 election. John Taylor was re-elected, and went on to become Speaker of the House during the debates over the Missouri Compromise. Comstock celebrated by changing the name of his newspaper to the *People's Watch-Tower* and solemnly pledging to "watch ... with sober and discreet vigilance, against all encroachments upon the rights and privileges of the 'people.'"[29] The victory of the People's Party, he wrote, showed that it was still possible for "farmers, plain, honest and virtuous men" to take government back from "the court lordlings, law speculators, note shavers and usurers, who are our cruel oppressors." If the people would but stand firm, democracy would triumph, as in "the days of our primitive innocence and simplicity."[30]

Envisioning politics as an epic struggle between the rich and the poor, with the soul of the nation at stake, gave meaning and grandeur to the everyday indignities of being poor in a world of privilege. Brownson adopted this view and made it his own. The rhetoric of the People's Party contained most of the major points that would characterize his political thinking for the next twenty-five years: that democracy was endangered by privilege, that privilege was exercised particularly by lawyers, banks, and corporations, and that the inalienable right of the people (understood as all free, white, adult male residents) to choose their own leaders should take precedence over any conventional or constitutional mechanisms that may have been established.[31] These principles remained the basis of Brownson's politics through his association with the Workingmen's Party in the late 1820s and the Jacksonian Democrats in the 1830s. As he learned more of history and political philosophy, his political statements became more elaborate and sophisticated, but his opinions did not change in any fundamental way until the upheaval in his political and religious beliefs in the 1840s. In many ways, they never changed. In 1875, the year before he died, he wrote:

> The working classes ... are as a rule the most loyal and honest part of the community ... The danger to our Republic comes precisely from the non-working classes, from bankers, brokers, speculators, stockholders, and jobbers, the great industrial chiefs, and railroad kings, and against this danger there is and can be no legal or constitutional protection, indeed no protection at all, so long as wealth is the passport to distinction or the mark of respectability, and poverty is treated as disreputable and criminal.[32]

Priestcraft

Brownson was as much dismayed by Ballston's secularism as by its materialism. In religion, as in politics and social structure, Ballston was a very different place from the world of Brownson's childhood. In Royalton he had encountered Congregationalists, Methodists, "Christians," Universalists, and Baptists. These groups differed, sometimes quite passionately, about theology, but they shared a common religious heritage and a common understanding of the central place of religion in personal and social life. None doubted the importance of the question, "What must I do to be saved?" In Ballston, Brownson encountered for the first time a large number of people for whom religion was simply not a major concern. Ballston Spa was known for licentiousness, not for piety.[33]

The Congregationalists, Methodists, and "Christians" who had dominated the scenes of Brownson's childhood were all absent from Ballston Spa.[34] Until 1817, the only church in the village was a fervent but small

Baptist congregation that predated the development of the resort and remained largely apart from it. A neighboring Episcopal church held services in Ballston Spa during the summer for the benefit of the resort's visitors. The two new church buildings that graced the village center in Brownson's day were built at the initiative of the landlord, Nicholas Low. In 1816 he gave the Baptists a lot on the main street. The following year he donated a lot for an Episcopal church and induced the congregation from Ballston Centre to relocate to the spa.[35] As Low was not known for his piety, he may have been motivated by the wish to provide religious services as an amenity for his guests.

Early in his stay in Ballston, Brownson became infected with the prevailing attitude of worldliness and indifference. The "long familiar conversations" with Jesus that had cheered his childhood, and the intimation of heaven that had accompanied his conversion, receded from his memory. Within months of his arrival in Ballston, he "had left off prayer and was living forgetful of him who was continually showering down mercies upon me." When he thought of religion now, "the gloominess of christianity – parting with playmates – the taunting of the licentious – presented themselves to view as its attendants, and my heart withheld the assent!"[36]

Brownson not only felt alienated from religious experience; he entertained dark suspicions about religion itself. Confused by "the contradictory opinions I heard advanced, and the doubts and denials to which I listened," he began to fear that "all religion was a delusion – the work of priestcraft or statecraft."[37] In this he was probably influenced by the anticlericalism of his new employer, Horatio Gates Spafford, who bought the *People's Watch-Tower* from James Comstock in 1820. Spafford published the paper, which he renamed the *Saratoga Farmer*, for one year – the only interruption in Comstock's thirty-six-year career as publisher.[38] During this time Comstock remained as editor and printer, and Brownson continued as his apprentice.

Spafford was a self-taught scholar and inventor of great energy and ingenuity, but prone to errors of judgment which gave him, as his biographer admitted, "an unrivalled capacity for turning every scheme into loss and ruin." Prior to coming to Ballston, he had published a short-lived magazine and written books on geography, philosophy, agriculture, and a sentimental novel. His most substantial achievement was his *Gazetteer of the State of New York* (1813). His habit of making extravagant claims for the importance of his inventions and sending them to dignitaries such as ex-presidents Jefferson and Madison and the Emperor of Russia ensured that his one really substantial discovery, an improved method of making steel which anticipated the Bessemer process, would go unrecognized. He came to Ballston for the waters following the failure of a land speculation scheme in western Pennsylvania. It is something of a mystery how he was able to buy a newspaper, since he was too poor in 1820 to pay his dues to the American Antiquarian Society.[39] Certainly neither Comstock nor Spafford had much ready money. Both printed frequent notices urging subscribers to settle their accounts with rags (used in papermaking), firewood, or farm produce.

The *Saratoga Farmer*, like its predecessor the *People's Watch-Tower*, supported the political ambitions of John W. Taylor, opposed the influence of lawyers and banks, and preached peace and temperance. The most significant difference between Comstock and Spafford was in the area of religion. Comstock advocated the spread of Christianity in any form. He reported all "Religious Intelligence" in tones of bland approval. Spafford devoted much less space to religion, and what he did include could be sharply critical.[40]

Spafford was a Quaker and, on his own terms, a religious man, but he disapproved of organized religion and of clergy, believing them to be enemies of liberty. He opposed government support for churches, suggested that the Indians should be taught the "arts of civilization" without being pressured to adopt Christianity, and asserted that common schools were more valuable than theological seminaries.[41] In his private correspondence he seems to have expressed his opposition to "priestcraft" quite bluntly. A letter to Thomas Jefferson enclosing a copy of his *Gazetteer* elicited this reply: "I join in your reprobation of our merchants, priests, and lawyers ... In every country and in every age, the priest has been hostile to liberty. He is always in alliance with the despot, abetting his abuses in return for protection to his own."[42]

Brownson's writings, up to the time of his conversion to Catholicism, reveal a similar distrust of "priests." Like Jefferson and Spafford, he accused the clergy of perverting the religion of Jesus into an instrument of oppression, and feared that the orthodox clergy had designs on political power. Much of Brownson's anticlericalism was based on the idea that the clergy, like lawyers and bankers, were "nonproducers" who lived on the labor of the working class. Even when he was himself a member of the clergy, he continued to inveigh against the evils of priests and priestcraft. When he wrote his essay *The Laboring Classes* in 1840, he was serving as a Unitarian minister, but this did not prevent him from calling for "the complete and final destruction of the priestly order."[43] During his Universalist ministry, cynicism about the motivations of the clergy was a commonplace in his newspaper writing and even in his sermons. In an 1828 sermon "On the Moral Condition of Mankind," he ascribed both social inequality and mental slavery to the privileged position of the priestly class:

> Formed by the persons who afterwards lived upon its revenue, [religion] had no idea of the equality of the human family ... Inequality increased among the wretched children of men; a privileged class arose to fatten on the labors of the ignorant, the timid and the credulous. The priest leagued with the despot ... Instead of firing the soul with a desire to be happy ... they taught that evil was unavoidable and that to complain would be to murmur against heaven. They discouraged free inquiry and stamped a fatal anathema upon the exercise of thought ... The pride, indolence, contempt, fanaticism and intolerance produced by these are the disease and the reason why our moral health is not recovered.[44]

In Ballston Brownson learned to distinguish between what he would later call "the gospel of Jesus" and "the gospel of the priests." According to the true Christianity of Christ, Brownson wrote, no one can enter the kingdom of God "who does not labor to bring down the high, and bring up the low; to break the fetters of the bound and set the captive free; to destroy all oppression, establish the reign of justice, which is the reign of equality between man and man ... No man can be a Christian who does not labor to reform society."[45]

In contrast to the radical gospel of Jesus, the gospel of the priests buttresses the status quo instead of challenging it in the name of justice and compassion. Concerned to protect their own privileged position, priests put the narrow concerns of the institutional church ahead of the welfare of humanity. In his sermon "On the Moral Condition of Mankind," Brownson parodied the kind of preaching that "endeavor[s] to silence the murmurs of those discontented wretches who [wish] for a better order of things and to reconcile the unfortunate to their sufferings."

> To the poor the priest came with his face full of sorrow and eyes suffused with tears. "Ah me," said he, "what a weary land is earth, full of briars and thorns; misery is the lot of mortals here; vain the attempt to be happy. Wealth is a mere bauble; power is a vexation; and pleasure is worse than mourning. God has wisely made these distinctions in society; he had, through his providence, appointed some to be masters; but there could be

no masters without servants ... there can be no priests without altars and sacrifice, and no preachers without hearers, consequently you must learn to obey, listen to us and believe what we teach... You are unhappy now: ah, thank God for that, you will be more happy hereafter."[46]

When Brownson wrote in *The Laboring Classes* that "priests are, in their capacity of priests, necessarily enemies of freedom and equality," he was only saying what he had heard from Horatio Gates Spafford twenty years earlier.[47] *The Laboring Classes* achieved great notoriety when it appeared at the height of the presidential campaign of 1840, but the ideas in it were not new. Brownson's hatred of inequality, injustice, and privilege in all their forms, and his condemnation of a religious establishment that failed in its Christian duty to oppose them, had their roots in his formative years as an apprentice journalist in Ballston Spa.

CHAPTER 3

Universalism and Skepticism

I fell in with new sectaries, universalists, deists, atheists, and nothingarians, as they are called with us, who profess no particular religion.

– Orestes Brownson, *The Convert*

Universalism in Ballston

Brownson's move to Ballston was the beginning of a complex and ambivalent relationship with Universalism that would, in one form or another, dominate his religious life from his mid-teens to his late twenties. Apart from a hazy recollection of his mother's early teachings about a loving God, and an inclination to be skeptical about the Calvinist scheme of salvation, he knew little about Universalism before arriving in Ballston. Reunited with his family, he found that, as he later wrote to Edward Turner, "all my associates were inclining to Universalism."[1] His mother was a Universalist, and his older siblings had been brought up in that faith. His aunt and her family were active in Ballston's tiny Universalist society.

The upper Hudson valley was not prime Universalist territory. Carried to central and western New York by Yankee migrants from the interior of New England, Universalism for the most part passed over the long-settled areas of eastern New York. Ballston, however, is only thirty-five miles from Bennington, Vermont. Especially before the development of the mineral springs, it functioned culturally as an outpost of western Vermont. In the 1780s, the Universalist evangelist Michael Coffin served a circuit that included Ballston, Whitehall, and Cranville, New York, as well as Clarendon and Pawlet, Vermont.[2] The Universalist General Convention met in the area twice around the turn of the century: in Bennington in 1795, and in Hoosick Falls, New York, twenty-five miles from Ballston, in 1806.[3] A Universalist society was organized in Ballston in 1809.[4]

Among the Universalist emigrants from Vermont who settled in Ballston around 1800 were Relief Brownson's sister Asenath and her husband

Obadiah Delano.[5] Asenath Delano, Brownson wrote, "initiated me into the mysteries of Universalism," introducing the classics of Universalist literature with her "brilliant and enthusiastic commentaries." No doubt she was as pleased to discover that one of her new-found nieces and nephews took a precocious interest in religion as he was to find an intellectual mentor in Ballston. Under his aunt's guidance, during his fourteenth and fifteenth years Brownson read Charles Chauncy's *The Mystery Hid from Ages and Generations, or Salvation for All Men*; Joseph Huntington's *Calvinism Improved*; and Elhanan Winchester's *Universal Restoration*, his *Lectures on the Prophecies*, and his 350-page poem, *The Process and Empire of Christ*.[6]

This selection of books, all written during the 1780s and 1790s, indicates that the Delanos' Universalism was of a rather old-fashioned type, little changed since they left Vermont twenty years earlier. Universalism in Ballston still followed the eighteenth-century model: the small lay-led society, the occasional visit from a traveling evangelist, the sharing of Universalist books and ideas within family and friendship circles.[7] There were probably no more than a few Universalist families in Ballston when the Brownsons settled there around 1817. The Universalist society had peaked in the first decade of the century, and was already in decline. By the time Stephen R. Smith recorded its brief existence in the 1840s, it had "long since lost its identity and merged in neighboring societies" – chiefly that of Saratoga Springs, which called its first minister in 1825 and hosted the Universalist General Convention in 1827.[8]

Ultra Universalism

Brownson was neither particularly captivated nor particularly distressed by the Universalism of Winchester, Chauncy, and Huntington. If his encounter with Universalism in Ballston had been confined to these writings and his aunt's commentaries, it would probably have made little impression on him. He later confessed to finding Chauncy's work "rather dull and heavily written," and retained a clearer recollection of Winchester's epic poem (which he judged "not equal to the *Iliad*, *Paradise Lost*, or the *Divina Commedia*") than of his theological works. He was most impressed with Huntington, whose "free, easy, flowing, and attractive style" he admired. In *The Convert* he gave a two-page summary of Huntington's argument, which suggests that he either remembered it very clearly or had recently consulted a copy – something he did not trouble to do with any of the other Universalist books he mentioned.[9]

There was little in any of these works to surprise or trouble a youth who had listened to the competing arguments of Congregationalists, Methodists, Baptists, and "Christians," and chosen the moderate "Christians." Brownson's experiences in Royalton had made him adept at negotiating contradictory religious claims, more likely to be stimulated than distressed by the prospect of a good religious argument. If he had found the notion of universal salvation less persuasive than the "Christian" doctrine of the destruction of the souls of the impenitent wicked, surely he could have refuted it, as he claimed to have refuted the determinism of Jonathan Edwards when he was nine.

Nonetheless, Brownson's encounter with Universalism in Ballston touched off one of the deepest religious crises of his life. In *The Convert*, he wrote that Universalism had "shaken my early belief in future rewards and punishments, and unsettled my mind on the most important points of Christian faith."[10] He placed the blame for his religious declension squarely on his family's Universalism: "With the aid of Universalist books, pamphlets & conversation," he told Turner, he was "soon a Deist, and before I was seventeen an Atheist."[11]

Why should his encounter with Universalism in Ballston have had such a devastating effect? An important clue is found in his reference to the effect of Universalism on his belief in "future rewards and punishments." None of the works recommended by his aunt would have shaken his belief on this point. Winchester, in particular, insisted most strongly that all creatures would be restored to a state of holiness and happiness only "after such as were rebellious had suffered in proportion to their crimes."[12]

The champion of "no future punishment" Universalism was Relief Brownson's one-time pastor, Hosea Ballou. Ballou's *Treatise on Atonement* (1805) represented a significant departure from the theology of the earlier generation of Universalists. According to the historian of Universalism Russell Miller, Ballou "gave Universalists for the first time a reasonably coherent theological system" (albeit a deeply unorthodox one).[13] He rejected doctrines generally considered fundamental to the Christian faith, such as the Trinity and vicarious atonement. Brownson conceded that Ballou's *Treatise on Atonement* "entitled him to rank among the most original thinkers of our times." He thought Ballou expressed his views "with wonderful acuteness and power, in language clear, simple, forcible, and at times beautiful, and even eloquent."[14]

Elhanan Winchester

Hosea Ballou

At the heart of Ballou's theology was his doctrine of human nature. He entirely rejected the idea that human beings, because of their own sins or the primordial sin of Adam, were deserving of divine punishment. Indeed, he did not accept the usual meanings of the terms "sin" and "punishment" at all. Human beings, in his view, were fallible because they were mortal. In creating humanity, "God saw fit, in his plan of divine wisdom, to make the creature subject to vanity; to give him a mortal constitution; to fix in his nature those faculties which would ... oppose the spirit of the heavenly nature." This carnal nature, prone to ignorant misjudgments about where true happiness lies, causes humans to commit actions which transgress divine law and result in misery. We may call these transgressions "sin" and the resulting misery "punishment," but for Ballou these terms did not carry the connotations of moral responsibility and divine judgment that they do in traditional theology. He frankly admitted that his system denied free will and made God responsible for sin. But he did not consider this a serious problem since, for him, sin was an inescapable part of mortal life. It did not affect the ultimate goodness of either the creature or the Creator. "God may be the innocent and holy cause of that, which, in a limited sense, is sin; but as it respects the meaning of God, it is intended for good."[15]

Ballou's "ultra" or "no future punishment" form of Universalism follows naturally from his understanding of sin. He denied that God ever inflicts suffering as a punishment, either in this life or in the afterlife. Since suffering is the natural consequence of sin, if there is no sin in the afterlife, there will be no suffering. In such a system, there is no need for Christ to offer himself as a sacrifice to satisfy divine judgment. Ballou asked, "If the Almighty govern all the affairs of mankind, according to his own appointment; if he were never disappointed; suffer no violation of will; but does, in all things ... support his own eternal system of divine goodness, what room do we find, for the necessity of atonement?" He answered that the task of the Mediator (his preferred term for Christ) was not to reconcile God to humanity, but to reconcile human beings to God – to free them from the blindness of sin, and allow them to see the divine love and goodness hidden beneath the apparent evil and suffering that plague human life.[16]

It was not Brownson's aunt, but a neighbor who introduced him to *A Treatise on Atonement*.[17] Perhaps the older Universalists in Ballston had reservations about Ballou's teachings. In his letter to Turner, Brownson referred to his mother and aunt as "Restorationists," the name taken in the 1820s by a group of Universalist ministers who opposed Ballou's theology and challenged his leadership in the denomination. Though it is unlikely that Universalists in Ballston were familiar with the term "Restorationist," Brownson's use of the word suggests a difference of opinion between the middle-aged followers of Elhanan Winchester and the younger generation, represented in the Brownson family by "a brother that was brought up under Mr. Ballou's preaching" (probably Daniel, the only one of the Brownson children old enough to have remembered Ballou's ministry in Barnard). Though Brownson did not accept all of Ballou's arguments, *A Treatise on Atonement* made a deep impression on him. It changed him, he said, from a "Restorationist" (that is, a Universalist of the old "Calvinism improved" type) to a "Universalist" (a follower of Hosea Ballou).[18]

It would take Brownson many years to sift through Ballou's treatise, rejecting some ideas, modifying others, and incorporating others more or less intact into his own belief system. An examination of the sermons and essays that Brownson wrote during his period as a Universalist minister shows how thoroughly he had absorbed Ballou's ideas, and even much of his language. Like Ballou, he argued that God "made us as he saw fit" and that our failings are the natural result of our constitution: "A limited and imperfect being like man, propelled to action by wants and appetites not to be resisted, must naturally in many things go wrong."[19] One of Brownson's sermons includes a paraphrase of Ballou's refutation of the claim that sin, being a transgression of an infinite law, is deserving of infinite punishment.[20] In an exchange of letters in a Universalist journal in 1828, Brownson championed Ballou's view that there is no such thing as love for God apart from gratitude for blessings received.[21]

Brownson adopted Ballou's ideas on atonement, and retained them even after breaking off his connection with the Universalists. His article "Justification," published in a Unitarian journal in 1831, contains an accurate précis of Ballou's theory of atonement or reconciliation:

> God loved man, but man loved not God ... We, not God, received the atonement, which was not a satisfaction paid to divine justice, but a commendation of our Father's love to us ...
>
> But we dislike the term atonement. As that word is now used it detracts from the goodness of God, destroys the freeness of his grace, and places us under obligation only to the son who purchased the divine love ... We prefer the term *reconciliation* ... Man was not reconciled to God ... could not enjoy the Divine Goodness, he could not appreciate his Father's love, nor enjoy the bounties of Providence, consequently he must be miserable. Christ came to remove this difficulty. He came a messenger from the throne of love.[22]

The Problem of Evil

Ballou's *Treatise on Atonement*, like virtually all Universalist literature and preaching in the early nineteenth century, was aimed at people coming from orthodox Calvinism. In order to be able to accept the good news of universal salvation, Universalists reasoned, people must first be brought to understand the weaknesses of the traditional doctrines: their logical inconsistencies, their objectionable implications, and the tenuousness of their scriptural support. The true nature of God, the universal loving Father, could only be revealed by destroying the false doctrines and assumptions promulgated by the orthodox churches. Hosea Ballou, in particular, went about this work with great gusto, exercising all of his wit, charm, and argumentative power in the effort to undermine orthodox faith.

The problem with this approach in Brownson's case was that he had no orthodox faith to undermine. He did not believe in election, reprobation, and eternal damnation. He did not need to be shown the weakness of those beliefs, nor exhorted to apply reason to religious questions. He was dealing with quite a different religious problem. He was struggling to defend his faith – that sense of the nearness of God that had been such a comfort to him during his childhood – against the challenges of Horatio Spafford's cynicism and Ballston Spa's worldliness. He was looking for reasons to believe, not reasons to disbelieve. That is why, despite all of the exciting new ideas that he encountered in the thought of Hosea Ballou, he found Ballou's version of Universalism an inadequate religious foundation on which to build his life. In *The Convert*, he classed *A Treatise on Atonement* with "some popular works openly warring against all revealed religion, indeed against all religion, whether revealed or natural." These works, he wrote, "had a pernicious influence on my mind. They unsettled it, loosed it from its moorings, and filled me with doubt."[23]

The "pernicious influence" of *A Treatise on Atonement* may have had less to do with Ballou's ideas than with his style of expressing them. Though Ballou was aware that "some may think me too ironical, and, in many instances, too severe, on what I call error," he did not hesitate to hold up sacred subjects to ridicule. In *A Treatise on Atonement* he made fun of the devil, the Trinity, the idea of atonement as satisfaction of a debt, and the Calvinist idea (memorably expressed by Jonathan Edwards's student and disciple, Samuel Hopkins) of "being willing to be damned for the glory of God."[24] Ballou's admirers thought his style witty, but his detractors, including some of his fellow Universalists, considered it unseemly and disrespectful. Adin Ballou, the distant cousin who later became one of the leaders of the Restorationist movement, wrote that Hosea Ballou and his followers "ridiculed revivals of religion; held all spiritual experience to be superstitious or fanatical; and expended nearly all their effort in proving, argumentatively, the naked tenet of universal salvation, as if that were the whole of the gospel of Christ."[25] Such a style was not calculated to comfort a mind beset by doubts.

Brownson's doubts came to center on the problem of evil. In an undated fragment written during the Ballston Spa years, he gave vent to a passionate cry of bewilderment and pain:

> Call you this God's World? To me it seems more like the devil's world, in which Ahriman, the prince of darkness is supreme. If God made it, and is all good and all powerful, why does he suffer it to be governed, ruined rather, turned topsy-turvy by his enemy whom he could crush, extinguish, with a look? why, if he made all equal, and is equally good to all, does he suffer inequality to prevail everywhere? If he is good, the good in itself, and is the maker of heaven and earth and all things therein, visible and invisible, whence comes evil?[26]

To this urgent question, the Universalism of Hosea Ballou offered him no satisfactory response. Ballou dealt with evil by more or less denying its existence. What appears to us to be evil, he taught, is merely the result of our limited understanding of God's beneficent purposes. Citing the Bible passage in which Joseph tells the brothers who sold him into slavery, "Ye thought evil against me; but God meant it unto good," Ballou commented, "But will this rule do, says the reader, to apply to all sin? I answer without hesitancy, that I fully believe it." In another commentary on the same passage he wrote, "Perhaps the reader by this time, is ready to say, according to this reasoning, there can be no such things as *real evil* in the universe. If, by real evil, he meant something that ought not to be ... I cannot admit of its existence."[27]

But what beneficent purpose could require God to inflict so much suffering upon his creatures? Ballou could only suggest that it was so that they might better appreciate its absence:

> Food for the body would never please the appetite, unless we first experienced hunger; the cooling spring would not be sought for, if men were never thirsty; health could never be prized, could we not contrast it with sickness; ease is appreciated, by the remembrance of pain; and a physician would never be wanted, if it were not for our infirmities; a Saviour would never have been praised, by his redeemed, had they never been in bondage.

Sin, likewise, was required by the scheme of salvation: "If sin and guilt had never been introduced into our system, the plan of grace, by atonement, could never have been exhibited."[28]

Brownson found this line of reasoning unconvincing. In 1828 he wrote this reply to the proposition that "if there had been no suffering, God's mercy could never have been exhibited in relieving it":

> Now I have long been familiar with this kind of reasoning, but have always been unable to perceive its force. We may as well say ... if a man had never broken his skull, the value of trepanning would have been a secret; but for me, I had rather have a whole head if I never learn the value of the surgeon's skill.

Of the idea that humankind will be happier for having been sinners and been redeemed, than if they had never sinned at all, he wrote, "I do not like this sentiment."[29] In another article he was more blunt: "'God ... has, in his wisdom, deemed it proper to inflict terrible evils on his children that they may know how to appreciate enjoyments,' it is said, and from time immemorial this stupid doctrine has been preached to justify tyrants in their usurpations and priests in the maintenance of their craft."[30]

These questions would continue to trouble Brownson for many years. Eventually he concluded that the meaning and purpose of suffering is a mystery, not given to mortals to know. Scripture tells us that God is good, and with that we must be content. The task of humankind is not to fathom the ways of the Creator, but to improve human society in such ways as lie within our power. "[God] made us as he saw fit. It does not become us to ask why he had made us as he has ... The question why Deity organized nature as he has is improper."[31] As yet, however, Brownson had neither philosophic resignation in the face of the unknown, nor faith in the power of human effort to overcome injustice. He remained tormented by unanswerable questions: Is there a God? Is God good? *Whence comes evil*?

To answer these questions, Brownson turned to books on "natural theology," an approach to religion that rejects revelation as a source of information about God and relies instead on what can be deduced from observation of the natural world. Brownson probably began his reading with William Paley's *A View of the Evidences of Christianity* (1794) and *Natural Theology* (1802).[32]

Paley's works were popular with evangelical Christians and Universalists alike. Around the same time Brownson was struggling with his faith, a young man named Thomas Whittemore confessed to Hosea Ballou that he was troubled with doubts as to whether the Bible was the Word of God. "You evidently have not looked into this subject critically," Ballou replied. "Get Paley's work on the evidences of Christianity." Whittemore did, and came to the conclusion that "There are proofs of benevolence in all the works of God. There is no evidence, anywhere in nature, of cruelty or partiality in him." He was so much reassured that he decided to take Ballou's advice and become a Universalist minister.[33] Whittemore's reaction was typical. Most readers of Paley were comforted by the idea that the basic truth of the Christian religion could be corroborated by external evidence, independent of the assertions of the Bible and the authority of the church.

Brownson belonged to a minority on whom Paley's arguments produced the opposite effect. "My doubts were first awakened by reading Paley's *Natural Theology*," he wrote in 1832. He craved a more logically complete proof of the existence of God than these works could provide, and was shocked to discover that the entire superstructure of belief in the existence and benevolence of God rested on such a weak foundation. Describing how Paley's well-meaning efforts started him down the road to atheism, he warned that "belief may be lost, or not produced, if we attempt to prove there is a God by arguments which are not sound, or by a method of reasoning which is essentially defective." Such reasoning, he thought, "*may* confirm him who already believes in an Almighty Architect, but it will never convert the atheist." Nor, he might have added, would it be very persuasive to one who felt as if he was living in "the devil's world, in which Ahriman, the prince of darkness is supreme."[34] With growing horror, he plunged into the classics of natural theology – John Tillotson's *Of the Principles and Duties of Natural Religion* (1683), John Locke's *The Reasonableness of Christianity, as Delivered in the Scriptures* (1695), Samuel Clarke's *Demonstration of the Being and Attributes of God* (1705) – only to find that they were no more persuasive than Paley.[35]

Brownson turned next to an examination of the nature and powers of the human mind. Perhaps, having failed to deduce the existence of God from the evidence of nature, he hoped to convince himself that the fault lay in the inherent limitations of his powers of deduction. The major work on this subject was John Locke's *Essay Concerning Human Understanding* (1690), which he had read back in Royalton. Locke taught that knowledge arises from sensation and reflection, thus reinforcing the contention of natural theology that knowledge of God must come from the external world. Brownson also mentioned having read works by the Scottish "common sense" philosophers Thomas Reid and Dugald Stewart. These probably included Reid's *Inquiry into the Human Mind on the Principles of Common Sense* (1764) or *On the Intellectual Powers of Man* (1785) and Stewart's *Elements of the Philosophy of the Human Mind* (1792). In *The Convert*, Brownson cited *Lectures on the Philosophy of the Human Mind* (1820), by Stewart's disciple Thomas Brown, as the book which "drove me into speculative Atheism."[36]

Paley and the other writers on natural theology had convinced Brownson that God was not to be found in the external world. If, as Locke and the common sense philosophers insisted, sensory perception of the external world was the only sound basis for knowledge, then, he reasoned, his subjective sense of the presence of God must be a mere illusion. He wrote of this period, "The more I read the stronger grew my skepticism. Inclination, interest, early habit, and even a lively sensibility to devotion, struggled against it in vain. I stood upon the precipice, I looked down the abyss of atheism, ready to take the awful plunge."[37]

Yet he did not take the plunge. His religious feelings, though weaker than in the "hallowed days" of his childhood, were never entirely extinguished. Unable either to believe or to disbelieve, he felt that he was wandering "in a labyrinth of doubt, with no Ariadne's thread to guide me out to the light of day."[38]

CHAPTER 4

Presbyterianism and Despair

Of all Protestant theories, Calvinism, though the most revolting, is the least inconsistent with itself.

– Orestes Brownson, "The Bible Against Protestants"

Becoming a Presbyterian

Shortly after his nineteenth birthday, with his religious crisis still unresolved, Brownson left the printing office and entered Ballston Academy – the last formal education he would ever have. After two years as an apprentice and one as a journeyman, he had saved enough money to fulfill his ambition of continuing his education. Ballston Academy offered both an English and a classical curriculum to students ranging in age from ten to the mid-twenties.[1] Henry Brownson claimed that his father acquired "some Latin and less Greek," but this allusion to Ben Jonson's famous comment about Shakespeare should not be taken literally. It is unlikely that Brownson studied either Latin or Greek at the Academy, though he did once attempt, with little success, a couple of sentences in Latin in his diary.[2]

After leaving the printing office, which had been his only real home for the past three years, Brownson suffered greatly from loneliness. The diary that he kept during his nineteenth year is full of laments for his friendless state. "O Heaven if aught on earth thou grant me, grant me a friend," he prayed. "O let me when adversity presses hard upon me when misfortunes overwhelm me let me find some kindred soul to whom I may reveal the sources of my grief, some affectionate bosom to sooth my afflictions with the balm of kindness!"[3]

> Mark the friendless man! He live alone in the midst of thousands. Day and night successively bring pleasure to those surrounding him ... but alas no pleasure for him, he meets no welcome look no glad voice strikes his ear the musick of the grove is a melancholy plaint that distracts his mind ... No one says to me we are friends let us by mutual love soften the cares of life and smooth the rigours of fate.[4]

Cut off from both human companionship and the consolations of religion, with no trusted mentor in whom he could confide, Brownson sank into a deep depression.[5] In *The Convert* he reconstructed his mental state in the fall of 1822: "I know not what to believe. I know not what to do. I know not whence I came, why I am here, or whither I go. My life is a stream that flows out of darkness into darkness ... My heart is sad, and I see nothing to hope for, or to live for. For me heaven is dispeopled, and the earth is a desert, a barren waste."[6] In this miserable state, he grasped at a desperate remedy: he embraced the Calvinism he had been steadfastly resisting since he was eight years old.

In *The Convert*, Brownson described his first impulsive visit to a Presbyterian church. This was not the church in Ballston that he later joined, but a small congregation without regular preaching, formed less than three years before, following a revival in the neighboring town of Malta.[7]

> One day, when I was about nineteen years of age, I was passing by a Presbyterian meeting-house. It was Sunday, and the people were gathering for the service. The thought struck me that I would go in and join with them ... It was long since I had been in a house of worship. The singing was, perhaps, not very good, but it affected me, even to tears ... I went out from that meeting-house much affected, and feeling that I had missed my way. As I pursued my journey, I could not help asking myself what I had gained by my speculations, and why it was that I must have no sympathy with my kind; why I must stand alone, and find no belief to sustain me, and have no worship to refresh me.[8]

A few days after this first visit to a Presbyterian church, Brownson went to see Reuben Smith, the minister of the Ballston Presbyterian Church. In keeping with the church's practice – typical of New Light or evangelical churches – he was required to "tell his experience," that is, to satisfy the minister and the Session of the church that he had experienced the saving grace of God. He related the story of his "Christian" conversion and subsequent backsliding, expressed a desire to rejoin the religious community, and was accepted for membership.[9]

In *The Convert* Brownson claimed that at the time he joined the church, he was as unconvinced as ever of the Calvinist theology which the church espoused. He was, however, so distressed by the direction in which his reason was leading him that he grasped at religious authority – any religious authority – as a bulwark against atheism.[10] Reuben Smith disputed this account, saying that Brownson had not professed "peculiar views" in his examination before the Session, and would not have been accepted for membership if he had. He suggested that Brownson's concern with religious authority was "the merest dream of after years," that is, of the period after Brownson's conversion to Catholicism.[11] But though Brownson probably did not reveal his "peculiar views" at the time of his examination, it appears that he did join the church with mental reservations. In his letter to Turner, written a decade before he converted to Catholicism, he wrote, "I did not believe Presbyterianism. But I had resolved to surrender <u>Reason</u>, to be guided by <u>authority</u>."[12] His diary from his Presbyterian period bears out his contention that he "had never believed or professed to believe, except on the authority of the Presbyterian church," the specifically Calvinist doctrines taught by the church.[13] He willed himself to accept the teachings, but that is not the same as believing them.

If he did not believe its doctrines, why did Brownson join the Presbyterian Church? He told Turner that he "was found by a presbyterian clergyman," but in *The Convert* he indicated that he initiated the contact with Reuben Smith.[14] His emotional response to the service he attended in Malta suggests that he hoped to find companionship and a supportive community, but that does not explain why he chose to join the church in Ballston Centre instead of the small congregation whose service had moved him to tears.

Brownson may have chosen the Ballston Presbyterian Church for a very simple reason: because he knew people who belonged to the church. This factor is generally overlooked, because Brownson made such a point of his loneliness and isolation. But he did have relationships in Ballston. In *The Convert*, just a paragraph after he asked "why it was that I must have no sympathy with my kind; why I must stand alone," he wrote:

> Was I not told in the outset that, if I followed by own reason, it would lead me astray, that I would lose all belief, and find myself involved in universal doubt and uncertainty? Has it not been so? In attempting to follow the light of reason alone, have I not lost faith, and plunged myself into spiritual darkness? I did not believe what these people said, and yet, were they not right? They were.[15]

If he was truly as alone as he claimed, who were these mysterious "people" who had tried to warn him of his danger?

Brownson's closest relationship in Ballston was with his former employer, James Comstock. He had worked closely with Comstock for three years and may have lived in his household. He was probably acquainted

John W. Taylor

with Reuben Sears, Comstock's brother-in-law and business partner. And he certainly knew – at least by reputation – John W. Taylor, the hero of the People's Party, Speaker of the U.S. House of Representatives in 1820-21, and founder of Ballston Academy.[16] All three of these men were pillars of the Ballston Presbyterian Church. All three held moderate to liberal views on religion. They were interested in the spread of "Christianity" (meaning, probably, some form of Reformed Protestantism) but disinclined to quibble over fine points of doctrine.

John W. Taylor, the most prominent of the three, was also the most deeply religious. He had entered college with the intention of becoming a minister, but switched to law when confronted with the rigors of orthodox Calvinist theology. As a young man living in the logging settlement of Hadley, New York, he had organized a religious society, which was rejected by the Albany Presbytery for denying "that God before the creation of man ... appointed a certain portion of any race to everlasting misery."[17] During the period when Brownson knew him, Taylor belonged to the Presbyterian church (later in life he became an Episcopalian), but his favorite projects were interdenominational. In 1815 he was among the founders of the

Saratoga County Bible Society. In 1819 he organized a Union Sunday School which met at the Baptist church in Ballston. The students in his adult Bible class included James Comstock, Reuben Sears, and their wives.[18]

Reuben Sears was an ordained Presbyterian minister, though he never accepted a pulpit outside Ballston. He preached in the Ballston Presbyterian Church when the church was without a minister in 1815-16 and again in 1829-30.[19] He was no dour Calvinist divine, but a genial booster of Ballston and its mineral springs. In his *Poem on the Mineral Waters of Ballston and Saratoga* (1819), he celebrated "the polish'd multitudes" who "fill up and throng / Our little towns, and o'er these rural scenes / Splendor, and life, and gaiety diffuse." In another of his poems, he celebrated Philosophy, "Thou dost exalt the human race / To man imparting dignity and grace." He credited philosophy, not religion, with teaching the difference between right and wrong, subduing unruly passions, giving strength to bear sorrow and disappointment, and filling the soul with peace and contentment.[20]

Brownson's mentor and employer, James Comstock, was a member of the Presbyterian church and a teacher and director of the Union Sunday School.[21] He seems to have been comfortable in the Reformed mainstream, but was tolerant of widely divergent forms of Christianity, from Universalism to Roman Catholicism. The "Religious Intelligence" columns of his newspapers, with their reports of revivals, notices of meetings of Bible and missionary societies, and anecdotes of the conversion of Jews and Turks, show a general orientation toward evangelical Protestantism, but no particular denominational bias. He gave equal space to the proceedings of the General Assembly of the Presbyterian Church and the London Yearly Meeting of Friends. He even noted with approval the activities of Jesuit missionaries in China, expressing the hope that Protestants would follow their example.[22] Like his newspaper reporting, his book printing and publishing business was denominationally and theologically diverse. He printed books, sermons, and reports for Universalists, Methodists, and Baptists as well as for Presbyterians.[23] In fact, he is sometimes erroneously referred to as a Universalist, because the first book he printed was an edition of a Universalist work, Elhanan Winchester's *Lectures on the Prophecies*.[24]

Taylor, Sears, and Comstock lived upright but essentially worldly lives, balancing their concern for the next world with significant achievements in this one. As such, they would have made attractive models for Brownson at the outset of his adult life. He, too, had worldly cares in addition to his religious troubles. He was acutely aware of his limited education, and frustrated by his circumscribed prospects. In his journal he noted briefly, "Believe Ambition the greatest temptation," then crossed out "temptation" and wrote "destroyer of happiness."[25] If he took Taylor, Sears, and Comstock as typical of the membership of the Presbyterian Church, he had every reason to expect to find in the church a mild and tolerant form of Reformed faith, perhaps something like the liberal Congregationalism of his foster family back in Royalton.

It is impossible to know how much Brownson's decision to join the Presbyterians was influenced by the example of these men. Did Comstock ever counsel him about religion, or suggest that he might find answers to his questions at the Presbyterian church or the Union Sunday School? Brownson did not say so; but Brownson was in the habit of exaggerating his friendlessness. For all we know, Comstock might have been urging him for years to consult the Presbyterian minister about his doubts. At the very least, Brownson knew before he attended his first Presbyterian service that it was the church of people he respected and admired. It was natural, therefore, for him to be curious about what the church had to offer; natural for him to yield to the impulse to go in to a service; and natural for him to follow up his positive experience at the church in Malta with a visit to Reuben Smith.

A Troubled Youth among the Presbyterians

In joining the Ballston Presbyterian Church, Brownson had united with a form of religion that was most unlikely to bring him the peace he sought. Reuben Smith was a kind, fatherly, and, in his way, tolerant man; he warned against excessive "zeal for non-essential points of doctrine" and taught that those "not belonging to us in denomination ought not to be wounded in their feelings."[26] Unhappily for Brownson, however, he preached a doctrine that combined the most uncompromising features of Calvinism and evangelicalism.

As an orthodox Calvinist, Smith believed that God had selected for salvation only a portion of the human race: "The condition of the Father to [Christ] was, that *'a seed should serve him'* ... This seed, thus given to him, were ... called *his people – his sheep – his chosen ones*, long before they came into existence." The means by which God called the chosen ones was regeneration, "a radical and immediate change" initiated by God. Without regeneration, the human heart is hopelessly corrupt. Smith decried the notion that "natural morality" could suffice for salvation. "What necessity could there be, on such a supposition, for the gift of a Saviour? Would he have made the sacrifices he did, if mere morality could have saved the sinner?"[27]

On the other hand, Smith was an evangelical who presided over five revivals between 1816 and 1823.[28] His writings evince an anxiety about salvation which seems at odds with the doctrines of unconditional election and irresistible grace. His preaching sounded the notes of danger, guilt, and dread:

> Do not tell us you can do nothing for your new birth, and therefore you are excusable – that even to-day it have been declared, it must be of God. If it be so, that does not remove your danger: If it be so, your guilt remains ... you must be born again, sinner, and dreadful is your danger – awful and imminent is your cause of alarm, if you be not![29]

Smith laid great stress on the importance of self-examination to determine whether or not one was among the elect. In his lectures for the newly converted he wrote:

> *What importance is ... attached to the work of self-examination!* A leading object of religious examination is to determine this great question, if possible, whether we have experience of regeneration. But what a question this is! ... it has the most stupendous consequences attached to it; for, says the word of God, except a man *do* possess this change, he cannot enter the kingdom of heaven. ... If this whole world were at stake – if the examination we were about to make should determine whether it was to be burnt up tomorrow, it could not be a question of so much moment as that we attempt to settle when we set down to examine ourselves.[30]

Brownson, an eager pupil, quickly began to profess these beliefs as his own. In December 1822 he began keeping a spiritual diary, in which he conscientiously berated himself for his sins and shortcomings, and lamented the coldness and indifference of his heart. Instead of reading Thomas Paine and John Locke, on Smith's recommendation he was now studying self-examination manuals such as *The Almost Christian Discovered* (1661) by the seventeenth-century Puritan Matthew Mead, and *Closet Companion* (1790) by the English Evangelical minister George Burder. These works encourage the reader to search his heart for evidence of regeneration while simultaneously reminding him that, as Brownson exclaimed in his diary, "Nothing is more deceptious than the heart of man!" In February 1823 he wrote, "O my soul ... hast thou learned that sin is the origin of death? and that unless thou art been washed in the regeneration thou will feel its sting forever? does thou still feel the sting of death? hast thou no peace with God? if not, where art thou Man – Believe self examination an all-important thing."[31]

Brownson tried hard to persuade himself that in the Presbyterian church he had found a refuge from loneliness and unbelief. About two months after joining the church, he wrote in his diary, "Doest thou not feel thy heart to glow with gratitude to this great Preserver? Yes, for he ... has taken my feet from a horrible pit and placed them upon a sure foundation."[32]

By rejecting his mother's Universalism and joining his father's church, Brownson was signaling his desire for independence from his mother and her family. This must have been a disappointment to the family, especially to the aunt who had tried so hard to win him for the Universalists, but his relatives did their best to be gracious. His cousin Loring Delano wrote rather stiffly, "You appear to have changed your principles of Religion. I hope that you have changed for the better which I have no reason to doubt but you have." Loring's younger brother Moreau, who was the same age as Orestes and the cousin he was closest to, wrote in a more sympathetic vein. Focusing on the hope of relief from his cousin's painful doubts, he wrote, "I rejoice to hear that you have been brought to a knowledge of the Lord Jesus Christ and hope that you will continue to live in the love and knowledge of him for in that consists all the real happiness that is to be found in this world or the world to come."[33]

Yet membership in the Presbyterian church did not resolve Brownson's doubts. It merely added new layers of perplexity to his religious difficulties. Despite his best efforts he could not really believe in the view of God and humanity put forth by his new church. He attended Smith's lectures "for the better doctrinal instruction of the rising generation," but there was an important difference between him and the other members of the class. Most of the young people whom Smith regarded "in the endearing relation of spiritual children" had recently undergone a conversion experience. The lectures were designed to instruct them in the rudiments of Reformed theology and the responsibilities that came with their new condition.[34] Brownson, however, had no such recent assurance of salvation to buoy him up. He absorbed the warnings and threatenings of evangelical Calvinism without having tasted any of its joys. To his original, still unresolved doubts about the nature and existence of God was added the fear that the Calvinist view might be right, in which case he could find no very hopeful grounds for counting himself among the elect.

As time went on, a new fear emerged: that the Calvinist view was *not* right, and that he had done a great wrong in allying himself with it. His guilt and shame over having joined the church is a measure of how deeply he had absorbed the Universalist view of "the orthodox" as an oppressive power. He seemed to feel that uniting with them was not merely a mistake but a betrayal. "I soon regretted what I had done," he told Turner. "I thought I had done a great sin, in becoming a Presbyterian. It preyed upon my mind, so long and so painfully that insanity was the result, for a time." His son Henry, on reading his father's diary of the Presbyterian period, agreed, "Evidently he was losing his wits."[35]

"Insanity" is too strong a term for Brownson's mental condition, but it is clear from his diary that he was suffering from depression. "Would to heaven my heart was more insensible than steel or endowed with power adequate to the scenes which haunt it," he exclaimed. "I languish in despair. What can alleviate a mind burdened with painful recollection?" He noted the instability of his moods, "one moment ... nearly happy the next black despair reigns triumphant." In his happier moments, Brownson could look on his black moods with a degree of philosophical detachment: "There is a certain melancholy heaviness which sometimes hangs over my mind and clouds all my prospects ... Nothing when it approaches can avert it. It comes and goes of its own accord."[36] At other times the gloom was inescapable:

> O Contemplation! ... When thinking over all the miseries of life how thou raisest the swelling tears to sympathize for others woes! Now to rest – but O my God grant that these sad forbodings which hang over my soul may disappear and one ray of hope may beam afresh upon a melancholy heart.[37]

Beneath this last entry, "How sad the above!" is written in a different handwriting – either that of the older Brownson or, as Patrick Carey suggests, that of his son Henry.[38]

For one in Brownson's state of mind, Calvinistic introspection was about the worst possible spiritual discipline he could have practiced. The minister's assurance that "despair can never gain a foothold" in the regenerate heart, though meant to be encouraging, was a dangerous doctrine for one already in despair.[39] The doctrine of total human depravity resonated with his unhappy state of mind, as in this New Year meditation:

> Reflect, O my soul on what has employed thee during this year ... hast thou done nothing which causes shame and regret? nothing which makes thee mourn and condemn thyself, as vile in the sight of God – nothing which makes thee abhor thyself "in dust and ashes" and cry "unclean unclean"?

> Yes, I have sinned every day, every hour, yea and every breath has been drawn in inequity every thought and every imagination of my heart has been evil only evil and that continually.[40]

In his meditation on *The Almost Christian Discovered* he wrote, "who among us does not, when temptation offers, find himself possessed of principles at which humanity shudders and which he himself would not have believed to have been in the breath of any individual not even in the most abandoned malefactor."[41]

In these and other passages from Brownson's diary, he made use of formulaic expressions gleaned from the Bible and other religious books, sermons, lectures, and hymns. Other entries show the influence of the sentimental novels that he read, then castigated himself for reading. (Such books were "calculated to vitiate the mind and to corrupt the morals," he noted in his diary. "Instead of fortifying the mind against the attacks of vice, they lay it open for the reception of every romantick scene."[42]) One may wonder, then, whether these entries express genuine emotional distress or fashionable romantic melancholy. Although Brownson did experiment with literary genres in his diary – which includes fragments of fiction, essay, and poetry – his descriptions of his mental state, both at the time and afterward, indicate that his unhappiness was real and painful.

Flight

Brownson left the Presbyterian church after about nine months (not "a year or two" as he wrote in *The Convert*) in June or July 1823.[43] In *The Convert*, he gave what amounted to three or four separate explanations for his disaffection with the church. All have been challenged, even by such sympathetic biographers as Theodore Maynard and Thomas Ryan. "As always he is perfectly honest," Maynard wrote of Brownson's account of his experiences among the Presbyterians. Nevertheless, "he conveyed an impression that is unconvincing … one cannot help feeling that he was exaggerating."[44] Even the credulous Ryan thought that "he laid the darker tints on a bit too heavily."[45]

The first explanation Brownson offered is that he found, almost immediately after joining the Presbyterian church, that its members were a nasty, hypocritical lot, "animated by a singular mixture of bigotry, uncharitableness, apparent zeal for God's glory, and a shrewd regard to the interests of this world." They pledged themselves to avoid those they judged to be unconverted, but only "as far as possible, without sacrificing [their] own interests." Under the guise of "fraternal affection," they spied and informed upon one another with sanctimonious glee. "I was not long in discovering that this meant that we were each to be a spy upon the others, and to rebuke, admonish, or report them to the Session. My whole life became constrained. I dared not trust myself, in the presence of a church member, to a single spontaneous emotion; I dared not speak in my natural tone of voice, and if I smiled, I expected to be reported."[46]

Naturally, the Presbyterians did not recognize themselves in this portrait. When *The Convert* was published, Reuben Smith indignantly responded, "That we ever made such a pledge, or used such language ... we utterly deny and repudiate."[47] And in fact, Brownson said only that he *expected* to be reported, not that he was. He remained a member in good standing for the duration of his stay in the church, and even something of a protégé of the minister, who encouraged him to consider becoming a minister himself.[48] Whatever his inward feelings, his fellow parishioners probably regarded him as a conscientious and pious young man. His description of the Presbyterians seems to owe more to his own overwrought state of mind than to his actual relations with the members of the church.

Brownson's second explanation has to do with the problem of authority. "The question with me was what not what, but whom I should believe; not what doctrines I must embrace, but what authority I was to obey," he wrote. "As to particular doctrines, they did not trouble me."[49] Having determined to abnegate his own reason and follow the dictates of the church, he would have persevered in doing so despite his personal discomfort, but the church failed to live up to its side of this implicit bargain: it would not relieve him of the responsibility of working out his own beliefs.[50] As Reuben Smith carefully explained on giving him a copy of the Westminster Confession, the Presbyterian church, like all Reformed churches, regards the Bible alone as the source of authority. Church councils, confessions, and the like may summarize what the church believes the scriptures to teach, but they do not themselves speak with ultimate authority. "This I regarded as unfair treatment," Brownson wrote. "It subjected me to all the disadvantages of authority without any of its advantages."[51]

Further pondering of the question of authority, he wrote, led him to wonder, "After all, what reason had I to regard this Presbyterian Church as the true Church of Christ?"

> If our Lord founded a Church and has a Church on earth, it must reach back to his time, and come down in unbroken succession from the apostles. But the Presbyterian Church is a recently formed body, not three hundred

years old ... Were these men [who founded it] authorized by an express commission from God? Did they act by authority? or did they follow their own private judgment, and against authority which they had previously recognized?

The conclusion was inescapable: "If Christ had a church on earth which he had founded, and which had authority to teach in his name, it was evidently the Roman Catholic Church ... There was no alternative. It was the Catholic Church or no church."[52]

The question here is whether this line of reasoning reflects Brownson's feelings at the time, or whether it is a critique of Protestantism which he worked out years later, after his conversion to Catholicism. If "it was the Catholic Church or no church," how was it that, within a few months of leaving the Presbyterians, he was considering rejoining the Universalists? How could he have committed himself, apparently whole-heartedly, to leadership positions in the Universalist and later the Unitarian church, if he had already rejected the legitimacy of the Protestant Reformation? Even if we accept his explanation that he did not seek out the Catholic church for another twenty years because of the anti-Catholic prejudices he had absorbed in the course of his Protestant upbringing, it may be doubted whether he really thought all this through in 1823.

The most plausible explanation for Brownson's rejection of Presbyterianism is the simplest: he left the church because he found its doctrines repellent and unconvincing. This explanation is, paradoxically, supported by two of Brownson's most implausible claims: that Reuben Smith told him, "time and again, not to ... read any book touching the grounds of my faith as a Presbyterian, or even to think on the subject," and that Smith found the Calvinist doctrine of election and reprobation "revolting to human nature" and "had tried in the General Assembly of the Presbyterian church, in 1821, to get it modified, or rescinded altogether, but failed by one or two votes."[53]

As many commentators have pointed out, these claims are, on the face of it, absurd. It is highly unlikely that Smith told Brownson not to read or think about theology, when he was holding classes on the subject, and preparing for publication his doctrinal lectures "intended principally for young professors of religion." The assertion that this obscure provincial pastor had tried to repeal one of the basic tenets of Calvinist theology (and had nearly succeeded!) is the most unbelievable of all. As Maynard put it, "belief snaps altogether" at this point.[54] Yet Brownson not only made these claims in *The Convert*, but reiterated them in the face of Smith's denial. "The facts are as stated in *The Convert*," he insisted. "In regard to the vote on the article or confession touching foreordination, the author merely states what his pastor, an old-school Presbyterian, we believe, told him. If the information is incorrect, the fault lies not with him, but with his informant."[55] Smith did not know what to make of this. "Is he willfully false?" he asked, "or can we adopt the charitable conclusion ... that he had probably forgotten, or retained only a hazy remembrance of what transpired."[56]

It is possible that neither Brownson's veracity nor his memory was at fault; he may have honestly, though mistakenly, believed that Smith had said these things. Smith wrote, "To deny that I ever offered such a motion in the General Assembly would be superfluous, since any well-informed Presbyterian would know, that a direct vote of this kind could never be thought of there."[57] Brownson, however, had never been a well-informed Presbyterian. He was not a product of the "New England way," but of the reaction against it. He did not belong to a religious culture that found Calvinism comprehensible. His haphazard religious education, cobbled together from broad but unsystematic reading and from a series of brief associations with disaffected liberal Congregationalists, "Christians," and Universalists, had introduced him to Calvinist theology only from the point of view of its critics. Never having seen it from a sympathetic insider's perspective, he lacked the background that Reuben Smith assumed in his congregation. This, coupled with his emotionally distraught state, might have been sufficient to cause him to misinterpret things that Smith said. His recollection of having been advised not to read or think about the grounds of his faith, for example, might have arisen from nothing more than a fatherly admonition not to distress himself so much, or a reminder that God's ways defy human understanding. If he failed to see the improbability of Smith's alleged proceedings at the General Assembly, it was because it was easier for him to believe that Smith found Calvinism revolting than to comprehend how anyone could find it acceptable, believable, and comforting.

Brownson's profound lack of sympathy with the Calvinistic world view could not be changed by "the act of an intellectual desperado" determined to renounce reliance upon his own reason and judgment.[58] In particular, the doctrine of total human depravity accorded poorly with the positive view of human nature he had absorbed during his childhood. True, human beings were prone to sin and error – even Hosea Ballou, for all his optimism, admitted as much. The unaided human intellect could not discover ultimate truth, and even such partial truths as reason could uncover were often overruled by unworthy passions. But to say that the human mind and will are subject to error and sin is quite a different thing from saying that human beings are incapable of doing or even of desiring to do good. Brownson wrote:

> The fundamental doctrine of Calvinism is, that man by his fall lost his natural spiritual faculties, and became totally depraved, incapable by nature of anything but sin ... A totally depraved nature is incapable of a rational act ... No, no, it will not do. We cannot build faith on skepticism; and just in proportion as we discredit reason, we must discredit revelation. Reason must be at least the preamble to faith.[59]

Whatever the faults or virtues of Reuben Smith and his parishioners, it would have been impossible for Brownson long to have continued in a tradition that cast doubt on the reliability of human understanding in the manner of the *Closet Companion* and *The Almost Christian Discovered*. Brownson was a natural intellectual. His belief in the value of human reason was beyond argument; indeed, it was what made argument itself possible. He might have decided to subordinate his judgment, for a time, to that of a respected father figure, but he could not be part of a tradition that considered reason itself to be illusory. As a result of his encounter with this tradition, the Presbyterians – who actually had a robust intellectual tradition, and the highest standards of ministerial education of any denomination in the United States – remained ever afterward for him the type of mental slavery. Years later he wrote in a Unitarian newspaper, "No one of right feelings but must be grieved at the bondage in which the general mind is held by the Presbyterian influence."[60]

By late July, 1823, Brownson's diary was recording renewed confidence in the powers of the human mind. By August the origin of human misery was once again an open question; evidently he had rejected the explanation that it was the result of original sin. He wrote, "Whenever I cast my eyes around me and discover the misery that every where exists I pause and in melancholy pensiveness inquire whether it be the unavoidable lot of our nature or the effect of our own misguided choice?"[61]

Leaving Home

There is in *The Convert* one final, revealing suggestion of what the Presbyterian church meant to Brownson, and why he left it. "The Church demanded I should treat her as a true mother, while she was free to treat me only as a stepson, or even as a stranger."[62]

Did this image of the Church reflect Brownson's feelings about his mother after their long separation? It is not hard to imagine that Relief Brownson might have demanded more in the way of filial affection than Orestes felt comfortable giving, while falling short of his ideal of what a mother should be. Both mother and son had had ample time to build up idealized images of each other during eight years of separation. When reunited, they discovered that their personalities, temperaments, interests, and skills were entirely dissimilar. Relief was barely literate. Her concerns, as evidenced by her letters, centered on the concrete details of day-to-day life. Orestes's fascination with abstractions, his reliance upon logical analysis, the books he read, even the vocabulary he used must have been almost incomprehensible to her. In emotional matters, the positions were reversed: she expressed her feelings in clear, direct, though conventional language, whereas he would struggle all his life to communicate his feelings. The result was mutual misunderstanding and disappointment. In his diary he wrote confusedly, "Parents jealous of for their children are continually destroying his happiness. Children disaffected wound his feelings and the fear that he shall not do perfectly right is a source of perpetual uneasiness."[63]

In adult life, Brownson's relationship with his mother consisted mostly of sending her small sums of money. Her letters to him run on two themes – humble gratitude for small favors and unsatisfied desire for more closeness – which made him feel guilty and defensive. He rarely visited her, though she wrote plaintively, "I want to see you and your family very much I fear I never shall in this world," and "We should have been quite happy & almost overjoyed to have seen you, for you are my youngest son, Orestes, & very dear to my heart." Though she assured him, "I feel under great obligations to you my Dear Son for what you have done for me in my old age poverty and affliction," he was uneasily aware that the gift of twenty or forty dollars, which seemed munificent to his mother, meant little to him. Despite her protestations, he thought himself "neglectful and undutiful."[64]

If he had hoped to find in the Presbyterian church a more satisfactory mother, or some sort of connection with his unknown Presbyterian father, Brownson was once again disappointed. The church turned out to be only another all too human and fallible mother, confusing and angering him with what struck him as unfair demands, demanding his loyalty but failing to earn it.

Brownson's separation from the Presbyterian church was a personal declaration of independence. Now almost twenty years old, he was ready to take his place in society as an adult. Immediately upon completing his studies at the academy, he took a job as a schoolteacher in the nearby town of Stillwater, New York. The following year he took a more definite step to distance himself from his family: like so many of his generation, he moved west. Life in the Ballston area had brought him little satisfaction. His apprenticeship had made him aware of his poverty but left him without the means to remedy it. The reunion with his family had been disappointing. Reason and liberal religion had led him to the brink of atheism, but his attempt at obedience and orthodoxy had brought only misery. He longed for a friend, but none had appeared. There was nothing to keep him in the area, so early in 1824 he left to take up a teaching position in Camillus, Onondaga County, New York, about a hundred and fifty miles west of his family's Saratoga County home.

CHAPTER 5

Journey to the West

Shall the cheerful circle of friends never hail me and bid me ... to the scenes of early life? Never greet thee O sun as thou risest over my native hills? ... For I have roamed from kindred and friends, joy of my youth & support of my life. To their soft caresses, their tender voices sounding with kindest accent, succeeds the savage yell & frightful raven's ominous call.

– Orestes Brownson's diary, summer 1824

Camillus, New York

When Brownson moved from Ballston to Camillus in the spring of 1824, he must have felt as if he was returning home. Like the Vermont towns in which he had grown up, Camillus was an agricultural community, only a generation removed from its frontier beginnings. It had been settled in the 1790s as part of a land grant to veterans of the Revolutionary War. In 1824 almost ninety percent of the householders were farmers. The population was about 6000, of whom about a third were school-aged children. Brownson was responsible for one of the town's 34 district schools.[1] He would have been expected to teach up to 60 students, of all ages and levels of ability, from toddlers to young men and women nearly as old as himself.[2]

With his extensive private reading and his year of study at Ballston Academy, Brownson was probably better educated than most district school teachers. Teaching was not yet considered a profession, though it was moving in that direction faster in New York than in most parts of the United States. Under the new state constitution adopted in 1821, an education fund had been established, which paid for about three months' worth of instruction in each of the state's 7000-odd district schools. Towns were supposed to match the funding received from the state, though not all did so. A report to the state legislature in 1826 recommended that teachers should have studied at a university or academy, that counties examine and license teachers, and that teachers be paid a living wage.³ As yet, however, teachers received very little cash salary, most of their compensation coming in the form of room and board in the homes of families in the district. Therefore, most teachers were young, unattached men and women who needed a stopgap for a year or two before settling down to a career or marriage.⁴

Little is known about Brownson's experience as a teacher, except that he did not find it particularly rewarding. In his diary, he quoted James Thompson's couplet, "Delightful task! to rear the tender thought / To teach the young idea how to shoot," with the comment, "But little pleasure find I in combating stubbornness, indocility, and natural dullness. It would have been nearer the truth in my opinion to have substituted 'tedious' or 'wearisome' instead of delightful."⁵ Still, he was successful enough as a teacher to obtain four teaching positions: in Stillwater during the summer and fall of 1823; in Camillus during the winter and spring of 1824; in Springwells, Michigan, during the summer of 1824; and in Camillus again in the spring of 1825.⁶

The most important result of Brownson's teaching career is that it brought him together with his future wife. Sally Healy was a daughter of the family with whom he boarded in Camillus. In Sally, Brownson found the friend he had fervently wished for. "O Heaven if aught on earth thou grant me, grant me a friend," he had written in his journal in 1823.⁷ Realizing that his serious nature unfitted him to sympathize with "this man's caprice that man's scorn – with this man's jest, and that man's laugh," he longed for "one confidential friend or some kindred soul with whom I can think and think without restraint."⁸ Sally became that confidential friend, a lifelong intellectual and spiritual companion. Henry Brownson described his mother as "better educated than was often the case in rural districts; fond of reading, especially in the Bible, in history and in poetry; and gifted with marvelous power of memory." He recalled that his father "often read his articles to his wife before publication, and attached great importance to her judgment; indeed, he often said that intellectually she was his superior."⁹ Orestes and Sally apparently talked of marriage as early as 1825.¹⁰ Any decision on marriage, however, would have to wait until he was settled in a business or profession.

More pressing than the question of his future career was the problem of religion. Camillus was in the heart of the "burned-over district" of western New York, where religious excitement was pervasive. Evangelical Protestantism was the dominant form of Christianity in the region. As usual, it was accompanied by its shadow, Universalism.¹¹ In the 1820s Universalism in

New York was in a period of explosive growth. Nathaniel Stacy, the pioneer Universalist evangelist of New York State, recalled that when he arrived in New York in 1805, he had found "one little society ... tottering alone." The Universalist clergy consisted of "three of the feeblest of the feeble advocates of [the] cause." By 1830, there were nearly 200 societies, over 80 ministers, ten associations and a state convention.[12]

In Camillus, Brownson found a flourishing Presbyterian congregation, which had just constructed a new church building; a small Methodist society; and a group of Universalists, without formal organization, served by an evangelist named Isaac Whitnall.[13] He was thus faced with the unhappy task of choosing among three religious paths, all of which he had already rejected. The Methodists' emphasis on the conversion experience and the terrors of hell had repelled him since childhood. His recent experience with the Presbyterians had shown him that, whatever he was, he was not a Calvinist. For lack of a more attractive alternative, he reluctantly began to reconsider Universalism. "When I was forced to admit that Presbyterianism had no authority in the matter," he wrote in *The Convert*, "I was necessarily forced back on the point whence it had taken me up, when I believed, so far as I believed anything, the doctrine of Universalism."[14]

Brownson's diary from 1824-25 suggests that he was proselytized by Universalists and anti-Universalists alike. "What misery is occasioned in society by discordance in articles of faith!" he sighed. He recorded his shifting moods as the argument over universal salvation raged around and within him. "Will all mankind be happy in another world?" he asked himself.

> Considering the question as it relates to revelation, I am surprised at the debates there have been. How men can differ so much in understanding a book which all have and all can read is to me incomprehensible. The opponents are men of the same morals, the same tastes, educated in the same manner by the same teachers. Ask if the sun is square or triangular both agree to pronounce it round, and each is confident that sugar is sweet and gall bitter. Why then this discordance on this question only.[15]

For a long time he was unable to choose one side or the other. Sometimes he seemed on the point of uniting with the Universalist minority: "Go not in the way of the multitude ... for they are preposterous." In the next sentence he drew back: "But I can see no reason for believing why the majority ... are more likely to be in error than a few ... Sentiments that have obtained common assent have been found to be productive of common good. And in general there is no more propriety in dissenting from them than there would be for a philosopher to refuse to [breathe] the common air."[16]

The diary also records Brownson's frustration at his own indecisiveness. Anticipating the criticism that would later be leveled at him by James Freeman Clarke and others, he offered a vignette of the religious seeker as a weathercock whose religious views shift with every change in the wind:

> The inquirer meets his friend. They converse on the subject of inquiry. Powerful reasons are alleged in favor of a particular sentiment. The inquirer can raise no objections. Freed from all restraint except an obligation to believe whatever has the appearance of truth (for he can judge only by appearance) he gives full credit to the opinions of his friend. Soon he meets another by [whom] different sentiments [are] proposed. The inquirer finds he had been premature in his belief, it is liable to objections ... Dissatisfied he seizes with avidity the next that [is] offered but soon renounces it in the same manner so he may go on ad infinitum.[17]

Springwells, Michigan

This was Brownson's situation when, in the late spring or early summer of 1824, he was offered a teaching position in the township of Springwells, Michigan, just outside Detroit. Leaving the religious question unresolved, he left New York and headed west.

Brownson stayed in Michigan for about three-quarters of a year, from the summer of 1824 to the spring of 1825. He probably intended to stay longer, perhaps to settle there permanently. Henry Brownson thought his father "went west with the idea of making Detroit his future home."[18] However, illness brought his stay to a premature end. Malaria, or "bilious ague," was endemic in the swampy, mosquito-infested lowlands along the riverbanks.[19] Henry Brownson wrote, "The Rouge River was little more than a sess-pool of malaria in August and September, and [Brownson] used to say that he could see the fever and ague spawn on that stream thick enough to cut with a jack-knife."[20] Brownson contracted malaria in the late summer or fall, and spent much of his time in Michigan ill or convalescing. Nevertheless, he remembered Michigan fondly. Forty years later, he was pleased to hear that Henry would be moving to Detroit, "a place somewhat dear to my recollection."[21]

Practically nothing is known about the circumstances that led to Brownson's moving to Michigan. Perhaps because the Michigan episode interrupted the main narrative of his struggles with Presbyterianism and

A view of Detroit in 1826. Note the spires of Ste. Anne's Church on the far side of the river.

Universalism, he did not mention it at all in *The Convert*. We do not know how or with whom he traveled to Michigan, who hired him as a teacher or how they made contact with him. Presumably he was engaged to teach at a "subscription" school – an informal arrangement by which a group of parents pooled their resources to hire a teacher for their children – for, except for a few educational initiatives of the Catholic church, all education in Michigan was by subscription until the first public school system was established in 1827.[22] Brownson must have taught a school of this type, but no details of his employment have survived.[23]

These unanswered questions are intriguing, because Detroit was an unusual destination for a young New Englander in 1824. It is sometimes assumed that Brownson moved to Michigan as part of the Yankee migration into the "Old Northwest."[24] However, Michigan did not attract substantial numbers of immigrants from New England until the 1830s. The population of Detroit actually grew more slowly between 1820 and 1830 than in the previous decade.[25] Whereas Ohio, Indiana, and Illinois had all become states by 1818, in March of that year the mostly French-speaking people of Michigan voted down a proposal to take the first step toward statehood by electing a territorial legislature. Even when a trickle of enterprising Yankees began settling in Michigan around 1823, they tended to bypass the Detroit area, with its pre-existing population of French Catholics, in favor of the interior wilderness, where they could establish new settlements similar to those they had left behind.[26]

In the 1820s the township of Springwells extended inland from the Detroit River, bounded on the south by the Rouge River and on the north by the border between Wayne and Oakland counties (present-day southwest Detroit, Dearborn, and Livonia).[27] Brownson lived well out along the river, eleven miles from the center of Detroit.[28] The predominant form of land use in Springwells was "ribbon farms," narrow strips laid out perpendicular to the river, extending from the riverbank into the forest. The population was largely French-speaking or bilingual; several of Detroit's most prominent French and Anglo-French families, such as the Livernois, Campau, and Knaggs-Labadie families, owned land in Springwells.[29] As a teacher and printer, Brownson would have been interested to learn that Springwells was the site of Michigan's first printing press, first newspaper (the *Michigan Essay, or Impartial Observer*, 1809), and early Michigan's most ambitious educational project, the Spring Hill School (1809-10).

Brownson later recalled that it was in Detroit that he saw his first Catholic church.[30] In the 1820s the Catholic church was the dominant religious and civic organization in the Detroit area. As late as 1825, the procession from Ste. Anne's to Springwells on the feast of Corpus Christi was a public festival for Catholics and non-Catholics alike, with the highest-ranking civilian and military dignitaries in positions of honor.

Ste. Anne's Church, Detroit, in 1818

Gabriel Richard

Father Gabriel Richard, the rector of Ste. Anne's Church in Detroit from 1798 until his death in the cholera epidemic of 1832, was one of the leading citizens of the Michigan Territory. Indeed, if Brownson did not meet him, it was probably because Richard was in Washington for much of 1824-25, serving as the territory's Congressional representative. It was Richard who had brought the printing press to Springwells, and had founded the *Michigan Essay* and the Spring Hill School.[31]

By the time Brownson lived in the Detroit area, Protestants had begun to arrive. The Methodists established a preaching station around 1810. In 1817 they built a log church on the Rouge River in Springwells – the first Protestant church in Michigan. Also in 1817, a group of Presbyterians, Congregationalists, Episcopalians, and Methodists banded together to form the First Evangelic Society of Detroit. Three years later the society built an interdenominational church, the First Protestant Church of Detroit, with a congregational polity, elders elected in the Presbyterian manner, and a Presbyterian minister who bore the Methodistical title of Bishop. In 1824 a separate Episcopal church was organized, and in 1825 the First Protestant Church became Presbyterian.[32]

It is unlikely that Brownson visited the Catholic church while in Michigan, unless on one of the public feast days when the entire community was invited. He probably also avoided the First Protestant Church, although its interdenominational membership meant that it was open to any Protestant.[33] He may, however, have flirted with Methodism, perhaps attending services at the mission church on the banks of the Rouge River. On Sunday, August 15, 1824, he copied into his notebook a verse from a Methodist hymn, "When Thou My Righteous Judge Shall Come," followed two days later by three additional verses.[34] There is some evidence that he received a visit from a Methodist preacher when he was ill with malaria that fall. Toward the end of his life, contrasting the Catholic and Protestant varieties of asceticism (much to the advantage of the former), he wrote:

> The most unhappy and disagreeable people we have ever known are your would-be pious Puritans, who know nothing of the sweetness and cheerfulness of the Gospel. We remember one of them, a minister, who came with unutterable groanings to visit us, when we were given over by our physicians, and thought to be dying. Not a word of the love and mercy of God had he to say, but talked to us of hell-fire and brimstone, till we could bear it no longer, and were forced to bid him "begone, and suffer us to die in peace."[35]

Brownson did not say when this incident took place, except that it was before he became a Catholic. If it was during his bout with malaria in 1824 – the only time he is known to have been seriously ill in his youth – then the minister in question must have been a Methodist.[36]

If Brownson did attend the Methodist church, he would have heard some of their celebrated hellfire preaching. An anecdote is recorded of a Methodist preaching at Detroit's Council House before the governor and other territorial officials: "You, governor! You, lawyers! You, judges! You doctors! You must be converted and born again, or God will damn you as soon as the beggar on the dung-hill."[37] This hardly seems like the kind of message that would attract Brownson. It must be remembered, however, that his religious options in Michigan were quite limited. He may have admired the Methodists' refusal to defer to worldly rank, and found their Arminianism less objectionable than the Presbyterians' predestination.

In the end, as in Royalton and Camillus, Brownson was unable to stomach the Methodists' emphasis on the torments awaiting the unregenerate. He remained without a church in Michigan, working out his religious questions privately and recording his thoughts in his notebook. The concerns that he expressed in the entries dated "Michigan" are the same as those that had occupied his mind in New York: the transience of earthly pleasures, the consolation of religion, and the baneful effects of superstition and prejudice.

Religion was not the only subject to occupy Brownson's mind during his stay in Michigan. In later years, he would write appreciatively of the austere beauty of the vast forest and of the region's distinctive French Catholic culture. At the time, these pleasures were overshadowed by the fact that he spent much of his time in Michigan alone and ill. Images of loneliness and abandonment fill the pages of his notebook. In one fragment, he described the thoughts of a man "alone in a meager cabin far in the woods beyond the residence of any human being." Several of the poetic extracts that he copied, and a short passage of original fiction, are written from the point of view of women seduced and abandoned by their lovers; perhaps he found this an apt metaphor for his friendless state. He also copied a verse from William Cowper's "The Solitude of Alexander Selkirk," about the shipwrecked sailor who was the model for Robinson Crusoe:

> My friends, do they now and then send
> A wish or a thought after me?
> O tell me I yet have a friend,
> Though a friend I am never to see.[38]

Beyond their possible personal application, the passages Brownson copied into his notebook show him making a determined effort to continue his self-education. In addition to passages from poems by Thomas Campbell, James Thompson, James Beattie, Edward Young, Erasmus Darwin, Isaac Watts, John Milton, William Cowper, Alexander Pope, and others, the notebook includes passages from Hugh Blair's *Lectures on Rhetoric and Belles Lettres* and Tobias Smollett's translation of François Fénelon's *Telemachus*, as well as Brownson's own notes on Adam Smith's *Wealth of Nations* and a biography of George Washington. It is impossible to tell how much his reading list reflected his own interests, and how much it represented the books that happened to be available to him. As in Royalton, he probably depended on borrowed books for much of his reading.

Brownson spent late 1824 and early 1825 recovering from malaria, then returned to New York. By March 1825 he was back in Camillus, where he returned to his teaching job and renewed his courtship of Sally Healy. The Healys and his other friends welcomed him affectionately, and filled his notebook with pages of poems on virtue, hope, and friendship.[39]

Effects of Brownson's Encounter with Catholicism

One of the great unanswered questions about Brownson's stay in Michigan is how much contact he had with the French Catholic population, and what effect this had on his later interest in Catholicism and French language and literature. With the possible exception of the Fénelon, none of his reading shows any French or Catholic influence. Since he could not at that time read French, he naturally concentrated his studies on the eighteenth-century British classics, supplemented with some recent American works. Still, it appears that his year in Springwells left him with a positive feeling toward Catholicism, and toward French Catholicism in particular. When his son was about to move to Detroit in 1867, Brownson advised him, "Doubtless there are still remaining in the city some old, wealthy, & respectable French families, with whom you will meet agreeable society" – suggesting that he himself had pleasant recollections of that society.[40]

What we do know is that, after his stay in Michigan, Brownson began to speak of the Catholic Church with respect, even affection. His earliest published writings on the subject appear in the *Gospel Advocate* in 1828. At this stage of his life he did not yet see Catholicism as a viable religious option. Like most Protestants, he thought of Catholicism (along with Judaism) as an obsolete religion, outgrown and superseded by a more advanced form of Christianity. Yet he rejected the common image of the Reformation as a heroic rebellion against Catholic tyranny. Instead, he spoke kindly of Catholicism as the parent of Protestantism – a flawed parent, it is true, but no less deserving of respect than human parents are, despite their shortcomings. His protective attitude toward Catholicism may be seen in one of his letters to the Presbyterian minister William Wisner, with whom he carried on a long journalistic debate during his Universalist period. The subject arose when Wisner was denouncing an Episcopal bishop for opposing evangelical revivals and prayer meetings. To show in what disreputable company this placed him, the Presbyterian wrote, "His allies and friends in this conflict, are the Deist, the Universalist, the Socinian, and the Roman Catholick." Brownson, speaking as a Universalist, objected to being classed with Deists, but otherwise expressed pleasure at being included in this company. In particular, he reproached Wisner for ingratitude to his Catholic forebears: "In my opinion, it would be better for you not to speak disrespectfully of the Roman Catholick. His church may have failings, but children should not divulge them."[41] In the next issue of the *Gospel Advocate*, Brownson returned to the image of Catholicism as the parent of Protestantism: "The church which was not improperly styled the 'mother of harlots' has begun her reformation and bids fair to outstrip her daughters in this laudable work."[42] Here Brownson's apparently anti-Catholic language not only contains a shaft aimed at Protestant churches (the "daughters" of the "mother of harlots"), but also shows an awareness of

Catholicism as a living faith, continuing to evolve, and in some ways more progressive than Protestantism.

During the 1840s, while his fellow Transcendentalists found inspiration in German philosophical idealism, Brownson followed his own path through the writings of French Catholic philosophers. These studies influenced his doctrine of the church and eventually paved the way for his conversion to Catholicism. When he began these studies Brownson was, by his own admission, "wholly ignorant of Catholic theology."[43] But he was also unusually free of anti-Catholic prejudice, so that a path which was closed to most Protestants of his time was open to him. One difference between him and most other New England Protestants was that, many years before, for a brief but important period of his life, he had lived and worked in a predominantly Catholic community. At a time when most American Protestants knew the Catholic church only as the villain of old stories about the Reformation and the Inquisition, Brownson had encountered it firsthand as a benign and living presence – the spiritual, cultural, and educational heart of a tiny outpost of civilization in the wilderness.

CHAPTER 6

Return to Universalism

> *I thus passed from so-called Orthodox Christianity to what is sometimes denominated Liberal Christianity. This was my first notable change ... In fact, it should not be regarded so much as a change as the commencement of my intellectual life, for I was as yet only twenty-one years of age.*
>
> – Orestes Brownson, *The Convert*

The Universalist Press

On his return to Camillus, Brownson took up the threads of the argument he had been having with himself since before he went to Michigan. The question was whether he could believe in universal salvation. After the failure of his attempt to become a Presbyterian, he was once again in need of a religious home. Might he, after all, find a place for himself as a Universalist?

Brownson approached Universalism cautiously, keeping aloof from Universalist meetings, but reading the Scriptures "and such Universalist publications as were then extant, or at least such as were within my reach."[1] Brownson's biographers have generally understood "publications" to mean books, sometimes confusing his re-examination of Universalism in Camillus with his earlier introduction to Universalism via his aunt's books.[2] In the 1820s, however, "Universalist publications" primarily signified newspapers.

The 1820s were something of a golden age for religious journalism. Changes in printing technology flooded the market with affordable, simple-to-operate printing presses, allowing clergy and evangelists of all stripes to produce modest periodicals at minimal expense. By 1830, the religious press had become, in the words of Nathan O. Hatch, "the grand engine of a burgeoning religious culture, the primary means of promotion for, and bond of union within, competing religious groups."[3]

Universalists participated enthusiastically in the proliferation of religious publishing. As Russell Miller noted in his history of Universalism, considering their limited resources and small numbers, "the publication activity of the Universalists, particularly in the periodical press, was little short of amazing ... an indispensable arm and extension of the denomination, way out of proportion to either numbers or strength." Between 1820 and 1850, Universalists launched 138 periodicals, though most were very short-lived.[4] In 1843 the Universalist minister Thomas J. Sawyer noted wryly that his colleagues seemed to believe that all that was needed to start a newspaper was "pen, ink, and paper, a pair of scissors, and credit ... to the amount of fifty dollars."[5] Since these papers were conceived as missionary enterprises rather than commercial ventures, and since the ministers who edited and published them often lacked business experience, they generally lost money. As regularly as they were begun, Universalist newspapers changed editors, merged, or ceased publication altogether. Still, they were a crucial means of reaching scattered Universalists in places too small and remote to have Universalist societies or regular Universalist preaching.[6]

The first, most ambitious, and longest running of the Universalist papers was the *Universalist Magazine*, a weekly founded by Hosea Ballou in 1819. (It lasted, through many changes of name, management, and format, until 1968.) In the early 1820s it was edited by Ballou and his disciples Thomas Whittemore and Hosea Ballou 2d.[7] Most Universalist newspapers of the 1820s were more modest efforts, issued monthly or biweekly and intended for a local readership. The various papers borrowed freely from each other, creating regional and national networks for the exchange of Universalist news and opinion. A typical issue featured a theological essay or sermon by the editor, or an exchange between the editor and a local "partialist" minister. The back pages contained minutes of conventions and association meetings, letters to the editor, poetry, obituaries, and news stories deemed favorable to Universalism. Tales of suicides brought on by hellfire preaching were popular, as were reports of excommunications and intolerance in orthodox churches.

Living in Camillus, Brownson would have been within the distribution area of three Universalist newspapers based in central or western New York: the *Rochester Magazine and Theological Review*, edited by John S. Thompson of Rochester; the *Herald of Salvation*, edited by Pitt Morse of Watertown; and the *Gospel Advocate*, edited by Thomas Gross of Buffalo. Besides these local efforts, several New England papers made their way to central New York. Hosea Ballou's *Universalist Magazine* had subscribers throughout New England and New York. The *Christian Repository*, edited by Samuel

Loveland of Reading, Vermont, was distributed by agents throughout New England and as far west at New Hartford, New York (near Utica). Brownson later recalled reading both the *Christian Repository* and the *Evangelical Repertory*, which was published for one year (1823-24) by Edward Turner of Charlestown, Massachusetts.[8]

The editors of the *Rochester Magazine*, the *Herald of Salvation*, and the *Gospel Advocate* were all "ultra Universalists." That is, they believed, like Hosea Ballou, that sin and its consequences were confined to mortal life; that the Bible passages that appeared to threaten hell really referred to some earthly catastrophe; and that what appeared to be evil was actually part of a beneficent, though obscure, divine plan. (In proof of this, they were fond of quoting Alexander Pope's *Essay on Man*: "All discord, harmony not understood / All partial evil, universal good."[9])

Though these papers added nothing new to his understanding of Universalism, they helped to restore Brownson's confidence in his ability to reason his way out of his religious difficulties. They held out the hope that reason, rightly used, could be applied to matters of religion without leading to unbelief. In the inaugural issue of the *Rochester Magazine*, the editor thanked "the benevolent Parent of intellectual nature, who has lighted up, in the human brain, the polar star of Reason, to direct our course ... between the scylla of unfeeling and irreverent skepticism and the dread charybdis of a yawning and gloomy superstition." He assured his readers that when he converted to Universalism, "his faith in the Christian religion was not weakened by the change of opinion." Orthodox Calvinism, he said, was more likely than Universalism to lead to infidelity, for it "depicts the Deity such an unfeeling monster, as to excite the love of Atheism in every benevolent heart."[10]

Brownson found such testimony persuasive and reassuring. Now, though he still bemoaned the cunning of his deceitful heart, he saw it not as evidence of innate depravity, but rather as the product of "superstition, bigotry and fanaticism" bred by churches that taught irrational doctrines and discouraged free inquiry. Superstition, he wrote, "fans the flame enkindled by the most disorderly passions that reign in the human breast."[11] He began once again to see human reason as adequate for the understanding of religious truth – at least for such understanding as was necessary and possible for human beings. Surely he need only use "the common sense allotted to him" and trust to God's justice and compassion for the rest. After all, God could not require of his creatures more wisdom than he had given them.

THE EVANGELICAL REPERTORY.

EDITED BY EDWARD TURNER,

Minister of the Universalist Society, Charlestown, (Mass.)

HOLDING FAITH, AND A GOOD CONSCIENCE......ST. PAUL.

VOL. I.   BOSTON, APRIL 15, 1824.   NO. 10.

For the Repertory.

A BRIEF STATEMENT OF REASONS FOR NOT BELIEVING THE
Doctrine of Endless Misery.
(*No. 1.*)

The writer of this Article is far from intending to exhibit all the objections to the doctrine of endless misery, or to produce all the evidence in favor of Universal Restoration; he only proposes to give a *brief* statement of some of the *principal* reasons which weigh against the one, and tend to support the other. In treating this subject, he intends to be governed by Christian candor, but still he will endeavor to state the objections in their full force.

1. *We do not believe the doctrine of endless misery; because it involves principles which shock every feeling of humanity, and are contradictory in themselves.* It is an essential ingredient in the doctrine of endless misery, that the suffering of the damned augments the joys of heaven! This is strenuously contended for by those who stile themselves *orthodox*, at the present day. They assert that the good of the universe requires the endless torment of a part of mankind, and that every degree of misery in hell will produce corresponding degrees of joy in heaven. I am sensible that the liberal part (if such they can be called) of the advocates for endless misery disclaim such principles, but still, I think their doctrine necessarily involves them. Although they generally reject the notion of God's universal decrees, they still contend that God overrules all things for good. This is not only contended for in direct form, but is a principle recognized in almost all their arguments. Now if all things are overruled for good, it is certain that the misery of the wick-

Brownson recalled reading the Evangelical Repertory, a Universalist newspaper published by Rev. Edward Turner.

On the question of universal salvation, he wrote: "For me who am but an illiterate youth to attempt to decide a question where Doctors cannot agree may seem the height of folly; but freedom of thought and opinion is our natural right ... I cannot see anything more wanting to decide this question than nature has given to every rational man."[12]

Despite the best efforts of the Universalist press, however, Brownson hesitated to declare himself a Universalist. He remained unconvinced that the Bible taught universal salvation. The most he could say was that he thought it "a far more rational doctrine than its opposite."[13] He had no trouble rejecting the "superstitious" belief that God had predestined any of his creatures to eternal torment, but this did not necessarily imply that all would be saved. In fact, some of the objections to Calvinistic predestination applied equally to universalism; neither doctrine left much room for free will.

The Biblical interpretations in the *Rochester Magazine* and the *Gospel Advocate* seemed to him strained and unconvincing. Was it really true, as the *Gospel Advocate* had it, that the sin against the Holy Ghost (Matt. 12:31-32) was the sin of denying one's own reason? Did the Hebrew and Greek words translated as "hell" in the Bible really signify only "that anxiety and trouble which are the effects of sin," as the editor of the *Rochester Magazine* explained?[14] The editors themselves seemed to be aware of the weakness of their Biblical interpretations; for though they obligingly provided Universalist explanations of the Bible passages commonly used against them, they also advised their readers not to pay too much attention to the strict letter of Scripture. "Particular passages" may be difficult to interpret along Universalist lines, the editor of the *Rochester Magazine* conceded; "yet no inference should be drawn from a few passages that would contradict the decisions of reason and the general tenor of scripture."[15] If Brownson were to accept Universalism, therefore, he would have to adopt a new understanding of the Bible: one which said, "The letter killeth, it is the spirit that giveth life, and we must not be held to a strictly literal interpretation. We must allow ourselves great latitude of interpretation, and look at the general intent and scope of the whole, rather than at mere verbal statements."[16]

This was not an unusual position for a Universalist to hold. For example, Adin Ballou, another reluctant convert to Universalism, expressed himself in very similar terms after searching the Scriptures for evidence of Universalism. For Ballou, however, this new understanding of the Bible was revelatory and liberating: he felt "a flood of light beaming on my mind and a host of new ideas taking possession of my understanding."[17] Brownson experienced no such joy, only a sense of loss. The Bible had been a comforting presence in his life for many years. Reading and memorizing it were among the happiest of his childhood memories. In 1824, while literally "traveling through the wilderness" in Michigan, he wrote eloquently of his love for the Bible:

> I find ... it conducive to my happiness. Traveling through this wilderness I want a guide, a compass. The Bible supplies their place. Discouraged by the many asperities of the road I want an animating vision of the country to which I am bound. This the Bible gives. Still disheartened and ready to faint I want a more intimate knowledge of the King of that country, his love, his goodness, & his nonchangeable nature ... [The Bible] guides through the labyrinth of life; moderates in prosperity, advises and supports in adversity; and gives joy in the hour of death; joy and assurances of a happier world.[18]

The truth, as Brownson later acknowledged in *The Convert*, is that he was not particularly attracted to Universalism. He was attracted to liberal Christianity, and Universalism happened to be the only form of liberal Christianity he knew.[19] He wanted a religion that valued and respected human reason, and Universalism did that. But what would it profit him, if he could strengthen his faith in universal salvation only by weakening his faith in the Bible as a revelation from God? For the moment, he was at an impasse.

The Restorationist Controversy

While Brownson was struggling to decide whether or not he was a Universalist, the denomination was in the midst of a crisis that has come to be known as the "Restorationist controversy." In its narrowest sense, the term refers to a theological question: will all souls experience immediate salvation upon death, or must they experience some period of probation or discipline before being, as the common Universalist phrase had it, "restored to holiness and happiness"? But the term is no more than a useful shorthand, for the differences between the parties ran deeper than any particular doctrinal point.

The controversy is generally considered to have begun in 1817, when Jacob Wood, a young Universalist minister in Charlton, Massachusetts, published a pamphlet, *A Brief Essay on the Doctrine of Future Retribution*, in which he attacked Hosea Ballou's theory of immediate universal salvation as unjust, absurd, "productive of immoral effects," "deleterious in its effects upon society," and tending to undermine religion by weakening the authority of the Bible. In order to explain away the Biblical references to future punishment, Wood charged, proponents of immediate salvation were forced to adopt an allegorical or figurative reading of the scriptures, which he dismissed as "sophistry." He accused no-future-punishment Universalists of "do[ing] away with the natural meaning of the scriptures, thereby loosening restraint, and strengthening the arm of infidelity."[20]

Theologically conservative Universalists such as Wood tended to see themselves as Christians first, beyond any narrow sectarian identity. They wanted to bring the good news of universal salvation to as many people as possible, a task which they felt they could accomplish more readily by building bridges to their orthodox neighbors than by antagonizing them. They hoped to win over other Christians to belief in eventual universal salvation by showing that finite punishment for finite sin was both reasonable and scriptural. They knew that the no-future-punishment position was so extreme as to alienate potential converts, and they were frustrated that the strident message of immediate salvation drowned out their own quiet evangelism.

Wood envisioned his *Brief Essay* as the opening move in a campaign to have the Universalist General Convention adopt belief in limited future punishment as an article of faith. He planned to bring a resolution to this effect before the Convention at its annual meeting in 1817. In case this failed, he sounded out some of his colleagues about the possibility of withdrawing from Universalist fellowship and forming a "Restorationist Association." In the end, finding little support for either of these proposals, he did neither. Though a majority of Universalist clergy probably did believe in some form of future punishment, they were not prepared to place this issue above the unity and inclusiveness of the Universalist denomination.[21]

The most Wood could accomplish was to arrange for two of the most prominent Universalist ministers, Edward Turner and Hosea Ballou, to debate the question of future punishment in the pages of a Universalist periodical called the *Gospel Visitant*. Once the most intimate of friends, Turner and Ballou were by this time somewhat estranged, but they entered into the *Gospel Visitant* discussion ostensibly as partners in a shared intellectual effort. The debate had the effect of widening the division between them. As the correspondence proceeded, Ballou abandoned the elaborate politeness of the opening letters and addressed his old friend in the sarcastic, belittling, hectoring tone that he was accustomed to use in his arguments with non-Universalists. The experience convinced Turner of the justice of Wood's complaints that Restorationists were treated disrespectfully by other Universalists.[22]

The *Gospel Visitant* debate, confined to a short-lived, small-circulation paper, was probably seen by few readers outside the immediate circle of the participants. The next phase of the controversy, however, coincided with the rise of a popular Universalist press, so that distant spectators like Orestes Brownson could follow its progress. In 1821, the issue of future punishment was aired in the largest-circulation Universalist periodical, the *Universalist Magazine* of Boston. The discussion of future punishment in the *Magazine* was not a formal debate but an unruly exchange of letters in which Hosea Ballou, Edward Turner, Jacob Wood, Paul Dean, and others mingled arguments for and against future punishment with personal insults and attacks on each other's honor and integrity.[23]

In September 1822, Turner, Wood, Dean, and three other ministers – Levi Briggs of Westminster, Massachusetts; Barzillai Streeter, Hosea Ballou's successor at Salem, Massachusetts; and the young itinerant Charles Hudson – met at Wood's house to draft a statement of the Restorationist position. In December, they published their work in the form of two articles in the *Christian Repository*. The first, "A Declaration to the World," proclaimed that Restorationism and immediate universal salvation "are distinct and different doctrines, and are incapable of being reconciled together," and that the doctrine of immediate universal salvation was subversive of morality. The second, "An Appeal to the Public," complained of the conduct of the no-future-punishment ministers, especially those who controlled the *Universalist Magazine*. Both articles were signed by Jacob Wood alone, though the Declaration, at least, had been approved by all six of the Restorationist ministers.[24]

The so-called "Appeal and Declaration" quickly became a *cause célèbre* in Universalist circles. By staking out a narrow theological position, and by threatening schism if their demands were not met, the six Restorationists had violated a long-standing Universalist principle: that no one who professed belief in universal salvation was to be excluded from membership on theological grounds. The denomination had adopted a formal profession of faith only reluctantly, in order to establish the legal standing of Universalism as a denomination. In 1803 the General Convention, meeting at Winchester, New Hampshire, had adopted a statement known as the Winchester Profession. Trying hard to balance the need for a corporate identity with respect for individual differences, the convention took pains to choose language acceptable to both unitarians and trinitarians, and to both believers and disbelievers in future punishment. This minimalist profession, less than 100 words long, reads in full:

> *Article the First*. We believe that the Holy Scriptures of the Old and New Testament contain a revelation of the character of God, and of the duty, interest and final destination of mankind.
>
> *Article the Second*. We believe that there is one God, whose nature is Love, revealed in one Lord Jesus Christ, by one Holy Spirit of Grace, who will finally restore the whole family of mankind to holiness and happiness.
>
> *Article the Third*. We believe that holiness and true happiness are inseparably connected, and that believers ought to be careful to maintain order and practice good works; for these things are good and profitable unto men.

A statement was appended, allowing particular churches or local associations to adopt "more particular articles of faith" for themselves, but recommending that they "exercise the spirit of Christian meekness and charity towards those who have different modes of faith and practice, that where the brethren cannot see alike, they may agree to differ."[25]

By subscribing to the "Appeal and Declaration," the Restorationists had transgressed the spirit of the Winchester Profession, and the Universalists' tradition of diversity and tolerance. In doing so, they had placed themselves so thoroughly in the wrong, in the eyes of most of their colleagues, that the justice of their original complaints seemed irrelevant. In June 1823, the six Restorationists were censured by the Southern Association, the regional Universalist association serving southern New England. In September, partly as a result of his involvement in the Appeal and Declaration, Turner was dismissed from his church. The 1823 meeting of the General Convention, held in Clinton, New York, was dominated by the controversy. Hosea Ballou 2d filed a complaint against Paul Dean, and Charles Hudson filed one against Hosea Ballou. They were tried before an ad hoc "Committee on Complaints" made up of ministers from New York State. Both were found innocent of any wrongdoing, but Dean resigned from fellowship with the Convention.[26] Many of the attendees found the proceedings distressing and embarrassing. The host congregation charged that, instead of fostering growth, the unseemly display of internecine wrangling at the Convention had cost them membership.[27]

The Clinton meeting marked the low point of the controversy. Shortly afterward, the Universalists moved to patch things up. In December 1823,

Turner, Streeter, and Hudson apologized and were reconciled with the Southern Association. In June 1824, Wood and Dean signed the same agreement, and Dean was admitted back into fellowship. These agreements marked a real, if temporary, resolution of the crisis. At the time, however, it was far from clear whether the Restorationists had been reconciled or had capitulated – especially since Briggs and Streeter left the ministry shortly afterward.[28]

Brownson was able to follow all of these developments through his reading of the Universalist press. At this stage in his life he identified with the Restorationists, for while he was not sure whether he believed that all would eventually be saved, he knew that he did not believe in the no-future-punishment form of Universalism. Beyond the specific issue of future punishment, he admired and respected the Restorationist papers, the *Christian Repository* and the *Evangelical Repertory*, and their editors, Samuel Loveland and Edward Turner. Both avoided the mocking tone that Brownson had found offensive in the works of Hosea Ballou. Loveland made a point of replying courteously to any correspondent – Universalist, Calvinist, evangelical, even Catholic – whom he believed to be interested in a sincere exchange of views, while firmly rebuking anyone who resorted to incivility or abuse. An editorial in the *Evangelical Repertory* warned against "a loose and light manner of preaching, calculated to excite levity in the young and thoughtless." Such preaching "leads the hearer to doubt the sincerity even of the preacher, and to suppose, that religion is valuable only as a source of amusement … [Religion] is of all subjects the most serious. It can receive no embellishment from human wit."[29]

Brownson also appreciated the Restorationists' attitude toward the Bible. They encouraged close and attentive study of the Scriptures, yet they were forthright in acknowledging that such study could be dangerous. Loveland wrote with sympathy and understanding of the distress that Bible study could sometimes produce in the conscientious seeker:

> If we meet with a sentiment in the Scriptures that seems to militate with our general and most pleasing view of God, it creates an uneasy sensation, and damps the lively flame that had been enkindled within. And it will be well when such a circumstance does not stagger and unsettle our faith, and lead us to conclude that the Bible is a mass of contradictions.[30]

Because they admitted the existence of divine judgment and discipline in the afterlife, the Restorationists did not feel the need to reinterpret Biblical passages as radically as did the ultra Universalists. This allowed them to use a more straightforward style of Biblical interpretation, less likely to strike Brownson as a tendentious twisting of the sacred text. In his essay on the parable of the rich man and Lazarus (Luke 16:19-31), for example, Loveland took issue with Hosea Ballou's idea that the fates of Lazarus and the rich man represented the acceptance of Christianity by the Gentiles and its rejection by the Jews. According to Loveland, the story refers to retributive justice after death, just as it appears to. Only the inference that the rich man's punishment will be endless is unwarranted.[31]

In reading Hosea Ballou's *Treatise on Atonement*, Brownson had objected to Ballou's belief that God is the author of all that happens in the universe, since this seemed to deny that human beings were morally accountable for their actions. For the Restorationists, free will was an issue of only slightly less importance than future punishment. In the first issue of the *Christian Repository*, Loveland announced two questions for discussion. One was, "Will any of the descendants of Adam be punished after temporal death, for deeds done before?" – the question of future punishment. The other was, "Does the fore-knowledge of God universally control the actions of man?"[32] The Restorationists answered that it did not. Turner wrote a series of articles on "Christian Liberty," arguing that intelligent creatures have freedom of the will, and that this freedom may be used as an occasion to sin.[33] When Ballou cited the story of Joseph's being sold into slavery as an example of apparent evil which turned out to be part of God's providence, Turner replied that God could override evil designs for good without making them any less evil. The doctrines of free will and future punishment were related, in the Restorationist view, by the idea that reformatory punishment is the cure for sin. Those who did not believe in such punishment, they thought, would be forced (like Hosea Ballou) to deny the existence of moral evil, or (like the orthodox) to deny that all sinners would, in God's good time, be restored to holiness and happiness.[34]

For all of these reasons, Brownson was deeply impressed by Restorationist Universalism as presented by Loveland and Turner. Years later, after both he and Turner had left the Universalist ministry, he told Turner, "Your little paper the *Evangelical Repertory*, your sermons published in the *Christian Repository*, have had no little influence in forming my mind."[35] If he were to become a Universalist, it would be as a Restorationist in the Loveland-Turner mold.

CHAPTER 6

The Moment of Decision

By the time Brownson returned from Michigan, he was clearly leaning toward Universalism. The later pages of his notebook are filled with arguments in favor of universal salvation. He copied a long quotation from Hosea Ballou 2d on the consolation that belief in universal salvation affords to the bereaved, contrasting the Universalists' comforting view of the afterlife with "a funeral discourse by an orthodox divine, to frighten a disconsolate family ... with the terrors of a dread day." He collected Bible passages supporting universal salvation, and argued that it is to the greater glory of God to save all miserable sinners rather than only a chosen few.

> Shall [the Savior] be contented with the first few that come? ... Will he be discouraged & faint by the way? Will he give over the search as wearisome & fruitless attempts with no success? Know ye the Lord fainteth not ... the word is gone out of his mouth & shall [not] return empty; it shall prosper in the thing whereunto he sent it.[36]

Still, he hesitated to declare himself unequivocally a Universalist. Pages of meditation on the Biblical passage "in thy seed shall all the nations of the earth be blessed" (Gen. 22:18, 26:4) end by concluding only, "This sounds something like Universalism."[37]

As Brownson hesitated, he learned from the Universalist press that the Restorationist controversy had been settled, apparently to the satisfaction of all parties. While he had been away in Michigan, the Restorationists' fortunes had improved dramatically. Edward Turner, who had been preaching at the town hall in Charlestown after being dismissed by his church, was now settled in Portsmouth, New Hampshire. Charles Hudson had advanced from part-time and temporary positions to a settlement in Hudson, Massachusetts. Turner had served as moderator of the General Convention in September 1824.[38] It appeared that denominational solidarity and tolerance had triumphed. There had been no schism. Modern Universalism was not as monolithic as Brownson had feared; the ideas of Hosea Ballou had not entirely supplanted those of Joseph Huntington and Elhanan Winchester, let alone those of Samuel Loveland and Edward Turner. Universalists were free to hold a range of opinions about salvation, the role of Christ, the Bible, and the place of Universalism within Christianity.

At last Brownson made up his mind. He had been searching for a middle way: a rational, scriptural alternative to the extremes of Calvinist orthodoxy on one hand, and Hosea Ballou's "modern" or "ultra" Universalism on the other. Loveland and Turner presented Restorationism as that middle way. Turner, for example, advised Universalists to "endeavor that, in avoiding one extreme, we do not run into another."[39] Now that the Restorationist alternative had been vindicated as a valid option within Universalism, Brownson was ready to throw in his lot with the Universalists. As he later explained to Turner, "I thought now I would make a compromise between reason and authority. I thought Universalism did it. I thought it rational, taught by the Bible and calculated to do good. With this conviction I became a Universalist preacher."[40]

Brownson finally declared himself a Universalist only after he had finished his teaching in Camillus and returned to his mother's house – and the bosom of his Universalist family – during the summer of 1825. At that time he resumed writing in the journal he had used during his Presbyterian period; perhaps it had been left behind when he moved west, and only rediscovered when he returned to Ballston. This brought him into a dialogue with his younger self. In 1823 he had written, "What end should regulate all our conduct? All sentiments of religion whether natural or revealed declare the glory of God to be the end." Two years later, he amended this to:

> All sentiments of religion whether natural or revealed declare the glory of God to be the end that should regulate all our conduct ... but ... what is the glory of God ... To glorify we must imitate his character. He is good unto all and his tender mercies are over all his works. To be like him we must possess the same benevolent spirit – God seeks the good of his creatures. The glory of God is therefore the good of his creatures. To glorify him we must seek their good.[41]

Brownson proclaimed his return to Universalism in his diary, in an entry carefully signed and dated, on August 12, 1825. In giddy pseudo-Latin, he wrote, "Amor est the Universalists Credo est Deus. Veritas filius Dei."* There follows this ecstatic credo:

> 1. I believe in one God, infinite in power and wisdom and of unbounded goodness, Creator of all things and absolute Governour of the universe.
>
> 2. I believe man is subject to vanity actuated by principles which are constantly involving him in unhappiness. All are alike subject to errour. All alike suffer the bitter consequence of their aberration. All have common wants – equal rights and equally regarded by Heaven.

---

* Roughly, "Love is the Universalists' creed is God. Truth is the son of God."

> I believe Jesus Christ is the Son of God. That the doctrines he taught are eternal truth. That he has exhibited the true character of God. That this character if exhibited to all men will reconcile all to their creator. That it will cause discord to cease sorrow and sighing to flee away.
>
> 3. I believe this character must be exhibited to all people, be preached for a witness to every creature and then every creature in heaven and on the earth and under the earth and such as be in the sea and all that is in them shall sing the songs of joy and peace forever and ever. Amen. Orestes A. Brownson.[42]

This would not, of course, be the end of Brownson's religious journey. Despite the momentary euphoria that accompanied his decision, his acceptance of Universalism was tenuous, reluctant, and incomplete. He had no intense conversion experience, such as other converts to Universalism described. Adin Ballou, for example, reported that when he became convinced that God would save all souls, "the heavens seemed to open above my head ... every doubt vanished, a vision of the final triumph of good over evil shone forth in majestic splendor, and my heart was filled with transports of joy."[43] Nothing like this happened to Brownson. He chose Universalism, despite his lingering doubts about whether the Bible taught universal salvation, because he believed it offered him the best hope of fulfilling his intellectual and spiritual needs.

Nevertheless, his acceptance of Universalism gave him a measure of peace. Shortly before he inscribed the Universalist creed in his diary he asked himself, "As long as there is no infallible standard [that] all with one consent agree to follow how shall we know what is the correct profession we should make?"[44] In *The Convert* he recorded his answer:

> The main thing could not be to discover and know the exact truth. That could not be what God required of us, for, if it had been, he would have furnished us with facile and infallible means of doing it ... So, even if Universalism should turn out to be not true, I need not disturb myself, if I developed my faculties, and conducted myself as a man. Consequently, as Universalism appeared to me the more reasonable of all doctrines known to me, I need not hesitate to profess and even to preach it.[45]

For a brief moment, poised between an outgrown past and an unknown future, Brownson was able to envision a compromise between faith and reason, and even to look on the possibility of error with equanimity. It was the tragedy of his life that such moments were so few.

Education for the Ministry

Almost as soon as he had made up his mind to embrace Universalism, Brownson began to prepare for the Universalist ministry. Now, at last, he would be able to realize a long-deferred dream. As he wrote in *The Convert*, "The earliest wish I recollect to have formed with regard to my future life was to be a minister of religion, and to devote myself to the work of bringing people to the knowledge and love of God. For this, I longed to go to school, to get learning, to grow up, and to be a man."[46]

Though ministry had been Brownson's childhood dream, it was in some ways a strange choice of profession, for he was still deeply suspicious of the clergy. In his diary he railed against "clerical machination and priestcraft" and referred to teachers of religion as "the crafty, the ambitious, and the designing." These attitudes did not augur well for his own career as a minister, or his relationships with his ministerial colleagues. In the brief period of euphoria that accompanied his return to Universalism, however, Brownson was willing to exempt the Universalist clergy from the charge of "priestcraft." Indeed, the idea of Universalism was for him inextricably tied to the idea of liberty of thought. As a Universalist minister, he hoped, it would be his task to encourage ordinary people to ask and answer their own religious questions, not to impose orthodoxy on a gullible public. "I deem it a duty not only incumbent on me but upon every individual who has the least share of common sense allotted to him to search diligently if these things be so."[47]

Undoubtedly, one of the strongest attractions that ministry held for Brownson was the opportunity it presented for him to acquire the rudiments of a liberal education. For years his diary had been filled with reflections on the evils of ignorance and the rewards of knowledge. On New Years Day, 1823, he wrote, "O grant that I may apply myself wholly to the acquisition of knowledge! for O how ignorant!" Later that same month: "I am at a loss what to call the world! I am ignorant of its materials! so ignorant that I am every day deceived with its appearances."[48]

After Brownson left the Presbyterian church, he transferred to education some of the hopes he had pinned on the church: that it would provide him with stability, ease his loneliness, and free him from his undisciplined passions and despairing moods. As he moved toward Universalism, he ascribed to education yet another power: the ability to stand against the forces of superstition. An educated person, adept in the use of reason, would not be forced to choose between "shuddering at the horrours of some hereafter" and "the horrid hope of annihilation."[49]

At times Brownson seemed to believe that knowledge was within his reach, if he would just make the effort to pursue it. "How heedless am I as thoughtless as though I had nothing to learn!" he reproached himself. "Say my soul are thou contented to yawn out thy life here in sordid ignorance? Shall others toil and win the prize and you sit inactive?" At other times he was inclined to blame his family, or his fate, for having deprived him of the opportunity to become one of "those towering geniuses which astonish the world." He seemed to be speaking of both himself and his pupils when he wrote, during his first term of teaching, "Considering that the greatest genius that ever lived was once but an 'embryo blossom' in no point superior to the common class of mankind I am surprised that parents take no more pains to draw out those hidden virtues of the mind."[50] Now he would have a chance to go back to school, to have a teacher to help him draw out those hidden virtues.

While staying with his mother in Ballston, Brownson had become friendly with Dolphus Skinner, the young minister of the newly-organized Universalist church in Saratoga Springs. Skinner recommended that Brownson study with his own mentor, Samuel Loveland, whom Brownson already knew and respected as an editor and a voice of moderate Restorationism. In addition to editing the *Christian Repository*, Loveland was minister of the Universalist church in Reading, Vermont, where he conducted an academy for young men preparing for the professions. About a dozen of his students became Universalist ministers; others became physicians and lawyers.

Late in the summer of 1825, Brownson wrote to the Universalist General Convention for a letter of fellowship as an evangelist. In September, he and Skinner traveled together to the Universalist General Convention in Hartland, Vermont, where Skinner served as assistant clerk of the convention, and Brownson was accepted into fellowship as a Universalist evangelist.[51] Brownson then continued on to Reading, where from October 1825 to June 1826 he prepared for the ministry under Loveland's guidance.

Brownson's preparation for the ministry was fairly typical of Universalist clergy of his generation. Universalist ministers were rarely college graduates. A common school education, a few months at an academy, and a year or so of apprenticeship with an established Universalist minister was more usual. Mocking the pretensions of the college-educated, Adin Ballou once described the Universalist clergy as "only a trifle better schooled, perhaps, than the humble Nazarene himself and his original twelve apostles, without a D.D. [Doctor of Divinity] among them, and little better than barbarians when compared with the graduates of Harvard College, and other polished literati."[52] At the same time, Universalists did not believe, as did some Methodists, Baptists, and "Christians," that education was irrelevant or even detrimental to the truly God-called preacher.[53] Most Universalists valued education, and pursued it to the best of their ability. Some self-educated Universalist ministers were astonishingly accomplished. Loveland, with only a common school education and one term at an academy, claimed reading knowledge of eleven ancient and modern languages, including Hebrew, Arabic, and Anglo-Saxon. In 1828 he published a Greek lexicon of the New Testament, for which he received an honorary M.A. from Middlebury College. When he died in 1859, he bequeathed a library of 1700 books to Canton Theological School.[54]

Loveland taught his students the rudiments of Greek, Latin, modern languages, history, and mathematics, as well as theology and moral philosophy. It was at Loveland's school that Brownson began to acquire his reading knowledge of French, which would be crucial to his later intellectual development. Loveland took an interest in his students' physical and social well-being as well as their intellectual development: his students recalled that he encouraged them to take long walks for the sake of their health, and corrected their manners when necessary.[55] Gilmore thought that one of the benefits of Brownson's education in Loveland's academy was "a certain civility and urbanity ... vital to him in later life as he sought to be accepted in intellectual circles in Boston and New York City."[56]

Ordination

On June 15, 1826, Brownson was ordained a Universalist minister at a meeting of the New Hampshire Association in Jaffrey, New Hampshire. Though the Restorationist controversy had supposedly been resolved, its effects were very much in evidence in all of the arrangements. The Restorationist party turned out in force for the event. Three of the six signatories of the Appeal and Declaration took part in Brownson's ordination: Paul Dean preached the sermon, Charles Hudson offered a prayer, and Edward Turner gave the charge to the new minister. Neither Dolphus Skinner nor Samuel Loveland, who had been most active in preparing Brownson for the ministry, took part in his ordination, but both had proxies there. Loveland was represented by his friend and co-editor of the *Christian Repository*, Robert Bartlett. Also present were Dolphus Skinner's closest friend, Lemuel Willis, and Warren Skinner, Dolphus's older brother.[57]

The two ordinations that took place that day were the first ever performed under the auspices of the New Hampshire Association.[58] A few years earlier, a new Universalist minister would have been ordained by the General Convention, or by one of its four regional subdivisions: the Western Association (serving New York state), Eastern Association (Maine), Northern Association (Vermont and New Hampshire), or Southern Association (Massachusetts, Connecticut, and Rhode Island). Since 1823, however, there had been a proliferation of local associations, all claiming the right to license, ordain, and discipline clergy. No overall constitution governed the relations between the General Convention, the regional associations, and the new local associations. Groups such as the New Hampshire Association were formed whenever and wherever a group of ministers decided to form one. The organizing principle behind the association movement was partly geographical, but also political and theological, reflecting the divisions within the denomination in the wake of the Restorationist crisis.

The ordaining body itself was a product of the controversy. The New Hampshire Association was one of three Universalist ministers' associations founded between 1822 and 1824, all claiming jurisdiction over the southern tier of New Hampshire and Vermont and adjoining areas in Massachusetts. The Franklin Association had been organized first, in 1822. It was ostensibly a local ministers' group serving three counties at the border of New Hampshire, Vermont, and Massachusetts. At the organizational meeting, however, there were only two local clergy – a physician who sometimes served as a lay preacher, and a young evangelist not yet ordained – and three members of Hosea Ballou's family, none of whom lived in the area. In 1824, Samuel Loveland and Robert Bartlett formed the New Hampshire Association, serving the same area as the Franklin Association, but with a Restorationist orientation. Meanwhile, the Ballou group had founded the Rockingham Association as a "missionary instrumentality" in the area around Portsmouth. The Rockingham Association evolved into a more inclusive group than either the Franklin Association or the New Hampshire Association. Dolphus Skinner and Lemuel Willis attended its meetings as well as those of the New Hampshire Association, and Edward Turner joined the association after he settled in Portsmouth in 1824.[59]

Brownson was thus beginning his ministerial career in a deeply divided and unsettled denomination. The issues of the Restorationist era – issues of theology, of ministerial discipline and fellowship, of freedom of conscience, of organizational structure – would dominate and eventually destroy his ministry. For the moment, however, he was launched into a growing denomination, full of hopes for the future. In his first published work, a sermon printed in the *Christian Repository* in August 1826, Brownson steered clear of all controversial subjects, and instead set forth his vision of the truly happy man:

> He is one ... who studies the law of God, carefully inquires his duty, cultivates the warm and generous emotions of religion, feels them in his heart, and acknowledges them in his conduct; one we may suppose who has enlarged his mind, expanded his heart with benevolence ... studies to remove the load of common misery, and to enable all to smile beneath the gracious bounty of our heavenly Father.[60]

Brownson had reason to be happy. For a young man not yet twenty-three years of age, with the disadvantages he had had to overcome, he had made remarkable progress toward making a place for himself in the world. Despite his limited access to formal education, he had acquired a broad intellectual background in theology, philosophy, and literature. He had developed a relatively stable religious identity and philosophy of life: he would never again consider any form of Calvinism or evangelicalism, nor – despite the way he and others later dramatized his conflict with his colleagues in the Universalist ministry – would he ever again be seriously tempted by atheism or "infidelity." He remained firmly within the liberal Christian camp until his conversion to Catholicism nearly twenty years later. He had recovered from his depression and regained his emotional equilibrium. Despite the lack of a stable family during his own childhood, he had entered into a relationship with a young woman with whom he would build a strong and enduring marriage. Now, with the promise of a new career before him, he could look forward to being in a position to marry her in a year or two.

By becoming a minister, Brownson had taken an important step toward establishing himself in a social and intellectual sphere where he could flourish. He had also separated himself decisively from his family of origin. While he went on to a career as a minister, a journalist, and a public intellectual, his mother and his sister Thorina remained in Ballston, eking out a living by keeping a few cows, occasionally turning to him for money to buy hay to get through the winter. His brothers and their families drifted west, looking, as his brother Oren put it, "to better thare condition but poorly have they done."[61] Letters from his twin sister Daphne, unhappily married to an intemperate and abusive husband, reveal poignantly how far Orestes had come from his origins. On their fifty-fourth birthday Daphne wrote, "oh Brother how wide the space between our persons, but not more so than that Between our sphere in life. God grant that I may Do something worthy of notice yet before I Die."[62]

Orestes Brownson's education as a Universalist minister assured him that he would not suffer Daphne's fate. He, at least, would be able to do something worthy of notice before he died.

CHAPTER 7

Universalist Ministry

Ah! Universalists are nothing but men, after all; and are subject to like passions with other men.

– Memoirs of the Life of Nathaniel Stacy

Brownson spent the three and one-half years of his Universalist ministry at a succession of small churches in New York State. After his ordination, probably through the patronage of Samuel Loveland, he obtained a temporary position supplying the pulpit in two small New York towns between Lake George and Lake Champlain, not far from the Vermont border: Fort Ann, where the Universalists, Baptists, and Methodists were building a shared meetinghouse, and neighboring Whitehall. This was followed by a settlement of nearly a year, from November 1826 to October 1827, in Litchfield, New York, near Utica. From October 1827 to December 1828 he lived in Ithaca, in the Finger Lakes region, preaching to societies there and in nearby Genoa.[1] At the beginning of 1829 he settled in Auburn, New York, as minister to the Universalist society and editor of a Universalist newspaper, the *Gospel Advocate*.

Little is known of Brownson's life during the early part of his Universalist ministry. Like most frontier Universalist ministers in his day, he probably did not support himself solely by preaching. Perhaps, as some Universalist ministers did, he supplemented his income by teaching. In any case, by the middle of 1827 he was financially secure enough to risk marriage. He and Sally Healy were married in Litchfield in June 1827.[2]

What, exactly, do we know about Brownson's Universalist ministry? Documentation for the period before the fall of 1827, when he began to write regularly for the Universalist press, is admittedly sparse. The small societies he served were quite ephemeral; most of them had passed out of existence by 1835, when the *Universalist Register* began printing lists of clergy and societies.[3] As far as we can tell, his ministries appear to have been successful while they lasted. In Genoa, Universalists organized a society with

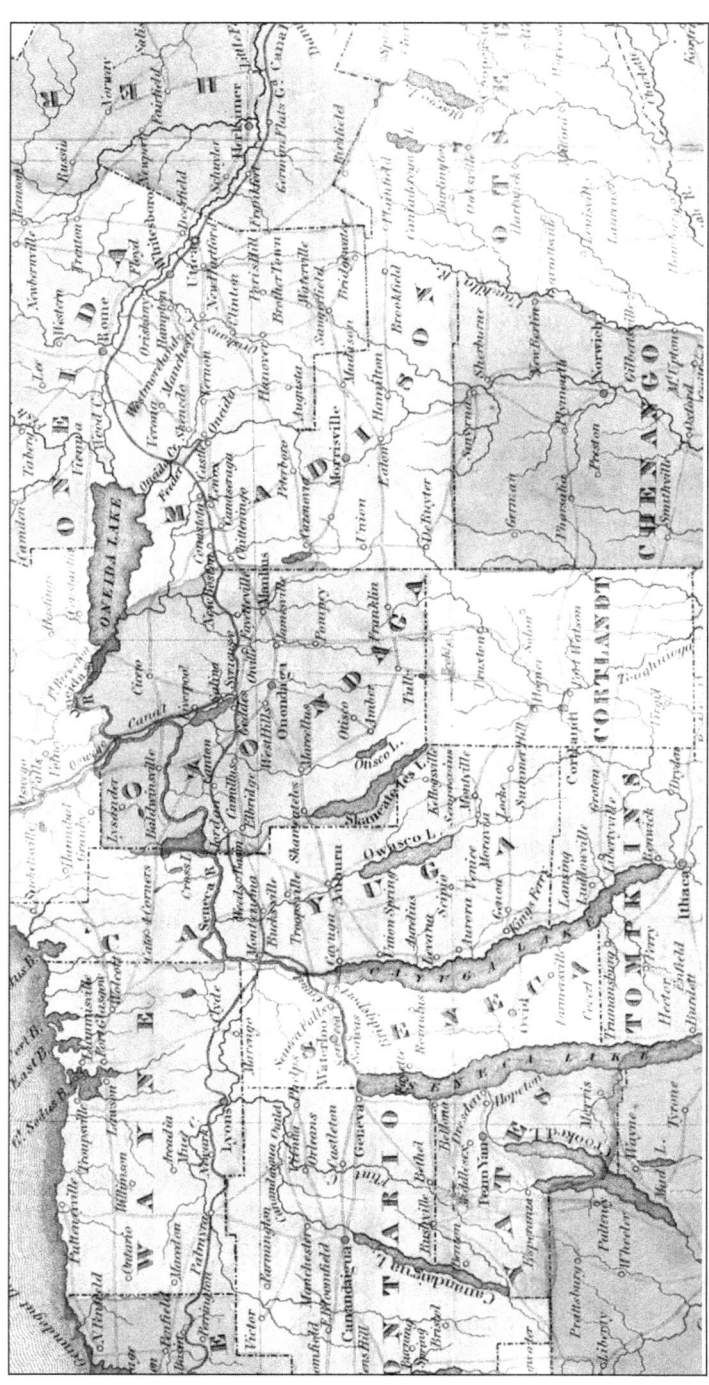

The geography of Brownson's Universalist career: This detail from an 1827 map shows the area of central New York State where Brownson spent most of his Universalist ministry. From November 1826 to October 1827 he was in Litchfield. (Litchfield is not shown on the map; it is located in southern Herkimer County, south of Frankfort and west of German Flats.) From October 1827 to December 1828 he lived in Ithaca, at the southern tip of Cayuga Lake, serving congregations there and in Genoa, to the north of Ithaca in Cayuga County. His final Universalist church was in Auburn, in Cayuga County just north of Owasco Lake. Northeast of Auburn, in Onondaga County, is Camillus, where he met his wife.

more than 100 subscribers in 1829, and built a meetinghouse in 1830. Over 130 years after Brownson's brief ministry, a local Universalist historian in Auburn reported that the Universalist society there had "flourished" under Brownson's leadership.[4]

We know quite a lot about the development of Brownson's political, philosophical, and theological opinions, especially during the latter part of his Universalist ministry. Beginning in the fall of 1827, his sermons, essays, and other writings were published in the *Gospel Advocate*, edited by his mentor and friend Linus Smith Everett. After Brownson succeeded to the editorship in January 1829, he used the paper almost as a private diary, recording his raw emotional responses and half-formed speculations along with his more well-developed ideas.

As he described it in *The Convert*, Brownson's Universalist career appears to have taken place in a kind of vacuum. Other people barely appeared in his account. The action takes place in Brownson's own mind and soul, as he struggles with the implications of belief in universal salvation. Contemporary documents, however, tell a different story, in which other people – particularly Brownson's colleagues in the Universalist ministry – figure prominently. Part of the story may be found in the records of the New York State Convention of Universalists. The conflict that brought his ministry to an end was reported in great detail in the Universalist press. Indeed, for this part of the story, the challenge is not so much to find information, as to construct a coherent narrative of a conflict that spilled untidily into every part of the paper: news, editorials, correspondence, sermons, essays, even advertisements and lists of sales agents.

The period of Brownson's Universalist ministry, neglected in most accounts of his life, was a time of great intellectual and spiritual development. During his years as a struggling young preacher, while doing his best to nurture his congregations and support his family, Brownson was working out his beliefs, finding his voice as a writer, and making a name for himself in the Universalist denomination.

Universalism in the Age of Evangelical Dominance

Brownson's Universalist ministry coincided with the climax of what is sometimes called "the age of evangelical hegemony" in American religious history.[5] Between 1800 and 1830, evangelical Protestantism enjoyed a greater degree of religious and cultural dominance than at any time before or since. To some extent, it was a simple matter of numbers: seven denominations, all with a common origin in the Reformed tradition, accounted for some 90 percent of American church membership in 1800. After 1830, immigration, especially of Roman Catholics, would erode this homogeneity, as would increased competition from new American alternatives such as Adventism and Mormonism.

Despite the formal independence of church and state, for most Americans in the early nineteenth century it was unthinkable that the government should or ever could be indifferent to the religious welfare of the people. As Supreme Court Justice Joseph Story wrote in his 1833 *Commentaries on the Constitution*, "The right of a society or government to interfere in matters of religion will hardly be contested by any persons, who believe that piety, religion, and morality are intimately connected with the well being of the state, and indispensable to the administration of civil justice." Government had a right and duty to "foster and encourage the Christian religion generally, as a matter of sound policy, as well as of revealed truth." The purpose of the non-establishment clause in the First Amendment was "not to countenance, much less to advance Mahometanism, or Judaism, or infidelity, by prostrating Christianity; but to exclude all rivalry among Christian sects, and to prevent any national ecclesiastical establishment, which should give to an hierarchy the exclusive patronage of the national government."[6] It assuredly was not intended to prevent citizens from selecting leaders and enacting laws in accordance with widely shared religious values. In a famous Fourth of July sermon in 1827, the Presbyterian minister Ezra Stiles Ely called upon the electorate "in this country, in which ninety-nine hundredths of the people are believers in the divine origin and authority of the Christian religion," to elect none but Christians to lead them. After all, "it deprives no man of his right for me to prefer a Christian to an Infidel."[7]

Though there was little opposition to the notion that the United States was a Christian nation, there was intense conflict over what form of Christianity the government should promote, and which of its citizens should be considered Christians. Justice Story doubtless meant to be inclusive when he enumerated the "great doctrines of religion" as "the being, and attributes, and providence of one Almighty God; the responsibility to him for all our actions, founded upon moral freedom and accountability; a future state of rewards and punishments; [and] the cultivation of all the personal, social, and benevolent virtues."[8] But this list excluded at least one class of people who thought of themselves as Christians, for not all

Universalists believed in "a future state of rewards and punishments." Were these people entitled to the privileges accorded to the Christian citizens of a Christian nation? Or were they aliens, to be tolerated, but nothing more? The question had immediate, practical consequences. During the 1820s, there was a lively debate over whether Universalists should be admitted to any privilege, such as holding public office or giving testimony in court, which required the swearing of an oath – the idea being that an oath was meaningless unless backed up by a threat (credible to the oath-taker) of eternal damnation.[9]

At least since the time of the Restorationist conflict, Universalists had argued about where they fit in the American religious spectrum. In the politically charged atmosphere of the late 1820s, the question took on new urgency. Faced with an apparently united, powerful, politically active evangelical consensus, Universalists and other religious minorities felt that they were fighting for survival. Their ability to secure their rights, and to have their voices heard in the debate over the place of religion in American life, seemed to depend on their being accepted as part of the Protestant mainstream. If the mainstream could be defined broadly enough, the more fervent evangelicals might be marginalized as extremists. The alternative strategy – to position themselves outside Ely's "ninety-nine hundredths of the people" and fight for the rights of the remaining one percent – would have been riskier and, for most Universalists, a less accurate representation of who they felt themselves to be. Virtually all Universalists had come out of mainstream Reformed churches. They had far more in common with Congregationalists and Baptists than they had with Catholics, Jews, or freethinkers.

One of the clearest expressions of what may be called the "mainstream" Universalist response to evangelical dominance is found in the editorials of William A. Drew, editor of the *Christian Intelligencer and Eastern Chronicle* in Gardiner, Maine. Though geographically remote from the power centers of the denomination, Drew exercised considerable influence over Universalist opinion by means of his weekly paper, which offered a digest of national and international news accompanied by analysis from a Universalist point of view. Drew's editorials chart the growing confidence of the evangelical movement during the late 1820s, and the correspondingly defensive attitude adopted by many Universalists.

At the beginning of 1827, Drew was sanguine about the prospects for liberal religion. In the half-century since the Declaration of Independence, he wrote, "the spread of liberal christianity and of the humiliation of what is called orthodoxy ... [have] opened the door for free and fearless inquiry – told people to *think for themselves*, and gave them the right to speak what they thought." A month later, however, he warned, "There is actually a silent and crafty but mighty effort now making throughout the union by the orthodox party, to get the Government under their influence." He was particularly concerned about "those *sectarian* institutions, multitudes of which have arisen up within a few years past." The very names of these institutions – the *American* Education Society, *National* Tract Society, *American* Bible Society, *National* Sunday School Union, and the like – revealed that "they sigh after a national religion and national power." Three months later he was warning Universalists to be careful how they used that right of free and fearless inquiry which he had once celebrated.

> We do not mean that there is no farther room for improvement or reformation ... That there are errors in the world, particularly of a religious character, we most solemnly believe, and hold it to be duty of every one to examine and reject them. – But we do not want people should consider *every* thing erroneous which has not originated with themselves, or sacrifice whatever of truth may heretofore have been obtained, to their own speculations.

Among the "incomprehensible subjects" on which he advised his readers not to speculate were "how God exists," "how the world was created," and "what are the properties of spirit and how it is allied to matter."[10]

Drew's news digests and editorials called attention to Ezra Stiles Ely's call for a "Christian party in politics";[11] to the controversy over whether Universalists should be allowed to give testimony in court; to efforts to enforce observance of the Sabbath; and to the activities of Bible societies, temperance societies, foreign missions, and Sunday schools. In reporting these projects, Drew sought to show that it was the more extreme evangelicals, not the Universalists, who were out of step with the evangelical consensus. For example, he denounced the American Bible Society as a sectarian instrument, but insisted, "We [Universalists] are not, nor will we be, behind any one, in a deep and lively anxiety for the distribution of the sacred scriptures." He argued that Universalists should be allowed to testify in court not because he opposed religious tests – indeed, he agreed that atheists should not be permitted to testify – but because Universalists "[believe] as strongly as any person in the existence of a God, in our moral accountability to him, in the holy Bible and in all the retribution which [they can] find mentioned therein." He urged his fellow Universalists to make common cause with the orthodox when possible, criticizing those who "suppose that ... every thing another party does, either in religion or politics, must of course be wrong, and that it is their duty to oppose and ridicule it."[12]

For most Universalists, insisting on their place in the mainstream meant claiming a position they felt to be rightfully theirs. Brownson did not share this "mainstream" perspective. His personal and family ties to the Reformed tradition were tenuous at best. His youth had been spent among Universalists, "Christians," and disaffected Congregationalists – none of them part of the evangelical consensus. His one brief, unhappy experience with an evangelical church had left him with a dislike and distrust of Presbyterianism that would last for the rest of his life. Intellectually, he found more to admire in the works of the freethinker Volney than in Paley's *Evidences of Christianity*.[13] He knew the Catholic church, not as the "mother of harlots" of Protestant rhetoric, but as an outpost of civilization in the Michigan wilderness. For Brownson, identifying with the Protestant mainstream would have meant joining with those he despised to oppress and exclude those he liked and respected. Such a course did not appeal to him, and he did not understand the appeal it had for others. Throughout his Universalist ministry, he would instinctively side with the outsiders, and would expect other Universalists to do the same.

Discipline, Freedom, and the New York State Convention

Brownson's introduction to the tumultuous world of New York Universalism came at the annual meeting of the New York State Convention of Universalists in May 1827. As he had only arrived in New York the previous summer, this was his first opportunity to attend an annual meeting of the Convention. He duly appeared at the meeting – and came away with an official reprimand and a threat of disfellowship. To understand how this came about, we must know something of the history of the state convention, and the controversy that Brownson unwittingly stumbled into.

The first to propose a state convention was the venerable Nathaniel Stacy, who had been preaching Universalism in central New York since 1805. As the number of Universalist clergy, societies, and associations in New York increased, Stacy became concerned about the adequacy of the ad hoc "visiting committees" which were the principal means of communication among the state's Universalists. He thought that a state convention, where delegates from local associations could meet on a regular basis, would be a more efficient and reliable way of exchanging information. He always insisted that he intended the convention only as a "center of communication." In his autobiography he wrote:

> I had no idea of creating a hierarchy, of investing this body with supreme or superior prerogatives, whereby it could impose creeds or rules of discipline on churches, societies, or associations ... No ecclesiastical power was to be invested in it, not even the power to grant letters of fellowship, or to confer ordination, as these powers belonged originally and exclusively to the churches ... All the power it could of right exercise was merely apellatory or advisatory.[14]

The Restorationist controversy had, however, given rise to a competing conception of a state convention. New York Universalists had been appalled by the behavior of Hosea Ballou, Paul Dean, and their respective supporters at the General Convention in Clinton in 1823. Shortly afterward, a group of Universalist ministers in the Utica area began to discuss forming a state convention as a means of preventing such scenes in the future. The connection between the founding of the New York State Convention and the debacle at Clinton was made explicit in the first entry in the Convention's record book:

> One circumstance leading to [the decision to establish a state convention] was the fact that in September [1823] ... two brethren in the ministry belonging to another state ... attended the "General Convention of the New England States and Others," holden at Clinton N.Y. in that year, and brought mutually against each other many bitter accusations and grievous complaints ... to the great grief and extreme mortification of almost all the members present.[15]

A convention of their own, these ministers reasoned, would distance them from their unruly brethren in New England and allow them to establish "a sort of ecclesiastical court or religious tribunal ... for settling and adjudicating any cases of contention or difficulty between the brethren in the ministry, or deciding on any charge preferred against any minister."[16] Accordingly, they set up an organization called the Conventional Association, which served as both a local ministers' group and a self-appointed committee for establishing a New York State Convention.

The Conventional Association's conception of a state convention as "a sort of ecclesiastical court or religious tribunal" was far more controversial than Stacy's idea of a "center of communication." By 1825 the Convention had become a serious source of discord among New York Universalists. Stacy wrote, "Up to about that time there had never anything taken place to cloud the sun-shine of our associational meetings ... or disturb the unanimity of action and harmony of feeling." But once the members of the Conventional Association began to agitate in favor of their version of a state convention, "a cloud [came] over us, and the thunders began to roll." Now when Stacy spoke in favor of a convention, he was called "Pope," "Bishop," and "tyrant," and accused of wishing to "impose creeds, confessions of faith, and rules of discipline, and the next thing would be a holy inquisition." In the midst of the uproar, the Conventional Association and a few other pro-convention associations organized themselves as the New York State Convention of Universalists and began to hold meetings, further inflaming the apprehensions of those who feared that the Convention meant to impose its authority upon them without their consent.[17]

The pro-Convention forces were led by some of the most respected elder statesmen of New York Universalism. In addition to Nathaniel Stacy, there was the aged William Underwood, Brownson's predecessor at Litchfield, a staunch supporter of the Convention and a leading member of the Conventional Association. The younger generation included Thomas F. King, William I. Reese, and Dolphus Skinner. After settling in Utica in 1827, Skinner became the most active member of the Conventional Association. In 1827 the Convention adopted Skinner's paper, the *Utica Magazine*, as its official publication.[18]

One of the most active participants in the Convention's first year – ironically, in view of his later career as a notorious "infidel" disowned by Universalist associations in New York and elsewhere – was Abner Kneeland, then minister of the Prince Street church in New York City. Kneeland led the "Utica Convocation," a group of ministers who objected to the power given to the laity and the associations by the original draft constitution. Few others shared Kneeland's concerns, but they tried hard to bring him into the fold. Kneeland was elected president of the Convention and was appointed to serve on the committee of discipline, to prepare minutes for the press, and to write the circular letter. However, issues of representation, membership, and jurisdiction remained contentious, and the Convention was not able to agree on a constitution.[19]

This was the situation when Brownson attended his first and only meeting of the Convention in May 1827. Up to this point Brownson had not paid much attention to the Convention and its problems, though he claimed to have started out as a moderate supporter of conventions in general. He belonged to the Conventional Association, but only because it was the local ministers' association serving Litchfield.[20]

A large part of the Convention's 1827 meeting was devoted to discussing a disciplinary case which, in the eyes of the Convention's opposers, exemplified the dangers they feared from a convention invested with arbitrary power. Richard Carrique, a Universalist minister from New England who had settled in Hudson, New York in 1824, had run afoul of the local ministers' association, the Hudson River Association. The nature of his alleged offenses is not recorded in any of the official documents, though it appears, from private correspondence, that it may have had to do with debts he owed to colleagues in the ministry.[21] In 1826 the Hudson River Association ordered Carrique to appear at the next meeting of the State Convention "to show reason why the fellowship of the Convention should not be withdrawn from [him]." Carrique had ceased preaching by the time the Convention met in 1827, but he wanted the record to show that he "[did] not acknowledge the jurisdiction of such a body." Instead of appearing, he sent a long letter, in which he challenged the powers and practices of the Convention.[22]

Carrique challenged the legitimacy of the Hudson River Association's actions in his case. He had already been investigated and cleared by the Southern Association before moving to New York. He had never joined the New York State Convention or any of its subordinate associations; by what right, then, did they presume to pass judgment on him? He wrote:

> It may however be the case in this land of boasted liberty and independence, that a few clergymen may form themselves into an association and have power to compel every preacher, who may live within the limits which they see fit to prescribe, to come into their fellowship, and under their discipline. If this is the case, the least that can be said is, that it is an arbitrary if not a dangerous power, and Universalists ought to pause and consider whether they are willing and disposed to submit themselves and posterity to the *yoke* of Clerical despotism.

Further, Carrique claimed, the discipline of Universalist ministers was notoriously inconsistent; others, including disciplinary committee member Abner Kneeland, had been dealt with much more indulgently on previous occasions. Finally, the Hudson River Association had failed to prove or even to accuse him of any specific misdeeds. Instead of substantiated charges, they offered only rumors, "set afloat by surmises, suspicions, and fears that the enemies of Universalism would say so and so, and these fears have continued to give countenance and circulation to those reports."[23]

Here, Carrique had identified the key weakness in the Convention's disciplinary process: it was entirely subjective. The Convention's aim was to avoid "mortification" by removing ministers whose actions threatened to bring Universalism into disrepute. But in the absence of an agreed-upon code of conduct for ministers – not likely to be forthcoming from a Convention that still had not been able to agree on a constitution – the definition of disreputable behavior depended on the discretion of the members of the disciplinary committee. Any kind of offense, from moral turpitude to theological nonconformity to personal conflict with a committee member, might trigger disciplinary action. The charges did not need to be proved; Carrique's case showed that they did not even need to be specified. Nor did it really matter whether they were well founded. Since the focus was on the reputation of Universalism rather than the rights of the minister, the appearance of wrongdoing was treated as harshly as the reality.

The assembled ministers heard, discussed, and, to some extent, acknowledged the justice of Carrique's criticisms. In the minutes they recorded that, as Carrique did not acknowledge the jurisdiction of the Convention, "we are willing the subject be dismissed from this body, and referred to one, the jurisdiction of which he does acknowledge." The Convention then passed on to other business: agreeing to sponsor the *Utica Magazine*, setting the date of the next meeting, and selecting officers for the coming year.[24]

At least one person present was not ready to move on. "Here," in the words of William Reese, who was acting as secretary, "a desultory conversation was commenced between Br. W. Underwood & O. A. Brownson on the subject of the organization and proper discipline of churches & societies." Underwood, who was chairing the meeting, could simply have ruled Brownson out of order. Instead, however, he entered into an argument with him, "Br. B. opposing all organization or discipline whatever, and Br. U. strenuously advocating the necessity and advantages of both." According to Reese, "the discussion grew warm and animated, and at length Br. B. became so excited as to use very harsh and abusive epithets to Br. U. even insulting him to his face in the presence of the council."[25]

From Reese's account, it is impossible to know the tone of Brownson's initial remarks. Perhaps he was dissatisfied with the resolution of the Carrique case, and thought the issues needed further discussion. Perhaps he was trying to annoy Underwood, with whom he seems already to have been on bad terms. (The letter of reprimand that the convention addressed to Brownson after this incident included the line, "We will not say any thing particularly of your treatment of Br. U. previous to this day," suggesting that there was a history of animosity between the two.[26]) Or perhaps, with his naive delight in philosophical conjecture, he conceived the Convention to be a sort of debating society, and wanted to discuss ecclesiastical discipline and organization in the abstract.

The Convention chose to treat the incident the way it treated most things: as a disciplinary issue. They placed all the blame on Brownson, portraying Underwood as an innocent victim. They passed two resolutions against Brownson: first, "that this Convention consider such principles subversive of good order and productive of evil to the Church, and cannot fellowship doctrines so pernicious and destructive of the harmony of the order," and second, "that unless [Brownson] correct his views or cease their promulgation within three months, the committee will suspend him from the fellowship of this body." The committee of discipline was instructed to prepare a letter of admonition to Brownson.[27]

The letter, which was dated the day after the meeting, was signed by Dolphus Skinner, William Reese, and Thomas King (although Nathaniel Stacy, not King, had just been elected to the committee of discipline, along with Skinner and Reese). The three young men, none more than a few years older than Brownson, addressed him in patronizing terms, imploring him "earnestly and affectionately" to reconsider his conduct. They were writing, they said, "not only from the respect we feel for all whom you have injured," but out of concern "for you also, believing that you must, in a greater or less degree, participate in the disadvantages arising from the impropriety of your conduct." In keeping with the Convention's concern for appearances, the committee reminded Brownson of the duty of Universalists to treat each other well "in order to the effectual building up of the cause of the Redeemer, and to silence gainsayers."[28]

The quarrel between Brownson and Underwood, petty as it was, was symptomatic of the issues that would cast a shadow over Brownson's entire ministry in New York. The Convention's instant judgment of Brownson as guilty and Underwood as innocent, and its summary use of disciplinary action without any formal complaint or inquiry, were typical of the way the Convention's inner circle used their disciplinary powers. Faced with a challenge from a brash newcomer to one of their own, the Convention closed ranks, protecting Underwood and putting Brownson on notice that he retained his fellowship with the Convention at the pleasure of the core members. The incident left Brownson with serious reservations about the advisability of a state convention – at least as then constituted.

Changing Alliances

Brownson's new-found opposition to the Convention brought him to the attention of Linus Smith Everett, the minister in Auburn, New York, editor of the *Gospel Advocate*, and a leading opponent of the Convention.[29] Hearing of the altercation between Brownson and Underwood, Everett determined to use the incident in his campaign against the Convention and, if possible, to recruit Brownson for the anti-Convention party.

Everett's opposition to the Convention was based on his fear that it would become an inquisitorial body enforcing theological conformity. When he heard of the Convention's treatment of Brownson, he believed (or affected to believe) that the Universalist Inquisition had begun. He wrote in the *Gospel Advocate* that the Convention had "sent forth an admonitory letter, plainly censuring a brother in the ministry for holding and propagating certain sentiments ... supposed by the convention to be erroneous, relating to the ordinances of baptism and the Lord's supper."[30] After Dolphus Skinner and others challenged the accuracy of this description of the incident, Everett wrote to Brownson, asking whether he thought that the Convention had "dictated in matters of conscience" and "whether you regarded the resolution as implying a censure of your *moral conduct* or of your *opinions*."[31]

In his reply, which Everett published in the *Gospel Advocate*, Brownson endorsed Everett's view that the Convention had "dictated in matters of conscience." He admitted that he had used "improper" language to Underwood, but dismissed that as irrelevant – he had apologized on the spot, and Underwood had accepted his apology. In reality, he said, he had been disciplined by the Convention for his opinions. The letter admonishing him for his behavior toward Underwood was nothing but a smoke screen, written so that "people may be led to think there was some immorality in the case."

Brownson did not go into detail about the opinions the Convention had found objectionable, but he listed four reasons why, he claimed, Underwood and his supporters considered them "heretical":

> 1. Because he considered their adoption would eventually "bring Baptism and the Lord's Supper" into disrepute, if indeed, they did not render the administration of them wholly impracticable.

2. Because they were contrary to the rule, adopted by the Convention, and also of the Conventional Association, of which I was a member.
   3. Because they were unscriptural;
   4. Because the preaching of them is premature. They may be correct but the state of the publick mind will not bear them.³²

This summary does not shed much light on what Brownson actually said at the meeting. Certainly there is nothing in the minutes about baptism or the Lord's Supper, or about any issues other than order and discipline.

The correspondence with Everett helped Brownson to articulate his grievances against the Convention. These points would be at the heart of all of Brownson's subsequent complaints against the Universalists. Simply put, these were: (1) Universalists claimed to support free inquiry and liberty of conscience, but in reality they censured clergy whose opinions they deemed to be too far out of the mainstream; and (2) they were hypocritical, more concerned with their reputation than with their commitment to the truth, and would punish a colleague for saying publicly what they themselves thought privately.

How maddening it must have been to Brownson, then, when Dolphus Skinner accused him of hypocrisy! As Brownson told the story, Underwood had warned him, in the course of the quarrel, that his opinions would make him unpopular. Not so, Brownson retorted; Underwood had been so unpopular in Litchfield that his successor ought to be able to curry favor with the populace just by disagreeing with him. Skinner then gravely cautioned Brownson against shaping his views so as to court popularity. Stung, Brownson *"repelled* the insinuation with warmth."³³

Brownson may have thought that was the end of the matter, but it was not. Six months later, Skinner repeated the same charge in the *Utica Magazine*.³⁴ Brownson was indignant. He could perhaps have forgiven Skinner for speaking as he did during the argument at the Convention, when insults were being exchanged freely; but now Skinner had deliberately defamed him in the public press. The readers of the *Utica Magazine* would not know the whole story, and would be bound to believe Skinner's aspersions. Brownson wrote to Everett:

> The charge of shaping sentiments to the prejudices of the people cannot be sustained against me, and those who know me have frequently told me that if I *would* bend a little to them, it would be better for me and perhaps for my doctrine. Whatever impression the Convention received, it had no reason to apprehend that I was afraid to declare my honest sentiments, nor

that I was pursuing the course I was, merely from *policy*. Br. Skinner should be ashamed of making such an insinuation, for *he* knows me too well.[35]

This was the point of no return in the relationship between Brownson and Skinner. Brownson had entered the Universalist ministry as Skinner's protégé: Skinner had encouraged him to enter the ministry, had recommended him to Samuel Loveland, and had accompanied him to the convention where he received his first letter of fellowship. We do not know much about the relationship between Brownson and Skinner from June 1826, when Brownson began his ministry in New York, to May 1827, when they clashed at the Convention. They may already have been somewhat estranged by that time, for Skinner and Underwood were close allies in the Conventional Association, whereas Brownson and Underwood disliked each other. After the quarrel at the Convention, and more emphatically after the newspaper exchanges of October-November 1827, Brownson and Skinner were bitter enemies. The rift between them would never be repaired.

If Brownson had lost a friend and mentor in Dolphus Skinner, he found a new one in Linus Everett. In October 1827, as if to cement his change of allegiance, Brownson accepted the position of pastor to a newly-formed Universalist society in Ithaca, New York, about thirty miles from Everett's headquarters at Auburn, and another in Genoa, about halfway between Ithaca and Auburn. Under Everett's guidance, he became active in the Cayuga Association, a center of opposition to the State Convention. The same month Brownson arrived to take up his new duties, the Cayuga Association voted "that this association does not approve the New-York Convention of Universalists as it now exists." Brownson composed the circular letter for this meeting: "To our shame be it spoken there are *Universalists*, who retain all the bigotry of the twelfth, amid the improvements of the nineteenth century ... We must remember that we are dissenters from former notions, and it will be absurdity itself for us to establish a creed and presume to censure another if his mind cannot come to it, or if it should by chance go beyond it."[36]

As soon as he was settled in Ithaca, Brownson began to write for the *Gospel Advocate*. Within a few months he had became a principal contributor, publishing sermons, letters, articles on current events, and his most extended literary works to date: long essays of ten to fifteen thousand words, which were printed in installments over periods of weeks or months. This was his first substantial opportunity to write for publication. It was the beginning of his long career as an essayist, religious journalist, and public intellectual.

Brownson's intimacy with Everett radically altered his position in the shifting pattern of alliances within the Universalist ministry. He had entered the ministry as an adherent of the Restorationist cause. Along with Dolphus Skinner and Lemuel Willis, he was one of the young ministers trained by Samuel Loveland and sent forth to preach the Restorationist message on the frontier. Restorationists Edward Turner, Paul Dean, and Charles Hudson had taken part in his ordination. He was bound to Dean by family connections, and to Loveland and Turner by ties of affection and respect.

Linus Everett, on the other hand, was a disciple of Hosea Ballou. He printed excerpts from Ballou's *Notes on the Parables* in the *Gospel Advocate*. His sermons closely follow the theology of Ballou's *Treatise on Atonement*.[37] When Everett was installed in Charlestown, Massachusetts, in 1829, Ballou gave the charge to the minister. In 1831, Everett became a co-editor, with Hosea Ballou and Hosea Ballou 2d, of a scholarly journal called the *Universalist Expositor*.[38]

Though Brownson never renounced his Restorationist allegiance or declared himself a follower of Hosea Ballou, his early articles in the *Gospel Advocate* show unmistakable signs of Ballou's influence. In a series that ran from April to September 1828, he expressed a view of good and evil that sounded very much like Ballou's. "If I do wrong," he wrote, "it is because I am ignorant. I am deceived with regard to my true interest." As for "right" and "wrong," they are nothing but the names we give to actions more or less likely to produce happiness. "What is a wrong action? One which brings misery. Why does it bring misery? Because it is wrong? No; but it is wrong because it brings misery." Since, in this view, good inevitably leads to happiness and evil to misery, there is no need for rewards and punishments beyond the natural consequences that attend any action. It is not surprising, therefore, that when Brownson adopted Ballou's understanding of good and evil, he also accepted his rejection of future punishment. "There are no just principles on which punishment can be defended ... Man, by transgression, brings misery upon himself; punishment increases it, and consequently must be unjust."[39]

From Brownson's point of view, his re-appropriation of Ballou's ideas was simply the latest of many attempts to come to terms with ideas – of good and evil, of human nature, of natural law and divine justice – that he had been wrestling with for many years. From the point of view of his associates in the Restorationist movement, it was something different: a signal that he had changed sides. When he allied himself with Everett and began expressing ultra Universalist ideas in his writings, the Restorationists decided that he was no longer one of them. Thus it came about that, when he visited Boston during the fall of 1829, he was invited to preach at Hosea Ballou's church, but not at Paul Dean's.

Brownson never thought of himself as member of a party. It probably did not occur to him that his Restorationist colleagues and mentors would see his change of opinions as a betrayal. Even if it had, he would not have allowed himself to be swayed by such considerations. One did not turn aside from the pursuit of truth out of concern for what others might think. That, for him, would have been the worst kind of betrayal.

CHAPTER 8

Changing Beliefs

All those with whom I came into relation, either denied reason to make way for revelation, or revelation to make way for reason ... The one class declaimed against reason, used reason against reason, and sometimes assigned, apparently, a very good reason why reason ought not to be used. The other class either openly denied all supernatural revelation, or ... brought it within the sphere of the natural order, and subjected it to the dominion of natural reason.

– Orestes Brownson, *The Convert*

When Brownson looked back over his life from the perspective of middle age, the aspect of his Universalist career that interested him most was the development of his thinking during his Universalist years. He said very little about the external circumstances of his ministry, but devoted most of three chapters of *The Convert* to a detailed examination of the intellectual, emotional, and spiritual consequences of belief in universal salvation. As presented in *The Convert*, these consequences were almost wholly negative. In the chapter "Universalism Unsatisfactory," he discussed five ways in which Universalism tends to undermine Christian faith.[1]

1. By teaching "that vice has no punishment, virtue no reward; that Judas, Pilate, and Herod will receive a crown of life as well as Peter, James, and John," Universalism offers no rationale for choosing good over evil. In fact, it destroys the very idea of moral agency. "What is the criterion of right and wrong? Both must alike be pleasing to God ... if he regards with equal complacency the sinner and the saint."

2. In order to counter the charge that Universalism is incompatible with divine justice, some Universalists go to the opposite extreme and deny divine mercy. Restorationists teach that, before a sinner can be saved, "he must pay the debt he contracts" – that is, suffer the natural consequences of his sins – "to the uttermost farthing." But this is tantamount to deism, or the belief that God "has made the world, adjusted its parts, given it a jog, and bid it go ahead and take care of itself."

3. The Bible does not consistently and unambiguously teach universal salvation. Therefore, Universalists must either disregard the Bible, or judge, by the light of reason, which passages are worthy of belief. This raises issues about the authority of scripture, for "in order to be able to judge by its own light the truth or falsity of a revealed doctrine, [reason] must know, independently of the revelation, all that it can teach us." It follows that revelation is superfluous and the scriptures "worse than useless."

4. Universalists feel no need for a savior. Whether they reject outright the idea of divine judgment and punishment, or reinterpret it as beneficent discipline, they have no need to be saved from its rigors. Jesus thus becomes no more than a good man, who tried, with limited success, to teach humanity wisdom and virtue.

5. Universalism is, ultimately, entirely without foundation. The most basic assumption of Universalism is that God is good. But if Universalists cannot accept the authority of scripture and do not believe in a personal God who actively participates in creation, they have no basis for asserting that God is good.

Brownson insisted in "Universalism Unsatisfactory" that "this was my reasoning at the time, not merely my reasoning now."[2] To some extent, his writings from his Universalist years bear this out. Nevertheless, "Universalism Unsatisfactory" gives a fundamentally misleading picture of his intellectual and spiritual state during his Universalist period. The points it makes – that Universalism is unscriptural, that it eliminates the need for a savior, that it denies the justice and mercy of God – are familiar anti-Universalist arguments, which early-nineteenth-century Universalists were accustomed to hearing and refuting. These arguments represent the starting point of Brownson's reasoning on these subjects, not his conclusions.

Just as it fails to do justice to the complexity of Brownson's thought, "Universalism Unsatisfactory" misrepresents the emotional tone of his Universalist writings. It presents Universalism as a dreary business, pervaded with loss. "Thus I had ... lost the Bible, lost my Saviour, lost Providence, lost reason itself," he wrote. "Surely I have a marvelous faculty in losing. Wonder what I have gained!"[3] His writings from this period, however, are bold, confident, sometimes belligerent, often fervent – anything but weary and despairing. In these writings, he challenged all easy answers and accepted ideas, a process he seemed to find exhilarating.

The account in "Universalism Unsatisfactory" is correct, however, in describing Brownson's increasing willingness to question – and sometimes to discard – traditional Christian doctrines. His impatience with the endless debates over future punishment led him back to the questions that had occupied his mind since his early teens: what do we really know about God, and how do we know it? How can this world, with all its sin and suffering, be said to be the creation of a just and beneficent God?

In 1825, as a reluctant convert to Universalism, Brownson had rejected the innovative theology of Hosea Ballou in favor of the conservative "Calvinism improved" of the Restorationists. Once he was settled in New York, events propelled him to take increasingly skeptical views of received truth. New associates such as Linus Everett encouraged him to reconsider the thinking of Hosea Ballou. It is unlikely, in any case, that the Restorationists' cautious approach to theology would have satisfied him for long. As he settled into his identity as a Universalist, his questioning mind and philosophical temperament inevitably reasserted themselves. The result was that, though he was one of the more conservative Universalists in 1825, by 1828 he had become one of the most radical. He was impatient with traditional doctrinal religion and its concerns. In one essay he dismissed "the existence of God, his providence, the accountability of man to him, and a future state of happiness or misery" as matters which "rest for the most part on that kind of evidence which we are but ill prepared to collate in this mode of existence." He wrote that "faith is less important than philosophy," and that the Bible must "submit to the supremacy of reason." As for Christ, his mission was "simply to reform mankind, not by any supernatural means, but by a simple operation, differing in degree, but not in kind, from the labors of every reformer."[4]

It is understandable that, while he was engaged in such a thoroughgoing re-examination of his beliefs, Brownson was uncomfortable repeating the party line of either the Restorationists or the ultra Universalists. Very likely he did reproach himself, as he said in *The Convert*, for "want of manliness and strict honesty" in continuing to preach what he no longer believed. But his determination not to profess more than he believed did not lead him either to give up preaching or to resolve to "leave alone all metaphysical or theological speculations."[5] On the contrary, between mid-1828 and mid-1829, he developed his own unorthodox but coherent religious philosophy. During his last two years as a Universalist, he engaged some of the most original and creative theological thinking of his career, comparable only to the period leading up to his conversion to Catholicism.

Justice, Mercy, and World-Reform

In order to understand the development of Brownson's thinking during his Universalist period, we must begin, as he did, with the question of future punishment.

"Few men ever reason out their own systems," Brownson wrote in *The Convert*.[6] His move from the Restorationist to the ultra camp, and his consequent re-examination of the question of future punishment, caused him to reflect on the various Universalist "systems." When he did, he could not help noticing their logical flaws and inconsistencies. On the question of God's justice and mercy – the whole complex of beliefs encompassed by the idea of "future punishment" – he was an astute critic of both the Restorationist and the ultra Universalist positions.

Brownson was irritated by the lack of precision in the Restorationists' use of the word "punishment." Restorationist Universalists tried to distance themselves from non-Universalists by explaining that they understood "punishment" as discipline imposed for the sinner's own good. However, in their eagerness to show that their version of universal salvation (unlike that of the ultra Universalists) did not allow malefactors to escape just retribution, they also insisted that each soul would receive, in the afterlife, a quantity of punishment precisely calibrated to the quantity of sin committed in life. These claims could not both be true, Brownson argued; to speak of punishment as deserved, and at the same time as reformatory, "is to talk without understanding oneself."[7] In any case, he could not believe that God would use such a crude instrument as the infliction of pain to accomplish the work of reformation. "Reformation is effected by enlightening the understanding; but how inflicting pain on the body can convey light to the mind, I am unable to perceive." Still less could he accept the idea of pain as a kind of currency which could be used to discharge the debt incurred by sin.[8]

On the other hand, he remained enough of a Restorationist to dismiss the ultras' claim that the unhappiness inherent in the possession of a sinful nature was punishment enough to cover any offense. According to this view, the greater the sin, the greater the suffering, so that the demands of justice are always satisfied. Brownson could not accept this view, which seemed to erase the distinction between the vicious and the virtuous. Surely, he thought, some souls enter the afterlife in greater need of reformation than others. If so, and if a sinner must suffer in order to be reformed, then "he must suffer after death or never be reformed. My reader will understand that I mean pain inflicted in addition to the natural consequence of the act."[9]

Thus, by the summer of 1828 Brownson could not be described as either a Restorationist or an ultra Universalist. He continued to accept the basic Universalist tenet that "God can and will make his children holy and happy."[10] But he began to question the wisdom of trying to understand exactly how God might accomplish this. If human beings could form no satisfactory vision of the afterlife, perhaps it was because God did not intend them to "fathom his wisdom or ascertain the depth of his designs." He advised Universalists to "call [their] attention from those things which we cannot know in this state of existence and place it upon those things which are within our sphere of observation and are immediately connected with our happiness or misery in this world."[11]

As Brownson later described it in *The Convert*, the moment when he was forced to "drop from the clouds, take my stand on the solid earth, and devote myself to the material order, to the virtue and happiness of mankind in this earthly life" was a moment of profound loss. "I had made nothing of my religious speculations," he wrote. "I had no choice in the matter ... as the other world disappeared from my view, nothing but this world did or could remain." With nothing left to trust or believe in but "my five senses, and what could fall under their observation," he felt "reduced ... to a mere animal."[12]

In his writings from 1828, the change does not appear either so tragic or so momentous. In turning his attention from the afterlife to the present world, he was not giving up "the hope of heaven," or renouncing his faith in "the invisible and the heavenly."[13] He was merely applying to the Universalists the same criticism he had previously leveled at the evangelicals. Almost a year earlier, in his first long article in the *Gospel Advocate*, he had written, "Whatever bliss there may be in store for us in that unseen world to which we are all hastening, the present is all we can call our own. We are now inhabitants of the earth, and our chief inquiry should be, how can we render it a pleasing and desirable habitation? I am a believer in life and immortality beyond the grave, but I am not ambitious of being one of that number who forget earth for heaven."[14] In other words, part of what had attracted Brownson to Universalism in the first place was the value it placed on virtue and happiness in this world. Its advantage over other forms of Christianity was that, by relieving its adherents' anxiety about salvation after death, it freed them to concentrate on the true essence of Christianity: the development of a more just society. When he decided that the problem of future punishment was insoluble, Brownson realized that the debate over this issue had distracted Universalists, including himself, from what ought to have been their main concern. The result of this realization was confidence, not despair.

In fact, Brownson seemed particularly ebullient that summer of 1828. He praised Universalism as a religion "calculated to give man not only the hope of endless felicity hereafter, but unbounded felicity here. It reconciles him to his God, to life, to his brethren ... gives vigour to the mind, additional loveliness to truth and greater activity to virtue."[15] In a sermon he counseled his hearers to inquire "what good work can we perform" rather than troubling themselves with "the abstruse and often unintelligible points of polemical theology." If they would follow the Biblical injunction to "*do justly, to love mercy, and to walk humbly with your God,*" they might "rest with the fullest assurance that the God who has given you while here so many proofs of his loving kindness and fatherly protection will be no less mindful of you wherever he shall be pleased to continue your existence."[16]

Having decided not to pry into matters which God has hidden from human understanding, Brownson turned his attention to a study of the natural and social world. To discover the laws of nature and to develop the institutions that would enable humankind to live in accordance with them, he advocated the study of "philosophy," which for him embraced all facts observable by the senses and all inferences drawn from them.

The problem that most strongly attracted his attention was the old one of social injustice, which had stung him as a youth at Ballston Spa, and which would one day find expression in his essay on *The Laboring Classes*. He developed Hosea Ballou's idea of evil-as-ignorance in a new and characteristic direction by understanding ignorance and knowledge, misery and happiness, in collective rather than individual terms:

> Individual ignorance is not always the cause of individual suffering. Suffering or misery proceeds, in my opinion, from the imperfect state of society ... I do not say that knowledge, however great, possessed by an individual only can make that individual happy. For should he understand the laws of nature himself and be determined to obey them ... he would, from his connection with others suffer for their disobedience. Hence when I say, "if man would obey the laws of nature," I mean that if ALL mankind would obey them, all would be happy.[17]

One of his last contributions to the *Gospel Advocate* was an extended description of how "evil flows as a necessary consequence from the present organization of things."

> It is the misfortune of the world to prize things in an inverse ratio to their real worth. The most useful profession is deemed the least respectable and the most worthless, the most honorable. The badge of labor, of useful labor, which should be the badge of merit, of distinction, of honor is by the strange perversity of men's taste the badge of degradation ...This makes those who are of the lower class, as it is improperly and cruelly named ... anxious to be idle and useless that they may be respectable. This not only leads to crime in the poor classes, but leads to that idleness and listlessness which are the chief causes of ... those practices which degrade and destroy the more wealthy and opulent.[18]

Brownson believed that human society, though faulty, was capable of improvement. Here he parted company from Hosea Ballou, who believed that the ignorance that led to sin and misery was the result of the position of humanity in the great chain of being. Brownson found this idea as depressing as the Calvinist notion of inherent depravity, and almost as difficult to reconcile with the goodness of God. Whether humans do wrong because they lack the will to do better, or because they lack the wit to know better, in neither case is there much hope for happiness on this side of the grave.

Brownson took a somewhat more hopeful view. He was inclined to attribute the faulty organization of society to inexperience rather than to irremediable incapacity:

> Man, when first permitted to breathe upon this "terrestrial ball," [was] an infant and like all infants destitute of knowledge ... Ignorant, not knowing aliment from poison, unacquainted with the constitution of things, unable to predict the consequences of his actions, he acted simply from impulse, unguided by the least ray of light he was equally liable to act wrong as right ... Commencing wrong we established wrong principles, gave wrong impressions to each other's mind, a wrong bias to the minds of children; erected society on a wrong basis.[19]

Just as a child may grow from helpless infancy to responsible adulthood, society might in time overcome the ignorance which created and sustained dysfunctional social institutions. "If ignorance be the cause of the evils which prevail in society, little discernment is requisite to know that TRUTH is the needed remedy, the balm in Gilead; the knowledge and practical application of it, all that can be required to restore society to the soundness of moral health."[20]

The Authority of the Scriptures

Brownson's investigation of the arguments for and against future punishment led him back to the question of what, if anything, we can reasonably claim to know about matters which lie outside human experience, such as God and the afterlife. Many of his essays from late 1828 and early 1829 dealt with this issue. It is worth examining these essays in some detail, because they are among the most controversial of his Universalist writings. When, later in 1829, Brownson was accused of having become an infidel, his opponents often cited these essays in support of the charges against him.

As Brownson pointed out in *The Convert*, Universalists tended to hold liberal views about the authority of the Bible – for example, favoring a metaphorical rather than a literal interpretation of passages dealing with hell and damnation, or arguing that the details of biblical language were of less importance than the overall sense of the whole. One of the reasons Brownson had hesitated to embrace Universalism was that he was afraid that the Universalist approach to scripture would deprive him of the comfort he had found in the Bible. By 1828, however, he had come to believe that the Bible was not all of a piece, and need not be accepted or rejected in its entirety. It must interpreted by the human mind, in accordance with ordinary human judgment. Following John Locke's *Essay Concerning Human Understanding*, he argued that all knowledge is based on intuitive perception, sensory experience, or the testimony of others. The Bible falls into the category of testimony, the weakest form of evidence. It cannot compel us to believe anything which contradicts the evidence of our senses or of our intuitive perception. To those who argued that the Bible, being the word of God, was a higher source of truth than any other, he replied, "Though God cannot lie, man, who can and often does lie, is the only authority we have for believing the Bible is the word of God."[21]

Though Brownson believed that the Bible contained much timeless truth, he thought it also contained things "which cannot be believed by a man of common sense. It does contradict itself. It does contain doctrines subversive of the best interests of mankind and dishonorable to its reputed author." Its authors may have "had mental greatness, perhaps superior to our own, but they were deficient in science or a true knowledge of nature ... though God may have spoken to them face to face."[22] Brownson believed that the truth in the Bible could be distinguished from the error by the use of human reason. This must be so, he argued, because both revelation and the means to understand it are gifts of God. In fact, it is only the capacity for reason that makes revelation possible at all. "It is as much sacrilege to detract from the worth of reason as from the worth of the Bible." Any assertion that could be disproved, either by the findings of science or the rules of logic, was false and must be discarded. "If the preacher enjoins a religion contrary to all facts we have discovered ... why, let mankind be irreligious; we think they will do as well as those who embrace such a religion."[23]

This does not mean that Brownson considered the Bible, as he said in *The Convert*, "worse than useless ... calculated to mislead, to perpetuate superstitious fear, and to prevent the world from rising to just conceptions of the love and goodness of God."[24] In proposing the use of reason to separate truth from error in the Bible, he was as concerned to salvage the truth as to discard the error. He warned that, if Christians did not prune away ignorance and superstition from their religion, they would "lose their influence and be cast aside as the refuse of the earth."[25] As an example of the danger, he pointed to the corrosive skepticism of such "liberal publications" as the *Free Enquirer*, edited by Frances Wright, the radical feminist and freethinker, and Robert Dale Owen, the son of the utopian socialist and atheist Robert Owen. Such publications might provide a useful critique of religion, but they threatened to sweep away what was true and valuable in Christianity along with what was false.[26]

Brownson was not a skeptic like Wright and Owen. He considered the Bible "infallible" on all matters that are "beyond our reason and not opposed to it."[27] Without it, we could know nothing about matters that lay outside the realm of the senses. "Nature can prove nothing separate from itself; and should it prove the existence of a God, that God would either be nature or a part of nature. This is the same as atheism. The Deity, according to the notions of all intelligent theists, is independent of the universe." Only revelation could redeem nature by pointing to a transcendent reality hidden from mortal eyes. "I believe in the existence of a God," he wrote, "but I do not believe it because I think *nature* sufficient to teach his existence, but because he has revealed himself to the world in his word ... I see nothing in nature which appears able to originate the idea of a God in my mind. But since revelation has informed me there is a God, everything in nature bears testimony to its truth."[28]

Not all of Brownson's readers understood or shared his interest in the origin of the idea of God. Some saw it as evidence of doubt or skepticism. His statement that "I see nothing in nature which appears able to originate the idea of a God in my mind" was later quoted as proof that he did not believe in God, although in context it is part of a statement of faith.[29]

Probably most of the readers of the *Gospel Advocate* would have preferred more positive assertions of Universalist belief, and fewer examinations of the philosophical underpinnings of that belief.[30] Brownson, however, saw his questioning, probing, and debunking as strengthening belief by freeing it from falsehood. In one of his last articles for the *Gospel Advocate* he wrote, "Christianity is either true or false, if it is true it has nothing to fear from free inquiry, if it be false, we ought not to wish to believe it. For ourselves, we have no fears on this subject. The greatest part of the last ten years we have devoted to solving the momentous question, Is Christianity true? We have satisfied our mind, our faith on that point is fixed, not by tradition but by investigation."[31]

The Mission of Christ

Brownson had little patience with traditional Christian doctrines concerning the nature and mission of Christ. He dismissed the doctrine of the Trinity as "unintelligible and unreasonable or contradictory," and the doctrine of vicarious atonement as the product of "ignorance or fraud."[32] The most ridiculous of all theological systems, in Brownson's view, was "the absurd system of religion, known in the world for the last fifteen hundred years as the Christian," a confused medley of Jewish and Persian prophecy, Greek philosophy, and "pagan idolatry." Like most reformers, Brownson wished to strip Christianity of its accumulated errors and return it to its primitive simplicity. True religion, he thought, should be accessible to all, something "the most stupid can comprehend and the most skeptical acknowledge convincing."[33]

For all his criticism of Christianity, Brownson never spoke of Jesus except in terms of the highest respect and devotion. Jesus was for him the great reformer, who drove the money-changers out of the temple and declared that it was easier for a camel to go through the eye of a needle than for a rich man to enter the kingdom of God. Nothing in Brownson's Universalist writings remotely resembles the position he described in *The Convert:* that Jesus "so far from saving [humankind] from sinning, actually prevents them from being saved, and becomes the occasion of their moral degradation and misery. I ought, then, to war against him, and do my best to deliver the world from its bondage to him."[34] On the contrary, he honored Jesus as both a spiritual leader and a social reformer.

As a Universalist, Brownson believed that the true mission of Christ was "to produce righteousness, to reform the world, to make the numerous family of man holy and happy." He did not believe this could be accomplished by vicarious suffering, for "the murder of an innocent person can never be very satisfactory to justice." Nor did it make sense to believe that "the righteousness of Christ will answer for us in the sight of God while we remain unrighteous ourselves." Such a belief was morally repugnant as well as absurd: "The very notion begins with a falsehood; it proceeds with cruelty and ends as it begun, in a lie." Christ's purpose was "to reform the abuses of his countrymen, to root out their prejudices, to *humanize* their minds, destroy their bigotry and intolerance, and to give them more enlarged views of God and man" – in other words, to point the way to a less sinful way of life, not to interpose himself between sin and its consequences.[35]

Brownson was aware that, by eliminating the supernatural element from the mission and methods of Christ, "most Christians will think I degrade the works of the Savior; that the mission of Christ ... is thus dwindled down to comparatively nothing." But he defended the dignity and importance of the purely human Christ and his reforming mission. "Was this a small object?" he asked. "To us it appears the most noble, the most magnificent, and the most desirable object which man can conceive. For this the philanthropist may labor with the warmest zeal and for this he may lay down his life."[36]

Divine Goodness and the Problem of Evil

Brownson wrote in *The Convert* that Universalism, by undermining the authority of Scripture, "runs itself out, and renders doubtful even its own premises," namely, the essential goodness of God and of creation. "How am I to be assured that God is good? I can prove his goodness only from nature, and in nature the evil seems to surpass the good."[37]

The problem of evil, or how to reconcile the imperfection of the world with belief in an all-wise, all-powerful, and infinitely loving God, had always been at the heart of Brownson's religious doubts. This was the problem that had driven him first to the brink of atheism, and then, in reaction, to embrace the uncongenial solution offered by the Presbyterian church. Now, as a Universalist, he faced the problem again.

> Everybody knows there is evil in the world. How did it come? Why does a good God allow it to remain? ... Everybody must admit that a good Being will not voluntarily produce misery or evil. An Omnipotent Being cannot

be compelled to produce it. If God be omnipotent, and produce it, we have a right to infer he does it voluntarily, from choice. Can he then be good?[38]

This time, however, the question did not lead him to despair. Instead, it led him to what is perhaps the most sophisticated solution to the problem of evil developed by any American Universalist of his time.

Brownson presented his solution to the problem in his "Essay on Divine Goodness." This essay, the culmination of his Universalist thought, was published in the *Gospel Advocate* in five installments, in February, March, April, May, and September 1829. He began the essay by dismissing some commonly offered solutions to the problem. He could not believe, like the Presbyterians, that all of creation was cursed for the transgression of man. "I detest that sickly disposition ... which can see nothing but misery and do nothing but exclaim, 'Ah me! How wretched is the world! All is vanity, undeserving a wish or a thought!'" On the other hand, he saw that to deny the existence of evil, as Hosea Ballou did, only presented the problem in a more acute form. "If the idea that this is an imperfect world be denied, and it is said that it is perfect, that is still worse; for then we must say, it is just such a world as Deity designed it; and as it produces misery, we must say he designed it, consequently he is not good." Brownson agreed with Ballou that sin brought about misery, but considered this at best only a partial solution. Many misfortunes fall on the just and the unjust alike. And in any case, to blame humanity would not exculpate God, who gave his creatures the power to make themselves miserable. "Would the father who loved his child give him the means of destruction?"[39]

Brownson next considered the related problem of free will and necessity. He considered the doctrine of free will, as commonly understood, "only an imaginary notion, advocated for the purpose of making man guilty before God, to give God the right to punish." But to believe that we are constrained by necessity is even worse, for this "either plunges us in atheism or charges our sufferings upon God." Both errors may be avoided by recognizing that human beings are neither all-powerful nor absolutely powerless to influence their fate. "Man is governed by laws of nature, that is, the various objects with which he is surrounded act upon him, as well as he upon them." Though constrained by circumstances (including personal and collective sin and error), "man has the power to improve his condition, to lessen the evils he suffers and to enlarge his enjoyments."[40]

It is in the ability of human beings to improve their condition that Brownson finally located the proof of the beneficence of God. "Man," he concluded, "is placed here ignorant, and compelled to learn his duty and his felicity in the severe school of experience."[41] Truth is cumulative and progressive; each generation has to expand and refine the knowledge bequeathed by their parents. Though the task is difficult, and attended by many failures, to a "progressive being" it is the only road to happiness. Human beings could never be truly happy in a static world, even a perfect one. Sin and misery, in fact, are inescapably bound up with human happiness. "We can propose no alteration in [man's] constituent principles without making him worse. The question why did Deity permit evil to enter his system is an improper one ... evil flows as a necessary consequence from the present organization of things." Despite all the sin and suffering that beset human life, still "man may be more happy than he is miserable; and ... we may pronounce the Creator of the world good in creating it."[42]

The purpose of life, then, was to labor, to learn, and to do one's part for the progress of the human race. This understanding became the central organizing principle of Brownson's life. Summing up the fourteen years between the end of his Universalist ministry and his conversion to Catholicism, he wrote, "The various systems I embraced or defended, whether social or political, ethical or aesthetical, philosophical or theological, were all subordinated to this end, as means by which man's earthly condition was to be meliorated. I sought truth, I sought knowledge, I sought virtue for no other end."[43]

In *The Convert*, Brownson presented his career as a "world-reformer" in a negative light: it was all that remained after Universalism had destroyed his faith in the Bible, the Savior, divine providence, and felicity in the world to come. "Certainly this did not perfectly satisfy me in the beginning; but it seemed to be the only alternative that was left me."[44] However, his "Essay on Divine Goodness" and other writings from 1828 and 1829 offer a different view of "world-reform." In this view, world-reforming is not a poor substitute for religion, but a positive expression of social, philosophical, and religious beliefs. If God had made the world imperfect so that human beings might find their highest good in perfecting it, then to improve the world was to carry out God's purpose. Far from feeling "reduced to a mere animal," Brownson celebrated the unbounded possibility for improvement as the very hallmark of the human race:

> The brute creation may have knowledge; the beaver may elicit skill and foresight in the erection of its house and the provision of its food; but the beaver of today is probably no wiser nor more provident than the beaver

of four thousand years ago. Not so with man. One generation improves upon another. The infant not only arrives to the wisdom of manhood, but man himself can add to his own acquisitions the stock accumulated by his predecessor, and transmit it to posterity to be still enlarged by those who succeed him.[45]

Brownson's This-Worldly Universalism

Brownson's reflections on the goodness of God and the perfectibility of human society thus led him to a distinctively this-worldly form of Universalism, less concerned with speculation about the unseen world than with removing the impediments that kept people from living a good life. To reform the world was the noblest possible mission in life, worthy of the Savior and of all who strove to follow in his footsteps. True religion was not a matter of right belief, but of right action. "The preacher's office is to point out to us what we should *do*, and persuade us to its performance."[46]

Brownson's agnosticism on the subject of future punishment, his insistence that the claims of revelation must be validated by reason and experience, and his emphasis on reforming society rather than speculating on the world to come, had made him one of the more radical of the Universalists – but still, emphatically, a Universalist. Even his most rationalistic arguments, such as his insistence on the subservience of scripture to reason, were marshaled in support of Universalist doctrine. Here, for example, is the illustration he selected to demonstrate that not even the Bible can compel belief in two mutually contradictory statements: "Should I be told that the Bible, as many suppose it does, declares the larger part of mankind will in another world be made miserable by their Creator, and that the Creator loves all his creatures, I should not believe both propositions; for they are absolutely in contradiction to each other."[47] There is no question which of the two propositions Brownson believed. Like the audience for whom he wrote, he believed in a loving God, who would not doom any part of his creation to eternal misery.

In his sermons and articles, Brownson proclaimed that tolerance and freedom of inquiry, humanitarian concern and social justice were specifically Universalist virtues. Since they did not write others off as "children of the devil," Universalists were free of the "ungenerous prejudices" that infected "petty religious associations." While the more orthodox denominations taught that "*morality* is no mark of piety," Universalists were sensible enough to judge people by their actions rather than by their doctrinal correctness.

Where other denominations said, "you join *our* church, believe what we tell you, and pay us liberally for the care we take of your soul; and eternal felicity shall be your reward," Universalism encouraged bold and independent thinking:

> Universalism is identified with the march of mind. It does not cramp inquiry, but allows free scope to the intellectual powers; – holds no part of nature as forbidden to be examined and no opinion however different from the majority improper to be expressed. Opposed to dogmatism, it asks its advocates to be modest in giving their opinions; displeased with bigotry and superstition, it requires its followers to study for enlarged and elevated views, whether speaking of Deity or of man.[48]

Brownson may have shared Robert Owen's commitment to a life of "mental independence," but he did not agree with Owen that free and fearless thinking could only be found outside of organized religion.[49] When he took over the editorship of the *Gospel Advocate* at the beginning of 1829, he did so as a champion of Universalism in the fight against orthodoxy.

CHAPTER 9

Accusations of Infidelity

> *There is no way except a man's own declaration by which you can ascertain what is his belief; now this we are denied. For though we should "assert a thousand times we believe in God," it seems we should not be credited ... We have asserted time after time that we believed in the existence of God, and we never have, to our knowledge, used a single expression which implies anything different.*
>
> –Orestes Brownson, "Mr. Reese's Letter"

Late in 1828, Linus Everett was called to the troubled Universalist church in Charlestown, Massachusetts, which had been struggling ever since dismissing Edward Turner in 1823.[1] Before departing for the East, Everett arranged for Brownson to succeed him both as minister at Auburn and as editor of the *Gospel Advocate*. Brownson entered into his new duties with high hopes that the paper, "so firmly established, and so liberally patronized ... will continue to maintain its character and command the attention of the liberal minded of all parties."[2] Yet within three months, his fellow Universalist ministers had begun to denounce him as an "infidel." Before the year was over, he had been forced out of the editorship, the ministry, and the Universalist denomination. To understand how this came about, we must examine in some detail the events of the critical year 1829.

January 1829: Brownson Becomes Editor

Brownson began his editorship of the *Gospel Advocate* by setting forth what he probably thought of as an unexceptionable Universalist program. In his introductory editorial, he pledged "to vindicate rational Christianity, to encourage genuine morality, and to ... protect the civil liberty [from] unhallowed designs to unite 'Church and State.'"[3]

This is not to say that he had retired from the field of religious controversy. In the same issue he confessed his liking for a good argument. "Diversity of sentiment ... prompts inquiry; gives energy as well as activity to the mind; prevents that monotony and that general stagnation of the intellectual stream, which would result, were mankind all of the same opinion." When people of faith are contending for their beliefs, he wrote, "a close observer will discover the angels of science, of virtue and felicity, rising from the midst of the contention and joyfully hovering over the contending parties." All he hoped was that the combatants would conduct themselves with dignity and propriety, and avoid "that animosity which embitters their controversies."[4]

While Brownson believed that vigorous debate could advance the cause of truth, the same could not be said of the internecine strife that had plagued the Universalists since the beginning of the Restorationist controversy. He hoped to devote his efforts to the search for "a system worthy our adoption," not to petty quarrels with those who should be his partners in the search.[5] One reason for optimism was the resolution of the dispute over the New York State Convention. In May 1828, after five years of wrangling, the Convention had approved a constitution, under which each local association was free to choose whether or not to unite with the Convention. The Cayuga Association voted not to join, and there the matter rested.[6] With the right to remain outside the Convention guaranteed, Brownson was not disposed to continue fighting against a *fait accompli*.

Despite this hopeful sign, Brownson was in a vulnerable position. In the contentious and faction-ridden world of the Universalist clergy, he was singularly without allies. Neither the Restorationists nor the ultra Universalists considered him one of their own. The fight over the New York State Convention had left him with many enemies and only one real friend, Linus Everett. Everett had done his best for Brownson, but once he left for Charlestown, Brownson was on his own. His resources were slender. The Auburn society, founded in 1821 with about thirty members, was still a small group, meeting irregularly in schools, the county courthouse, and other public buildings.[7] For such a small society to call a minister was a symbolic expression of their faith and hope for the future, but it did not indicate their ability to support a minister with a growing family. Like Everett before him, Brownson depended for most of his income on his editorial position with the *Gospel Advocate*.

Brownson's position as editor was nominally the same as Everett's had been. In practice, however, it was quite different. Everett was an established minister and a leader in local Universalist circles. He was an experienced editor and publisher, with the wherewithal to buy and sell newspapers.

(Between 1825 and 1848 he would serve as editor, and usually owner, of eight different Universalist and secular periodicals.[8]) He had a long history with the *Gospel Advocate*, including a stint as owner. In January 1827, he and another Universalist minister, Theophilus Fisk, had bought the paper from its founder, Thomas Gross of Buffalo. Six months later, Fisk was called to the Lombard Street Universalist church in Philadelphia. Everett, now sole owner and editor, moved from Buffalo to Auburn, taking the *Gospel Advocate* with him. In 1828 he sold the *Gospel Advocate* to its printer, Ulysses Freeman Doubleday. Doubleday, a founding member of the Universalist congregation in Auburn, was owner-editor of a secular newspaper, the *Cayuga Patriot*. Technically, Doubleday was now Everett's employer, but both men seem to have taken it for granted that Everett would retain editorial control of the paper.

The balance of power between owner and editor was bound to change when Brownson took over the editorship from Everett. Brownson was an impecunious and inexperienced newcomer of twenty-five – eleven years younger than Doubleday – stepping into a position he could not have achieved without Everett's patronage. Moreover, prior to coming to Auburn, Doubleday had lived in Ballston Spa. He had been the owner and editor of the *Saratoga Courier* when Brownson was a lowly apprentice printer at the rival *Independent American*.[9] Thus, despite his ostensible status as editor and minister, Brownson could not command the authority vis-à-vis Doubleday that Everett had. He was nothing but an employee, holding his position at Doubleday's pleasure, dependent on Doubleday's journalistic experience, and subject to Doubleday's editorial oversight.

February-April 1829: The Gospel Advocate vs. the Gospel Herald

Within two months of taking over as editor of the *Gospel Advocate*, Brownson was embroiled in a controversy, but it was not one he would have chosen. His antagonist was Theophilus Fisk, the Universalist minister who had once co-owned the *Gospel Advocate* with Linus Everett. Though he served a church in Philadelphia, that January Fisk had begun publishing a Universalist newspaper, the *Gospel Herald*, in New York. The issue began as nothing more than a squabble over newspaper business practices. Thus, it did not appear to be the kind of controversy that led to the discovery of religious truth. And it was carried on with all the acrimony and personal malice that Brownson had deprecated in his introductory article.

There was no obvious reason why Fisk, shuttling between Philadelphia and New York, and Brownson, over 200 miles away in Auburn, should have singled each other out as rivals. Like all Universalist editors, they were competitors for the limited Universalist readership. At the same time, however, all Universalist periodicals were partners in the shared enterprise of spreading the Universalist message. They supplied each other with news, reprinted each other's articles, and regularly printed prospectuses for new and proposed Universalist periodicals.

The trouble between Brownson and Fisk began with a letter to Brownson from John S. Flagler, a Universalist minister who served as an agent for the *Gospel Advocate* in York, Livingston County, New York.[10] "Dear Sir," it began portentously, "I believe it my duty, when I see any one in danger of being injured, to inform him of the danger." It went on to describe the danger to the *Gospel Advocate* posed by Fisk's *Gospel Herald*:

> They have sent me the first No. of the paper with proposals for subscribers, and as far as I can learn, they have taken advantage of your list of agents, by supplying them in the same manner. This kind of management appears to me as dishonourable as it is contemptible ... it looks to me too much like brother trying to supplant his brother.[11]

This kind of inflammatory language was characteristic of Flagler. One of the most adamant opponents of the New York State Convention, Flagler was powerful and influential in local Universalist councils, but unpopular with colleagues because of the stubbornness with which he maintained his opinions and the harshness with which he treated those who disagreed with him. Nathaniel Stacy, who had clashed with him over the New York State Convention, wrote, "You might as well stand and argue with the mighty waters of the cataract of Niagara ... as to attempt to remove him from a position he had taken." According to Stacy, it was Flagler who had initiated the campaign to characterize the Convention as a "holy inquisition" and to impugn Stacy's motives for proposing it. When the constitution of the Convention was approved in 1828, and the other anti-Convention ministers moved on, Flagler remained unreconciled. Stacy wrote in 1850 that Flagler "never, to this day, gave up his opposition; but being overpowered by the operation of the convention ... he was at length compelled to 'sit and grieve alone.'"[12] Perhaps, with the resolution of the controversy over the Convention, Flagler felt the need for a new battle to fight, or a new reason for Brownson to defer to his leadership.

On receiving Flagler's letter, Brownson consulted his publisher. Doubleday, it turns out, had his own issues with Fisk, stemming from Fisk's conduct as co-owner of the *Gospel Advocate*. Between them, Doubleday and Brownson decided on an aggressive strategy. In the February 21 issue of the *Gospel Advocate*, Brownson printed Flagler's letter (anonymously), along with three columns of complaints about the business practices of Fisk and two other Universalist editors. This article, and subsequent follow-up articles including one signed by Doubleday as publisher, explained in detail what Fisk had done to merit the adjectives "dishonourable" and "contemptible."[13]

Flagler accused the *Gospel Herald* of using deceptive pricing to "supplant" or "undersell" the *Gospel Advocate*. Brownson and Doubleday took up this theme, complaining of the way Fisk advertised his paper's bargain price – "FOUR HUNDRED AND SIXTEEN PAGES FOR ONE DOLLAR!" A year's subscription to the *Gospel Advocate* consisted of the same number of pages but cost $2.00 ($1.50 if paid in advance). In reality, Doubleday said, the *Gospel Advocate* was the lower priced of the two: it was printed on larger paper, "hence the price of Mr. Fisk's paper should be only about 87½ cents, to be as cheap as the Advocate."[14]

Next, Flagler accused Fisk of trying to steal away the *Gospel Advocate*'s agents. In the early nineteenth century, publishers of regional and national newspapers employed local agents to manage subscriptions, collect payment, and distribute papers. The agency system facilitated the business of requesting and paying for a subscription, which could be dauntingly complicated in the absence of a uniform national currency. In 1828 the *Gospel Advocate* had over 250 agents, two-thirds of them in western and central New York State. Other agents carried the paper west to Pennsylvania, Ohio, Indiana, Kentucky, Michigan, and Missouri, and south to Virginia, the Carolinas, and Alabama. Far fewer carried it eastward. On the entire east coast it had only one agent: Theophilus Fisk himself, listed as the agent in Philadelphia.[15]

Brownson and Doubleday took the position that, while it was perfectly acceptable to advertise a new publication to another paper's subscribers, there was an unwritten rule against approaching another paper's agents. Fisk had transgressed this rule by sending copies of his new paper "with proposals for subscribers" to agents such as Flagler. The *Gospel Advocate*, on the other hand, was scrupulous in adhering to the code:

> After we have at great expense established our agencies, and published a list of agents for the benefit of our patrons, we can but think it ungenerous and dishonourable not to say unjust and unchristian for another publisher to take advantage of it to crowd his paper into notice. The publisher of the Advocate has never so far debased himself as to be guilty of such ungenerous and unfair means to increase the circulation of his paper, and while he has any sense of what is due from one man to another he never will.[16]

In March, the *Advocate* published its list of agents, accompanied by a sarcastic footnote: "We continue to publish additional agents. Those editors whose papers are circumscribed in their circulation will know where to send."[17]

Doubleday's primary grievance was that Fisk was using inside knowledge acquired through his connection with the *Gospel Advocate* in the service of a rival newspaper. As former part-owner and paid "traveling agent" for the *Gospel Advocate* – a salesman who recruited local agents in return for a commission – Fisk had access to unpublished information, which Doubleday saw in starkly commercial terms. He believed that, by paying Fisk for his services as agent, the *Gospel Advocate* had acquired exclusive rights to whatever information he collected. When Doubleday bought the paper from Everett, he had purchased these rights. If Fisk was still trading on this information, he was in effect stealing from Doubleday.[18]

Doubleday questioned Fisk's right to engage in Universalist journalism at all. When Fisk sold his share of the *Gospel Advocate* in 1827, he had promised that he would not "be engaged in another paper which might interfere with the circulation of the Advocate." Doubleday interpreted Fisk's editorship of the *Gospel Herald* as a violation of his pledge. Fisk, however, thought the promise bound him "only while I remained in Buffalo, or while Mr. Everett continued as the proprietor of the Advocate."[19]

Were Brownson and Doubleday justified in claiming that Fisk had acted improperly? The case against Fisk is weakened, rather than strengthened, by the fact that the *Advocate* made similar complaints against other editors. Thomas Whittemore, editor of the powerful and venerable *Trumpet and Universalist Magazine*, had "resorted to the same underhanded methods," sending copies of his paper to the *Advocate*'s agents. Russell Canfield, former owner-editor of the *Religious Inquirer* in Hartford, Connecticut, had behaved toward his previous paper just as Fisk had toward his: he "sold out his share of the Inquirer at a high price, and now ... wishes all his former subscribers to patronize said paper. Is this just to those to whom he sold the

Inquirer?"[20] These examples suggest that there was no general agreement about the norms Fisk was supposed to have contravened.

Fisk replied to Brownson and Doubleday's charges in two long articles in the March 28 issue of the *Gospel Herald*. In the first, a four-column open letter to readers of the *Gospel Advocate*, he defended his journalistic ethics and laid the groundwork for counter-charges against Brownson. In the second he struck back by attacking Brownson's character, background, and loyalty to the Universalist cause. He berated Brownson for bringing Universalism into disrepute by making his complaints in public, and reminded his readers of Brownson's humble origins and recent promotion: "We are truly sorry if being enticed from obscurity and raised to the editorship of a paper, should have had the effect on Mr. Brownson of destroying every noble and generous sentiment of the heart."[21]

Then, in a more piercing blow, Fisk denied that Brownson was a Christian. Brownson's article, said Fisk, was "so injurious to the spirit and genius of Christianity, that I was almost led to rejoice, that Mr. Brownson had renounced his belief in Christianity, before he wrote the article to which I allude." Brownson's essays and other writings in the *Gospel Advocate* "very nearly deny the existence of Almighty God, and still more nearly, if possible, reject the truth of divine revelation." They were "directly opposed to Christianity," "injurious to the spirit and object of Universalism," and had made the *Gospel Advocate* "a secret agent in the cause of infidelity." For months, Fisk said, he had been reading Brownson's essays "with trembling anxiety, solicitude, and alarm." Meanwhile, "the unbelievers in this city have been glorying in the desolation they were making in the vineyard of the Lord, thro' the instrumentality of the Advocate Editor."[22]

The evidence Fisk adduced in support of these sensational claims was rather unimpressive. The charge of infidelity turned out to rest on three points. First, Brownson had denied that human suffering is inflicted by God, asserting that "Jehovah is good." Secondly, he had written, "Let every man be a philosopher," which, Fisk claimed, actually meant "Every man should reject Christianity." Finally, he had denied the existence of God. Fisk backed up this allegation by quoting out of context Brownson's statement, "I see nothing in nature which appears able to originate the idea of a God in my mind."[23]

Fisk's article concluded with what amounted to a call for the Universalists to expel Brownson from the denomination. As Brownson was neither a Universalist nor a Christian, Fisk demanded, how long would the Universalists allow him to shelter within their fold?

> Let it be distinctly understood that we do not blame Mr. Brownson for being a deist, or even an atheist – we blame no man for his opinion – but it is for his *secret* attempts to undermine the fair fabric of our holy religion under the guise of friendship! It is for this we censure him ...
>
> Why is it that those who reject Christianity wish to hide in its folds? why wear the cloak when it is so much despised by them? ... Are they ashamed of their real name, that they thus skulk into a corner? or do they expect to gain more proselytes by acting the Judas awhile – and going secretly about their nefarious designs, under the mask of friendship?

The article concluded with a call to arms:

> The time is come when every man must gird on his armour – when every Christian must prepare himself for "perils among false brethren." Let every man who wishes well to our holy religion, arise in the majesty of truth, and say, "Blow ye the trumpet in Zion."[24]

We cannot know what response Brownson expected when he launched his attack on the *Gospel Herald*, but it is safe to say that he did not expect this. As far as he knew, the issue was whether or not Fisk had taken inappropriate advantage of his former relationship with the *Gospel Advocate* to promote his new paper at the expense of the old. Suddenly, Brownson was facing allegations – particularly galling to one who prided himself upon his sincerity – that he was neither a true Universalist nor a true Christian, that he was sailing under false colors.

When Brownson forced himself upon Fisk's attention with his complaints about the business practices of the *Gospel Herald*, it was perhaps inevitable that Fisk would respond by attacking Brownson's theology. Fisk was a conservative Christian who loathed the tendency of liberal Universalists to subject scripture and tradition to critical questioning. Brownson was just the sort of Universalist that Fisk despised. Brownson concentrated his attention on this world, Fisk on the next. Brownson lauded philosophy; Fisk warned that the application of "vain philosophy" to religion "demolishes the whole superstructure, and Christianity is annihilated."[25] When Brownson suggested that human beings were responsible for much of their own misery, he thought he was vindicating the goodness of God. Fisk thought he was denying both divine sovereignty and divine justice.

Fisk believed that "all objections to miracles are founded in atheism," since to deny miracles is to make God subject to the laws of nature.[26] By this definition, a good many of his fellow Universalists were atheists, and he had no objection to saying as much. Atheism among the Universalist clergy was the kind of dramatic topic that Fisk favored in both his preaching and his journalism. Abel Thomas, his associate in the *Gospel Herald* and eventual successor at the church in Philadelphia, described Fisk as "essentially of the propagandist type, luxuriating in the fire, his audiences gathered by sensational topics and held by sensational manner."[27]

January-February 1829: The Kneeland Case

The theological, philosophical, and temperamental differences between Brownson and Fisk do not entirely account for the manner of Fisk's counterattack on Brownson. In order to understand why Fisk responded the way he did, it is necessary to take into account the great issue which had dominated the *Gospel Herald* during the first two months of Fisk's editorship: the dismissal of Abner Kneeland, on the charge of infidelity, from the pulpit of the Second Universalist Society of New York.

Abner Kneeland had been a Universalist minister since 1804. In 1814 he resigned from the ministry, citing financial considerations but also troubled by doubts as to revealed religion. He entered into a correspondence on this subject with his friend Hosea Ballou, which Ballou published in 1820 as *A Series Of Letters in Defence Of Divine Revelation*. Kneeland allowed himself to be persuaded and returned to the ministry in 1816. From 1818 to 1825 he served the Lombard Street church in Philadelphia – the same pulpit later occupied by Theophilus Fisk. By all accounts he was an able and successful minister, who attracted many new members to the church. He edited a Universalist newspaper, compiled a hymnbook, and participated in a celebrated four-day debate with the Presbyterian minister W. L. McCalla, in which he defended the ultra Universalist view of the afterlife.[28]

Toward the end of his Philadelphia pastorate, Kneeland came under the influence of the British communitarian Robert Owen, who was then preparing to establish his "Community of Equality" at New Harmony, Indiana. In itself Kneeland's enthusiasm was nothing out of the ordinary, for Owen was immensely popular during his first American tour. He met with President Monroe and president-elect John Quincy Adams, twice addressed Congress on the subject of his new social scheme, and persuaded several prominent educators and scientists to join the venture at New Harmony. But though many Americans were taken with Owen's vision of a rational, cooperative, and egalitarian society, most disagreed with his sweeping condemnation of the institutions that, in his view, created and perpetuated

Abner Kneeland

inequality: private property, marriage, and religion. Kneeland, however, responded enthusiastically to this part of Owen's message.

After moving to the Prince Street church in New York City in 1825, Kneeland became more outspoken about his unconventional religious views. Abel Thomas described Kneeland's preaching in New York: "Constitutionally a skeptic, and exulting in novel criticisms, he constantly evoked questionings which he could not answer."[29] He shared with this congregation his enthusiasm for Robert Owen's program of social reform, solicited members for an Owenite community, and read from the pulpit Owen's notorious Fourth of July oration, which includes such provocative statements as, "Religion, or Superstition, – for all religions have proved themselves to be Superstitions, – by destroying the judgment, irrationalized all the mental faculties of man, and made him the most abject slave, through the fear of nonentities created solely by his own disorganized imagination."[30] Kneeland's controversial preaching split the church. In 1827 he left Prince Street and set up the Second Universalist Society of New York, taking about half the congregation with him.[31]

Kneeland's radical preaching distressed some of his Universalist colleagues, who accused him of infidelity, even atheism.[32] In September 1827, he was examined by the Hudson River Association, the ministerial association for the New York City area, on the charge that "he did not believe in the Divine authenticity of the Christian Scriptures, or of Christianity." The association voted to reprimand him for having left the Prince Street church without sufficient notice, but acquitted him on the theological charge after he agreed to sign a "concession" stating his belief in the truth and authenticity of the Scriptures.[33] A year later he was still in good standing – indeed, he occupied a position of honor – in the Hudson River Association. At its 1828 meeting he served as moderator, preached two sermons, administered the Lord's Supper, wrote the circular letter, was elected as a delegate to the state convention, and served on the committee of discipline.[34]

This was the situation when Fisk inaugurated the *Gospel Herald* with a pledge to take an uncompromising stand against infidelity among Universalists. He announced that he would print "no communication, that tends to impeach the veracity of the Holy Scriptures – or to weaken our belief in Divine Revelation ... under any circumstances whatever, unless it be for the purpose of refuting it."[35] He mentioned no names, but at least some of his readers understood his strictures to be aimed principally at Kneeland. In Utica, Dolphus Skinner commented, "It would probably have been well for the cause of truth in New-York and its vicinity, had this course been pursued by all Editors in that city, for the last two years."[36] William Drew explained in the *Christian Intelligencer*, "We presume [Fisk] means to be understood that the new publication shall be of a different character from the *Olive Branch*" – a paper edited by Kneeland.[37]

If Fisk intended to use his paper to challenge Kneeland and call him to account for his "atheism," he was almost immediately presented with a golden opportunity: in January 1829, Kneeland allowed Frances Wright to speak at the meetinghouse of the Second Universalist Society. As Abel Thomas wrote, "A man of unquestioned reputation as to Christian faith, with little hazard ... might have invited [Frances Wright] or Mr. Owen into his pulpit to lecture on social reform; Mr. Kneeland did it at his peril, and at the peril of his cause."[38] In an impassioned appeal to the congregation of the Second Universalist Society, Fisk warned that, if Wright was allowed to speak from a Universalist pulpit, the shame would rest on all Universalists. "If you allow this dark shadow, this foul blot to rest on the fair fame of Universalists, will it not be a reproach to all? Will it not give rise to a thousand malicious misrepresentations on the part of orthodoxy? ... Every Universalist expects you to disown by your *deeds*, the slanderous imputation that Universalism and Atheism are identified."[39]

Frances Wright

Early in February, the trustees of the Second Universalist Society confronted Kneeland with a demand that he restrict his preaching to such safe topics as comparing universal salvation to endless misery. When he refused, they dismissed him, over the protests of a sizable minority of the congregation.[40] In the *Gospel Herald* for February 14 – before the final congregational meeting to confirm Kneeland's dismissal had been held – Fisk exulted, "Believers in the unlimited goodness of the Almighty, have risen in the majesty of truth, and have demonstrated to the world, that Atheism and Universalism are not identified. The glorious stand that has been taken by the Second Universalist Society, is worthy of all praise."[41]

In January, while the Second Universalist Society was still deliberating what action to take, Drew took up the case against Kneeland in the *Christian Intelligencer*. Where Fisk had merely called for the Second Universalist Society to dismiss Kneeland, Drew called for Universalists to unite in disowning and expelling him from the denomination. In an influential editorial, he wrote:

> We have seen enough to convince us, that his views differ so essentially from the denomination of Universalists, that he ought no longer to be considered as one of us. We would not, by any means deny to Mr. K. the right of believing the Sacred Scriptures to be false, or of publishing his

opinions on the subject, or of following with Robert Owen; if he is sincere in those views and these attachments, we would not even censure him, for every man has an undoubted right to think as he pleases and to speak as he thinks. We only say, that if he thinks the Universalists wrong in their belief of the Bible and in their opposition to deism, he ought peaceably to leave them or they ought to leave him. It is not right, it is not just, that any order of people should be made to bear reproach or to suffer on account of their connexion with an individual whose views and feelings are an essential departure from their own.[42]

Drew did not confine his feelings about Kneeland to the editorial page. On January 28, the Kennebec Association of Universalists, meeting in Bowdoinham, Maine, passed a resolution withdrawing fellowship from Kneeland. The resolution was offered by Dr. George Tinker, a layman from the newly organized Universalist society in Bowdoinham.[43] But the idea of such a resolution must have been inspired by Drew's article, if not instigated by Drew himself. Two other associations in Maine passed similar resolutions shortly afterward.[44]

Organizationally, the withdrawal of fellowship was meaningless, as Kneeland was not affiliated with any of these associations. However, it was a brilliant public relations move. The very fact that Kneeland was not a member of these associations increased the credibility of the resolutions, for lay people in Maine could hardly be suspected of any personal animus against Kneeland. Drew's predecessor as editor of the *Christian Intelligencer*, Russell Streeter, wrote approvingly, "It is not to be supposed that the Ecclesiastical Council at Bowdoinham would have formally withdrawn fellowship from Br. K. without the most palpable evidence of his pursuing a course injurious to truth. The members of that body – remote as they are from the scene of his operations – must have acted deliberately, from an imperious sense of duty."[45] Widely reported in the Universalist press, the resolutions created the impression of a nationwide groundswell of opposition to Kneeland's continued ministry.

Most Universalists found it difficult to reconcile Kneeland's claim to be a Christian with his radical questioning of every article of Christian faith. Kneeland, however, did not admit that his beliefs, or his doubts, put him outside the bounds of either Christianity or Universalism. He explained his position in a letter to Skinner's *Evangelical Magazine*:

> If I understand you, you would attach the same idea to *scepticism* as you would to *unbelief* ... Scepticism ... is faith, yes, true and honest faith,

however weak; and him that is weak in faith receive ye, Rom. xiv:1 ... Until I acknowledge myself to be an unbeliever, I claim, and shall claim, all the privileges of being a *believer*; though, if you please, one weak in faith.

Kneeland insisted that it was the Universalists who were separating from him, and not vice versa. "I still retain my former appellation," he wrote. "Whether my brethren will still own me as such, is another question, which will be for them to decide." If they decided against him, it would show that "Universalism has become a sect, and like other sects has its dogmas."[46]

If Kneeland hoped to force the Universalists to articulate the limits to their tolerance, he was disappointed. No formal proceedings were taken against him by the Hudson River Association or the New York State Convention. When he presented himself at the Southern Association meeting the following May, his old friend Hosea Ballou persuaded him to "suspend" his fellowship "until he shall be able to give entire satisfaction that the cause of the world's Redeemer – of God – of truth, and of righteousness, is the cause in which he is laboring."[47]

February-March 1829: Brownson as a Second Kneeland

The Kneeland case dramatically changed the issues, and the stakes, in the confrontation between Brownson and Fisk. In 1828, Brownson had praised Universalism as a religion free of "ungenerous prejudices": rational, non-dogmatic, accepting of theological diversity, and committed to unlimited free inquiry. The Kneeland case established that there were limits to the Universalists' tolerance, and that a Universalist whose views fell outside these limits might be asked, as Drew put it, "to leave [the Universalists] or they ought to leave him." Crucially, the case had created a new conceptual category – infidel Universalist ministers – with a set of signs by which they might be recognized, and a set of techniques for removing them from fellowship.

In the early spring of 1829, Brownson was not yet aware of the changes that the Kneeland case had wrought. Fisk, who had followed Kneeland's progress closely, thought he detected signs that Brownson was heading down the same road. By the time he wrote his article on Brownson, Fisk had probably seen the March 7 installment of Brownson's "Essay on Christianity," in which he wrote that the Bible "contains many good things – much knowledge of the human heart, and discloses many important facts. It also, if we determine as we do in other cases, contains much that appears, at best very doubtful."[48] This must have sounded to

Fisk very much like Kneeland's view of the Bible: "That the Bible contains much important truth, must, as we think, be plain and obvious to all who read it. That it contains much error ... must be equally obvious to all who critically examine it."[49]

A closer or more sympathetic reading would have shown that Brownson's views on the Bible were not actually very close to Kneeland's. In his essay, Brownson, noting the internal contradictions within the Bible and the problem of different manuscripts and translations, had concluded, "It seems wisdom to abandon the position, that every word of the bible is inspired."[50] This was not a particularly daring position for him to take; it was a line of reasoning accepted by many Universalists, though not by Fisk. It certainly stopped well short of Kneeland's conclusion that the Bible "is of no kind of consequences to any one NOW."[51] However, the superficial similarity between Brownson's and Kneeland's writing on the Bible made it easy for Fisk, who *did* believe that every word of the Bible is inspired, and who was annoyed with Brownson anyway, to assume that Brownson was another Kneeland, and to treat him accordingly.

Moreover, Brownson had gone on the record to defend Frances Wright. When Fisk reprimanded the Second Universalist Society for hosting Wright's lecture, Brownson wrote, "We do not know what Miss Wright preached, nor do we care ... We have been denied a house to preach our doctrine in because we were heretical in the estimation of the proprietors and we thought it hard, and we think it equally hard to refuse those we might deem heretical."[52] In March Brownson attended two of Wright's lectures. He found her to be "a lady of talents and no small philosophical acquisition," though he still disagreed with her views on religion: "We have not yet become so *enlightened* as to be pleased with universal skepticism, or with the cold unfeeling dreams of the Deist, or colder speculations of the Materialist."[53]

Having decided that Brownson belonged in the category of infidel ministers, Fisk applied the approach that had been used successfully against Kneeland. Fisk's article on Brownson ("we do not blame Mr. Brownson for being a deist, or even an atheist – we blame no man for his opinion") was modeled on Drew's editorial on Kneeland ("we would not, by any means deny to Mr. K. the right of believing the Sacred Scriptures to be false ... we would not even censure him, for every man has an undoubted right to think as he pleases").

April-May 1829: Brownson Defends Kneeland

The Kneeland case was bound to re-ignite Brownson's fears about the coercive power of Universalist ministers' associations. Like Richard Carrique in 1827, Kneeland had been condemned without formal charges or regular disciplinary procedures, without being informed of the charges against him or being given a chance to defend himself. It was just as Linus Everett and the Cayuga Association had feared: Universalist fellowship was in the hands of a self-appointed group, informal but nearly unlimited in power, from whose judgment there was no appeal. Anyone who offended or embarrassed this clique was liable to be harassed and hounded out of the denomination, let him be who he might. If age, prestige, a quarter-century of service, even the patronage of Hosea Ballou had failed to protect Abner Kneeland, what hope would there be for Orestes Brownson?

On hearing that Universalist associations were withdrawing fellowship from Kneeland, Brownson wrote, "With shame and bitter regret we have witnessed the cruel and unfeeling persecutions of this aged, and faithful and talented defender of liberal sentiments." For Kneeland's opinions, as for Wright's, he claimed to care little. What mattered to him was how Universalists treated a member who happened to hold unpopular views. If, after all, the Universalists were just another persecuting sect, Brownson did not see how they could claim to be superior to any other denomination. "Where is the blush to crimson our countenances when we speak of excluding one on account of his faith?" he asked. "Let us go and ask pardon of the orthodox for what we have written and published against them ... before we adopt their practice."[54] When the *Christian Intelligencer* printed a typically self-congratulatory story about someone being expelled from a Calvinistic church for professing belief in universal salvation, Brownson reprinted it in the *Gospel Advocate* with the comment:

> Dr. Wright was excommunicated from the Calvinistick church because he did not adhere to the faith that church prescribed, Mr. Kneeland from the Universalists because it was supposed he did not adhere to the faith of Universalists. Which was the worse. The editor of the Christian Intelligencer approved the course adopted toward Mr. Kneeland by his order, but ridicules the conduct of the Calvinists towards Mr. Wright ... Allow not in ourselves that which we condemn in others.[55]

Brownson believed that the persecution of Kneeland had started as an act of private hostility by an unnamed individual, possibly Fisk. "We are well aware how this controversy originated," he wrote. "In our opinion it was at first purely *personal*." It had spread from Kneeland's particular enemies to the Universalist clergy generally because they were cowards, "men [who] start at a shadow, and shriek at the rustling of a leaf." Kneeland stood condemned "because *somebody* thought, that if Br. Kneeland was not publickly disowned, the orthodox would say – what? why that Universalists fellowship a man whose faith is incorrect ... Our timorous friends were afraid the orthodox would call it Atheism, and that would prove ruinous to our cause." But why, Brownson demanded, should Universalists allow their message to be dictated by their theological opponents? "As for reproach from the orthodox, we expect, and we scorn it ... We are sick of this squeamishness. We want more independence of mind. If a man preaches Atheism, any fool may know he does not preach Universalism."[56]

At the root of the disagreement about how to respond to the Kneeland case was a deeper disagreement about the position of Universalism relative to the evangelical denominations. Brownson believed that the Universalists' timidity about associating with anyone who held unpopular opinions came from a feeling of weakness or inferiority:

> We are aware of the feelings of Universalists. We know very well they have a sensativeness [sic] peculiar to those who consider themselves the minority. We know they tremble at almost every sentiment that is advanced lest the orthodox gain some advantage over them. Hence they often treat with extreme illiberality the most deserving, because the most independent of their preachers. They do this not because they dislike the sentiments advanced but because they fear somebody else will.[57]

There was, in addition to a disagreement about values and strategy, a disagreement about the facts of the case. How strong were the orthodox? How weak were the Universalists? Among New York Universalists, Dolphus Skinner represented the view that the political activities and interdenominational organizations of the evangelicals posed a great danger to religious liberty in general and to religious minorities in particular. Between October and December 1828, he published a series of articles called "A Solemn Appeal to All Liberal Christians," in which he warned that the evangelical denominations were engaged in a "deep-laid and wily plot" to abolish separation of church and state, "prostrate the liberties of this nation," and establish their version of Calvinist Christianity as the official religion of the United States. If Universalists and other non-evangelicals "slumber a little longer, fold our hands in apathy and cry, *all is well* ...it will be too late for resistance."[58]

Universalist concern about a plot to unite church and state reached a climax between 1827 and 1830, when the evangelical churches mounted a massive campaign to petition Congress to suspend the transportation and delivery of mail on Sundays.[59] Even the most independent-minded Universalists were concerned. In September 1828, Kneeland wrote, "The mask of our opposers is completely thrown off, and their ultimate object can no longer be mistaken ... The machinations and craft of the enemy [must be] exposed, or the manacles of spiritual slavery will be fastened upon our posterity."[60] Brownson sounded a similar note at the beginning of his tenure as editor of the *Gospel Advocate*. The petition campaign, he said, "bears the mark of the beast, and is easily discovered to be the offspring of that pernicious spirit, which seems to have possessed the leaders of the Orthodox party in our country." If it succeeded, it would pave the way for "a union of Church and State, or rather for a usurpation of the Church over the State."[61]

Even at this early stage, however, Brownson was less inclined than Skinner to see the evangelical program as a credible threat. Perhaps this was because, whereas Skinner envisioned the United States as dominated by a monolithic orthodoxy, Brownson saw the country in more pluralistic terms. In a satiric editorial, he pointed out the practical difficulties of organizing operation of the Postal Service along religious lines:

> It is expected that all the Jews in the United States, with the Sabbatarians, will soon present a petition to Congress to stop the passage of the Mail, and the opening of the Post-Offices, on *Saturday* ... The Roman Catholicks may be expected to petition that the Mail be stopped on Ash *Wednesday*, and ... through the whole term of *Lent*, a period of forty days ...
>
> The different petitioners will sustain their respective prayers by the trite maxim of our government, that no preference is to be shown to one sect over another, and that the religious scruples of the different sects are alike to be respected.[62]

In January 1829, the evangelical petition campaign received a serious setback in the form of the *Report on the Transportation of Mail on Sundays* by the Committee on Post Offices and Post Roads. The committee found that transportation of the mail on Sunday did not interfere with the right of the petitioners to the free exercise of their religion, and advised them to seek to spread their religion, not by acts of Congress, but by the power of persuasion and the example of holy living.[63]

Brownson was reassured and jubilant at this outcome. He printed the report in the *Gospel Advocate* with the comment, "We feel proud that those we have selected to watch over our interests and to make laws to check our encroachments upon each other ... have given proofs of their determination to abide by it."[64] For Skinner, however, the resolution of the Sunday mail issue did little to allay his fears. In the fall of 1829 he was still writing of "an unholy league, a secret plot ... to demolish the fair temple of American liberty, unite Church and State, erect an inquisitorial tribunal, and establish a hierarchy in this hitherto free country."[65]

While Skinner continued to focus on the external threat, Brownson came to believe that the greatest threat to Universalism came from within, from the compromises that Universalists were willing to make to placate the orthodox. As he lost confidence in those Universalists who "conjure up monsters or giants at every step, armed for the destruction of our rights," he also lost his fear of what they feared. He thought the times called for watchfulness, but not for "idle fears ... [of] imagined dangers."[66] In place of overheated rhetoric about impending danger, Brownson used humor to mock the pretensions of the orthodox who imagined themselves more powerful than they were (and perhaps also of the Universalists who feared them). Under the heading "Horrid Impiety," he wrote of the Owasco River, which "winds along but a few rods from the Presbyterian Church" in the village of Auburn.

> The stream, it is said, is a confirmed Sabbath-breaker! Though sermon after sermon has been preached close by its banks, though prayer after prayer has been delivered for the sanctification of the Sabbath ... yet it continues to profane the holy day of rest of which God himself rested, by rolling the mass of waters collected in the Owasco Lake to the Seneca River ... Would it not be well to call a publick meeting to enquire if this daring impiety cannot be stopped?[67]

Skinner believed that Universalists and other non-evangelical Christians could secure their constitutional rights only by moving from the periphery of the religious landscape to the center. He looked forward to a time when joining a Universalist society would be perceived as just as safe, respectable, and ordinary as joining a Methodist or Presbyterian church.[68]

Brownson rejected that this entire line of reasoning. For him, it was the Universalists' liberalism that distinguished them from the orthodox. "Were we to ask what has given Universalists their present respectability, we should ... point to the freedom and fearlessness of their enquiries, to the boldness with which they have attacked existing errors, and to the independence they have ... exhibited." He declared that he would never abandon his commitment to think for himself in matters of religion. "We enlisted under the standard of free inquiry, with a determination to embrace TRUTH wherever found. We shall not desert our standard. If our brethren forsake it we shall regret their example but we shall not follow it."[69]

Nor did he. Even after he himself was branded as a deist, an atheist, and an infidel, he continued to defend both Frances Wright and Abner Kneeland in the name of free speech and freedom of the press.[70]

CHAPTER 10

Expulsion

As the body is rather injured than benefitted – rather weakened than strengthened – by partaking of poisonous or unwholesome food ... so the mind is equally liable to be injured by morally poisonous food – by spurious and unwholesome systems of religion.

– Dolphus Skinner, "Sermon on Modern Revivals"

April-July 1829: Brownson Defends Himself

On April 18, 1829, three weeks after Theophilus Fisk publicly accused Brownson of renouncing Christianity, the *Gospel Advocate* responded with two articles. In the first, Doubleday provided further detail about Fisk's alleged misdeeds as editor of the *Gospel Herald*.[1] By this time, however, the ground had shifted. If there had ever been a time to discuss Fisk's sins against the *Gospel Advocate*, the time had passed. The subject at issue was no longer Fisk's conduct as an editor, but Brownson's fitness to be a Universalist minister.

In the second article, Brownson replied to Fisk's allegation of infidelity. He began by asserting his zeal and loyalty for the Universalist cause:

> About four years since, the editor of this paper renounced his connection with the Presbyterians, turned from the prospects which that connection presented, and joined, with all his heart and with all the energies of intellect he possessed, the incipient cause of Universalism ... Few men have laboured with more industry or sacrificed more hours when rest was desirable, than he has, to aid the cause which he believed was dear to every philanthropist.[2]

Next he tried to bring logic to bear. He pointed out that Fisk was "ignorant of philosophy" – a charge that Fisk probably would not have denied – and had therefore misunderstood the points Brownson was trying to make. For example, Fisk had accused Brownson of denying that God may justly punish sin. Brownson replied that he "admits ALL for which Mr. T. Fisk or any other Universalist contends, viz. that pain may be inflicted on an individual for that individual's benefit." He had merely denied that such infliction could properly be called "punishment."³

Like his opponents, Brownson was not above a bit of sly innuendo: "We know not whether Mr. Fisk has any conscience or moral sense, except *policy*; if he has, we would give it one hint. We are *not* ignorant of his *private* views. But, as we suppose he wishes them to be private, we shall not give them publicity."⁴ In a defiant gesture, he appointed Abner Kneeland agent for the *Gospel Advocate* in the city of New York.⁵

After this exchange, Fisk preserved an almost unbroken silence on the subject of Brownson and the *Gospel Advocate*. The issue of Brownson's supposed infidelity did not go away, however. It is clear from Brownson's writings in the *Gospel Advocate* that he felt himself to be under attack during the spring and summer of 1829, along the general lines laid down in Fisk's articles. He wrote of readers who "fear I am deistical" and "call me heretick," and of "the ill advised measures of some of my brother editors and preachers ... who attempt to bear down a brother without cause."⁶

It must be said that the Universalist press contains little record of any such attacks. This is not to say that they did not occur, but they must have taken place behind the scenes rather than in the public press. In June, for example, Brownson complained that William Reese "says I am wild, inconsistent, absurd, and probably fighting under false colours; some of these charges he has preferred publickly and others perhaps more privately."⁷ Among other things, Reese had written to Doubleday to inform him that subscribers were complaining that the paper was less useful under Brownson's editorship than it had been under Everett's.⁸

Brownson responded to these attacks in a variety of ways, some effective, others childish and self-defeating. At various times he employed logical argumentation, protestations of innocence, counterattack, sarcasm, pathos, bluster. Since he replied publicly to provocations made in private, Brownson often appeared to be the aggressor. It was Brownson who insisted on keeping up the quarrel with Fisk, sniping at him for trivial breaches of journalistic etiquette and sarcastically congratulating him on "the strong claims he may have to be made grand Inquisitor when that office shall be established in this country."⁹ Fisk, for the most part, refused to be drawn. Only after several months did he respond, saying, "With Mr. Brownson and the Gospel Advocate I have done for ever. He may accuse me of murder or robbery – I shall not reply."¹⁰

We can guess that Dolphus Skinner and William Drew were among the "brother editors" Brownson considered his enemies, but neither of them said much about him on the record. Drew, in a rare reference, neatly captured the high ground, challenging Brownson's claim to be more liberal or tolerant than his opponents. In response to Brownson's defense of Kneeland, he wrote, "The Editor of the *Gospel Advocate* is so very *liberal*, that while he is willing to fellowship with Deists and Atheists, he is not willing that we or others should express a contrary inclination. Were he less illiberal in his liberality, and less pugnacious withal, we should feel more confidence as to the utility of noticing him further."[11]

While all this was going on, Brownson did his best to carry on the business of the *Gospel Advocate*. He published sermons by himself and other ministers, debates between Universalists and their orthodox opponents, and the usual letters, meeting notices, obituaries, poetry, and advertisements. There was no hint in any of this of the infidelity that his opponents claimed to detect, or that he himself would later confess. The views he expressed in 1829 were, if anything, a little more conservative than those of the year before. He did not precisely retreat from his liberalism and rationalism, but he gave more careful attention to explicitly theological subjects. In his "Essay on Christianity" he addressed such subjects as inspiration, miracles, scripture interpretation, and the Trinity. Most important from the Universalist standpoint was his "Essay on Divine Goodness," a detailed analysis of whether, and in what way, belief in the benevolence of God implies belief in the ultimate salvation of all.

There were moments when Brownson hoped that the accusations would die away. In the June 13 issue he wrote, "The black cloud we saw rising with threatening aspect has passed over without injury to my prospects. The Advocate has survived the storm."[12] After preaching at a meeting of the Black River Association in Watertown, New York, he wrote, "Universalists in this state, for these three or four years past, have been deeply afflicted. Division had come in among them, and brother become cold to brother; but that time is gone we hope, and we think we already see the sun of peace beaming from behind the dispersing cloud which has darkened our prospects!"[13]

June-August 1829: Brownson's Creed

Brownson was wrong about his prospects. Despite occasional small victories, the rumors and accusations kept coming. His frustration boiled over in the now-famous article "My Creed," published in June 1829. Reprinted in Henry Brownson's biography of his father, this article has subsequently been cited as evidence that, by mid-1829, Brownson no longer thought of himself as a Universalist, or even as a Christian.[14] Taken out of context, it is easy to see how it can be read that way. Four of the five points of the "creed" – exhortations to honesty, industry, generosity, and the cultivation of mental powers – are ethical rather than religious precepts. Only in the fifth point did he mention God, and then only to say, "I believe that if all mankind act on [the other four] principles they serve God all they can serve him – that he who has this faith and conforms the nearest to what it enjoins, is the most acceptable unto God." The article ended on a note of defiant irreverence:

> Now my reader, if you by believing that Jonah swallowed the whale, or the story about the witch of Endor, with various others of the same character, I say dear reader, that if believing these marvelous stories will make thee a better man ... then I have not the least objection, even shouldst thou believe that the moon is made of "green cheese." Now ye doctors of divinity hurl your anathemas. Let every man be HONEST.[15]

In the context of what Brownson had been enduring for the past several months, these do not sound like the words of a man who has lost his faith, but like the howl of a man who has been goaded beyond endurance. Those who cite it as evidence of Brownson's infidelity ignore what comes between the five points of the creed and the provocative peroration:

> This, O ye! who accuse me of Infidelity, is my creed – read it, obey it, and never again tell me I am a disbeliever ... I would quote Scripture, but people say I do not believe it, – how they should know I do not is more than I can divine. They have never derived that knowledge from myself for I have never had it to give.

This is followed by nearly a column of quotations from the Bible "to show my creed is scriptural." One to which Brownson particularly called his readers' attention was, "But if any provide not for his own, and especially for those of his own house, he hath denied the faith and is worse than an infidel" (1 Tim. 5:8) – a subtle rebuke to those Universalists who troubled their own house with quarrels and false accusations.[16]

"My Creed" was accompanied by an editor's note: "There are some who seem determined the publick shall believe the Gospel Advocate is an Infidel paper. I had written a long refutation of this charge with a design to present it to my readers, but upon second thought I believe I shall let it lie for the present." Instead, he challenged his critics to debate him openly if they thought him in the wrong. If any took up the challenge, he promised, "He shall have fair play, and the editor of the Gospel Advocate will reason the point, he hopes, to the satisfaction of the pious and to the convincing of those who are not *personally* prejudiced against him, that he is a firm believer in the Gospel of Christ."[17]

One who took up the challenge was William Reese. In 1829, as we have seen, Brownson numbered him among his enemies. Reese was, however, a fair-minded man. Challenged to state precisely what he found objectionable in Brownson's writings, he responded with five columns of detailed questions and comments. In his reply, Brownson argued that there was little real difference between his beliefs and Reese's. For example, both agreed that some parts of the Bible were inspired and others were not, though they disagreed over exactly which parts were which. He dismissed other points, such as whether inspiration should be called "supernatural" or "extraordinary," as insignificant semantic differences.[18]

The correspondence between Reese and Brownson, despite a certain defensiveness on both sides, was for the most part polite, respectful, and focused on the points at issue. In the end Reese accepted Brownson's explanations, declaring, "I am satisfied that you believe in the existence of God, as revealed in the scriptures, and in the Gospel of Christ." He did offer some friendly criticism. Without the "key" provided in the recent correspondence, he said, Brownson's essays and sermons were "ambiguous," and the light manner in which he wrote of sacred subjects "will never feast the mind of the devout Christian, nor convince a single sceptic of the truth of Christianity."[19]

Both Brownson and Reese had reason to be satisfied with the result of their discussion, but in the long run it did Brownson no good. He might win over an occasional critic who, like Reese, was willing to take the time and trouble to conduct a minute investigation into his antagonist's beliefs; but more casual readers would find his continued defense of Abner Kneeland, and his practice of printing letters and speeches by Kneeland, Frances Wright, and Robert Dale Owen, sufficient to give credence to the rumors about him.

Even among readers who did not find Brownson's sentiments objectionable, the steady stream of accusations and counter-accusations took its toll. The quality of the *Gospel Advocate* declined. Brownson devoted many pages to petty and, in some cases, obscure quarrels with his Universalist antagonists. General readers, looking for an exposition of Universalist faith or news about the political struggle with the evangelicals, could hardly have been edified by a series of articles in which Brownson, Reese, and Drew accused each other of "want of gravity."[20] A reader in Ohio wrote, "I have attended to the controversy between yourself and Mr. Reese, and cannot but lament that we should be forever splitting straws while the enemies of every species of freedom are inventing improvements on the Spanish Inquisition ... I see more cause for despondency in our own narrow notions and disunion, than in all the efforts of orthodoxy."[21] Brownson attached an editorial note agreeing with the writer, but the overall content of the paper undercut his case.[22]

September-October 1829: The Union of Papers

In mid-September 1829, Brownson set off on a six-week trip to visit Linus Everett and other friends in New England. On the way, he stopped at Utica, where he met with Doubleday and Dolphus Skinner to discuss the possibility of Skinner's buying the *Gospel Advocate*. Doubleday extracted from Brownson a promise that, "in case the Advocate was sold to Br. Skinner," he would not engage in a competing paper for a period of two years – a pledge similar to that Fisk had made when he sold his share of the *Gospel Advocate* in 1827. According to Doubleday's account of the meeting, Brownson heard of the proposed sale with equanimity and promised "that he would do nothing to injure the Advocate in the hands of brother Skinner, but would do all he could to benefit it."[23] The three parted on good terms, and Brownson continued on his way.

In view of the strained relations that had existed between himself and Skinner for the past several years, Brownson probably realized that his long-term prospects for employment on a paper owned by Skinner were not good. He therefore took the opportunity to do a little job-hunting while in New England. Skinner's friend and associate Lemuel Willis reported that Brownson tried to secure a position as a writer for either the *Christian Inquirer* in Hartford or the *Trumpet and Universalist Magazine* in Boston.[24] Thomas Whittemore, who edited the *Trumpet*, did not confirm that Brownson had asked him for a job, but said that he "supposed [Brownson] came to this neighbourhood, the focus of Universalism, to find employment." He added that he had heard a rumor that Brownson was to become co-editor of the *Christian Inquirer*.[25]

At this stage Brownson obviously still hoped to find a congenial position in Universalist journalism. Though he realized that it would be prudent to look for new opportunities, he does not appear to have had any immediate anxiety about his position with the Auburn church or the *Gospel Advocate*. On September 29 he wrote to Doubleday, telling of his progress "after taking my leave of you and your lady at Utica." He told of having preached in Hartford and gave a cheerful account of the state of Universalism in Connecticut. The letter ends, "I start to-morrow for Boston, and shall hasten back to my warm hearted friends at Auburn as soon as possible."[26]

The plans for the sale of the *Gospel Advocate* proceeded rapidly. On September 26, Skinner's *Evangelical Magazine* carried the notice, "The Editor and Publisher of this paper has recently entered into an agreement with the Publisher of the *Gospel Advocate*, Mr. U. F. Doubleday, for uniting that paper ... with the *Evangelical Magazine*, and publishing both together in one paper, at Utica, from and after the first of January next." The notice went on to say that the new arrangement had been "effected with the most amicable feelings."[27] Doubleday would later claim that he had sold the paper with Brownson's "consent and approbation."[28] It is clear, however, that Brownson was not aware of the full extent of the agreement between Doubleday and Skinner. He certainly did not know that Doubleday had offered to sell the *Gospel Advocate*, and Skinner had agreed to buy it, for the express purpose of removing Brownson as editor. In a biographical sketch of Skinner, Lemuel Willis wrote:

> The *Gospel Advocate*, a paper published at Auburn, by Mr. Doubleday, [was] under the editorial charge of O. A. Brownson, then professing to be a Universalist: but like Abner Kneeland when he edited the *Olive Branch* in the city of New York – a professedly Universalist publication, but containing semi-infidel thoughts and sentiments and fully indicating the tendency of his mind, contained articles of a decidedly infidel character. This fact was the cause of great dissatisfaction on the part of many and especially Mr. Doubleday; who, finally, to get rid of Mr. Brownson, as a dernier resort, proposed to Mr. Skinner to sell the *Advocate* to him.[29]

On October 6, Brownson wrote to Doubleday again, this time from Charlestown, Massachusetts, where he was staying with Linus Everett. "My visit has been so far attended with high satisfaction to myself," he wrote. He had visited Bunker Hill, met Hosea Ballou, and preached in Charlestown and at Hosea Ballou's church in Boston. He delighted in the church music, and conceded that the Lord's Supper, "an institution which I have generally considered of no great practical benefit," might have its advantages. In fact, he was pleased with everything he saw in Boston, except the spectacle of a schoolboy being flogged.[30] On his way home, on October 25, he wrote from Albany, where he had preached to the Universalist society. There, too, the prospect was pleasing. "Every thing we saw, indicated to us that the day of redemption for Albany has come nigh, and her deliverance from gloomy orthodoxy is at hand."[31] Whatever misgivings he may have had about the proposed sale of the *Gospel Advocate*, Brownson clearly expected his job to be waiting for him when he came home. These are not letters that a man who has just lost his job would write to the employer who had fired him.

On the return trip, Brownson again stopped at Utica. There he learned that Skinner had indeed bought the *Gospel Advocate* and that he intended to merge it with the *Evangelical Magazine*, eliminating Brownson's position as editor. Brownson did not yet, however, understand his true situation, for he immediately asked Skinner for a job. According to Skinner, Brownson offered to "travel about the country, and preach, get subscribers, collect arrearages, and write for the paper."[32] Willis wrote that Brownson "entreated Mr. Skinner to let him become an assistant editor of the *Evangelical Magazine and Gospel Advocate*. But Mr. S. would have no skeptical writers employed in conducting the paper, and, therefore, declined to accept his services." According to Willis, "the course pursued by Mr. S. in regard to this matter was the cause of driving Mr. B. from our ministry and denomination."[33]

Willis thought Skinner wanted to get rid of Brownson because of Brownson's "skeptical" or "semi-infidel" writings, but it is unlikely that Skinner's motivation was primarily theological. Skinner himself was a liberal Universalist, closer theologically to Brownson than to conservatives like Theophilus Fisk. Like Brownson, Skinner spoke feelingly about the goodness of God, but lightly and mockingly of such traditional Christian doctrines as vicarious atonement (which he called "absurd in the extreme," "degrading to Divine benevolence," and "unfavourable to gratitude, piety, and devotion"), the Trinity, and the Catholic doctrine of transubstantiation. Also like Brownson, he described the mission of Christ in rationalistic and humanistic terms. In the sermon which he chose to introduce himself to the readers of the *Gospel Advocate* as the new editor, he wrote:

> The principal object of [Christ's] mission was, to instruct and enlighten mankind – to teach them the true and amiable character of God, that

Dolphus Skinner

they might be reconciled to him – in short, it was "to bear witness unto the truth"...

The sufferings of Christ were of no further benefit to man, in themselves considered, than they served to commend and manifest the love of God, that shone through him, to the world of mankind.[34]

Skinner's conduct toward Brownson had more to do with denominational loyalty and discipline than with theology. Skinner's outstanding characteristic, throughout his career, was his devotion to institutional Universalism. Though not yet thirty years old in 1829, he was beginning to assume the position of guardian and gatekeeper for Universalism in New York State. He arranged for Brownson to be removed from the editorship of the *Gospel Advocate* because he believed him to be a liability to the paper and to the Universalist cause. Instead of presenting a clear and persuasive statement of Universalist belief, Brownson filled the *Gospel Advocate* with his private doubts, half-formed ideas, and philosophical speculations. He embarrassed his colleagues by quarrelling in public with other Universalists. He could not even be relied upon to teach the doctrine of universal salvation. In "A Gospel Creed," the explicitly theological companion piece to the secular "My Creed," Brownson wrote that he considered universal salvation to be "an inferential doctrine rather than one positively taught" in the Bible. Reasoning from the goodness of God, he thought it "almost certain" that all will finally be saved, but admitted that "I deem it a matter not positively decided."[35]

Doubleday and Skinner were not the only ones displeased with Brownson's performance as editor of the *Gospel Advocate*. One "worthy patron of the Advocate," who had been in the habit of using the paper to help him argue the case for Universalism, told William Reese that he now used the *Religious Inquirer* instead.[36] A reader in Ohio canceled his subscription, saying he did not understand "how a professed preacher of the Gospel can be an admirer of Miss Frances Wright, and make quotations from her infidel writings." To this Brownson replied airily, "We enquire for truth and care not who assists us to find it ... If that article be Infidel, be it so, we would to God there were more *such* infidelity in the world."[37]

If Brownson did not mind losing subscribers, Doubleday and Skinner assuredly did: Skinner out of zeal for the Universalist cause, and Doubleday for this reason and also because Brownson's follies were costing him money. When Doubleday presented him with an opportunity to take the *Gospel Advocate* out of Brownson's hands, Skinner jumped at the chance – not because he thought Brownson was an infidel (indeed, at this point Brownson seemed just as likely to stray in the direction of orthodoxy as of infidelity) but because he considered him incompetent and unreliable, and the subscribers were complaining.

October-November 1829: The Free Enquirer

Brownson's meeting with Skinner, at which he found out that the *Gospel Advocate* had been sold, offered his services to Skinner, and was turned down, took place in Utica on October 27, 1829. It happened that Frances Wright was also in Utica that day. Brownson attended her lecture and stayed to speak to her. By the end of the evening, he had accepted a position as "corresponding editor" for the *Free Enquirer*.[38]

Brownson's term as editor of the *Gospel Advocate* still had two months to run, and he determined to put a good face on the situation and take his leave as graciously as possible. Back in Auburn, he began putting together the November 14 issue of the *Gospel Advocate*. He included the sermon he had preached in Boston, his report on Universalism in Albany, the latest round of letters in the ongoing controversy between pro- and anti-Kneeland factions in New York City, and the usual articles on revivals, tract and Bible societies, and Sunday mail. He also included a brief statement about the forthcoming union with the *Evangelical Magazine*. He expressed his sadness at having to "take his leave from the kind friends who shall have followed him through the volume," and apologized for any offense he might have given them. "The union is a friendly one, and brought about by the most amicable means, and the writer of this trusts it will be for the general good of the cause," he wrote. The new editor was "a man of moral worth, good abilities, and a sound, orthodox Universalist ... He takes the *Advocate* with my good wishes for his success, and however different may be his course and mine hereafter, I shall always feel proud of his friendship." He even reminded the subscribers to settle their accounts in preparation for the transfer to the new owner.[39]

One thing that Brownson did not reveal was his arrangement with the *Free Enquirer*. All he said about his plans was, "His future course he is not at liberty to state, but he will add that if he lives the publick will learn what that course is" – a cryptic remark which could be interpreted to mean either that he did not know what he was going to do next, or that he had a surprise in store. Without mentioning that he had agreed to work for Frances Wright, he printed a substantial excerpt from a lecture in which she dismissed religion as irrational and a waste of time and money. Though most of her criticism was aimed at evangelical societies and revivals, she did not spare the Universalists.[40] This item was accompanied by a dissenting opinion by Skinner: "We think the general prevalence of her principles, with the destruction of all existing institutions, would cast mankind into a dark and tremendous ocean, without compass, or chart, or polar star to guide, without a helm to govern, or any haven in view where the wanderers would find a safe haven."[41]

The amicable relations between Brownson and his former employer did not last long. On November 7, as Brownson was completing his work on the forthcoming issue of the *Gospel Advocate*, the *Free Enquirer* printed the news that Brownson had "dropped from the clouds upon the solid earth," renounced religion, and joined the *Free Enquirer* staff.[42] This was apparently the first that Doubleday had heard of this arrangement, and he was outraged. He was no longer prepared to allow Brownson to stay until the end of the year – or even to the end of the current issue. On the next-to-last page of the November 14 issue of the *Gospel Advocate*, a thick horizontal line marks the abrupt end of Brownson's editorship. Beneath the line is a notice signed by Doubleday:

GOSPEL ADVOCATE. 369

month of January. To facilitate the work, we have contracted to have it printed on Treadwell's Power Press; and we have got through 150 pages. We expect it will make from 350 to 500. A copious Index will accompany it, by means of which, with very little trouble, the reader may turn to any subject embraced in it. If there are any who have not returned the subscription papers for this work, they are requested to do so forthwith.—*Trumpet.*

A society of Universalists, consisting of fifty three members was formed in Pultney, Vt. on the 3d ult. Another has just been gathered in Guildford in that State.

After this number of the Advocate was nearly prepared for the press, it was thought advisable to leave out the name of O. A. Brownson as editor. Mr. B. has ceased to be a Universalist preacher, and commenced lecturing in favour of Miss Frances Wright's notions of philosophy and religion. If he does not avow Atheism, he does not profess to be a Theist. He cannot, therefore, consistently advocate the truth of Christianity, the future salvation of all or any of the human family, nor the existence of a God, or of any intelligent power to us invisible. Whether his present course be the result of conviction or of mental aberration, we consider it widely inconsistent with the plan of the Gospel Advocate. He has already apprised the publick that Nature does not teach the existence of a God. The reader must know, if revelation be rejected, what this declaration amounts to, and we therefore omit repeating terms, which might be considered harsh or unfriendly.

The publisher of the Advocate always has believed that Nature taught the existence of a God. When we see the trees of the forest prostrated by the resistless hurricane, we see power without any visible marks of intelligence. But when we see the timbers nicely prepared and fitted so as to form an elegant mansion, we know that the skillful workman has been engaged, and that his intelligence not less than his physical power, was necessary to adjust the different parts of the building. And look at man! He did not form himself; and yet his bones, muscles, nerves, veins, and arteries, are all nicely calculated to answer particular purposes. The same may be seen in the great variety of animals. We farther observe that all their members are calculated for their peculiar condition—for defence or flight, and also for procuring subsistence.

Besides, the common sense of mankind in general has ever decided that there is an intelligent power manifested in the order of Nature; and we can see no use in attempting to unsettle this fundamental principle. It is true that this intelligent power is not cognizable by any of our senses, and hence must be excluded from Miss Wright's system of "knowledge." Nor can we see electricity, magnetism and many other things, which are discovered only by their effects on the material universe, and yet the best philosophers have not rejected them as dreams of the imagination.

We regret that we have been compelled to take a course that may be unpleasant to the feelings of Mr. B. We do it however without any unfriendly motives to him or any disposition to engage in controversy with any person whomsoever.

After three more numbers, the Advocate will pass into the hands of Br. Skinner, whose talents, prudence and stability are unquestionable.

U. F. DOUBLEDAY.

UNION OF PAPERS.
NEW ARRANGEMENT.
A weekly paper for One Dollar and Fifty cents.

The EVANGELICAL MAGAZINE, now in progress of the Third Volume at Utica, and GOSPEL ADVOCATE, now in progress of the Seventh Volume at Auburn, will on the 1st of January, 1830, be united, and published at Utica, N. Y. under the title of

Evangelical Magazine
AND GOSPEL ADVOCATE.

It has been deemed expedient by all concerned, that these two papers should be united, and hereafter published in one. By this arrangement, subscribers will receive a much larger proportion of matter for the same price, and the interests and harmony of the friends of liberal christianity be greatly promoted. Utica, being the centre of a large and central state in the Union, and embracing every possible facility of communicating with all parts of this state, and with the great bodies of Universalists, East and West, is decidedly the best location for such a paper that could be selected.— As we have the assurance of receiving the aid and contributions of the principal and most talented Universalist writers in the state, as well as the continued aid of former correspondents, we hope by patience, perseverance, and unremitting exertions on our own part, to make this one of the most interesting (as well as cheapest) papers in the connexion; and to sustain for it all the reputation heretofore acquired by the two papers; one of which has been before the publick for about seven years, and the other about three.

The *Evangelical Magazine and Gospel Advocate* will—as heretofore—be devoted principally to the inculcation and defence of Liberal Christianity, or the doctrine of God's impartial and universal grace, and the ultimate holiness and happiness of all his intellectual offspring: To sermons and essays, doctrinal, moral, and practical: To brief expositions and commentaries upon the Scriptures: To religious intelligence, poetic effusions, and miscellaneous matter: And last, but not least—to the determined defence of civil and religious liberty, against the craft of spiritual tyrants, and the wiles of the self-styled " orthodox" clergy, who are—many of them at least—aiming at nothing short of the total extinction of the light which guides

---

The Gospel Advocate, November 14, 1829. The horizontal line near the top of the first column marks the end of Brownson's editorship.

> After this number of the Advocate was nearly prepared for the press, it was thought advisable to leave out the name of O. A. Brownson as editor. Mr. B. has ceased to be a Universalist preacher, and commenced lecturing in favour of Miss Frances Wright's notions of philosophy & religion. If he does not avow Atheism, he does not profess to be a Theist. He cannot, therefore, consistently advocate the truth of Christianity, the future salvation of all or any of the human family, nor the existence of a God, or of any intelligent power to us invisible. Whether his present course be the result of conviction or of mental aberration, we consider it widely inconsistent with the plan of the Gospel Advocate.

The notice continued with a detailed description and refutation of Brownson's supposed beliefs, in which Theophilus Fisk's influence is obvious. Brownson, wrote Doubleday, "has already apprised the publick that Nature does not teach the existence of a God." The notice concludes with an assurance that "After three more numbers, the Advocate will pass into the hands of Br. Skinner, whose talents, prudence and stability are unquestionable." The remainder of the issue was filled with a reprint of the prospectus for the new *Magazine and Advocate*.[43]

By the time the next issue of the *Gospel Advocate* went to press, Skinner had taken over the editorial duties. Brownson's contribution was restricted to two short letters. One is a bit of unfinished business, which testifies to how suddenly and unexpectedly his life had changed. While in Boston, he had seen a new hymn book by Russell and Sebastian Streeter, and had promised to do what he could to promote the book. "As I am no longer a Universalist," he wrote, "it is not probable I shall take it upon me to supply universalist societies with hymn books, but feeling myself bound in honour to discharge my promise … I wish you to allow me through your paper to recommend Messrs. Streeter's Hymn Book."[44] There is also a letter from Brownson defending Frances Wright and a refutation by Doubleday, the whole correspondence being reprinted from Doubleday's secular paper, the *Cayuga Patriot*.[45]

It is not clear at exactly what point Brownson lost his position with the Auburn Universalist society, nor whether he resigned or was dismissed. It is not clear, either, what happened to the society after Brownson's departure. A new Universalist society was organized in Auburn in 1833, but there was little overlap between the new leadership and the original founding members.[46]

Brownson took formal leave of the Universalist denomination in an open letter "To the Universalists" in the *Free Enquirer*:

> Brethren: Four years last September, O. A. Brownson received from your general convention at Hartland Vt. a letter of fellowship as a preacher in your denomination; and the June following he was set apart to the work of the ministry by solemn ordination at Jaffrey N.H. Since that period he has labored with unremitting assiduity in the acquisition of correct knowledge and in the promulgation of truth, in such manner and in such portions as his judgment assured him would best accelerate human improvement. With what acceptance, it needs not now to enquire; suffice it to say, he has had his friends and his enemies; more of the former than the latter, he confidently hopes.
>
> From the Universalists he has received many favors, many proofs of fraternal affection, which are remembered, and will be, long as human kindness has power to move his heart. His late visit among his Universalist friends in the eastern states has given him matter for grateful recollection ... The recent expression of their confidence has endeared them to his heart; and it is with a momentary pang he says to his Universalist brethren that his connection with them by any other ties than those of common humanity and fellow being must hereafter cease, and that his fellowship with the Christian ministry is ended.

Brownson insisted that he had no quarrel with Universalism or with religious belief in general. What he was rejecting was the spirit of sectarianism, which he considered responsible for the poor treatment he had received at the hands of the Universalists. "I do not renounce my former religious belief, nor do I denounce the denomination to which I was attached. I but say, I am no longer to appear the advocate of any sect nor of any religious faith."[47] In a companion piece printed the following January, he enlarged on his disappointment at finding that even the Universalists, though "more benevolent and more forbearing than any other denomination," had put the demands of sectarian rivalry before the claims of charity and truth. After suffering from the "restraints" imposed by Presbyterianism, he said, he had "[settled] down in the full conviction of the truth of universal salvation. Then I felt to rejoice, because I thought I should be at liberty to use my reason and indulge charitable feelings to the world."

> But even a member of this sect will find that, though he has a wider range, he still has his enclosures. Not so much because they fear the individual may be lost, as that his wanderings may give the orthodox or other sects occasion to cast some expressions upon the one to which he belongs. The Universalists, in many instances, censure me for leaving them ... because it may prove injurious to them as a denomination or sect. Were it not for

this, they would receive me as a brother, and have as much good feeling toward me as ever. This is the case with all sects; and it is one reason why persecution has been practiced.[48]

November 1829-January 1830: The Aftermath

Branding Brownson as an infidel had left the Universalists in an embarrassing position. Many Universalists, including Skinner, were in the habit of contending that the "monstrous absurdities" of Calvinism were responsible for driving people to deism or atheism. Once convinced of the truth of Universalism, however, "he whose face was before averted with disgust and horror, will turn and listen; he who was about to reject the whole of Christianity as unworthy of his notice, will joyfully embrace it."[49] Now the Universalists had to explain why, in that case, both Brownson and Kneeland had apparently become infidels while serving as Universalist ministers.

In order to counter the implication that Universalism was a "slippery slope" leading to infidelity, Skinner suggested that Brownson was mentally unstable. "We hope and fervently pray," he wrote,

> that, so far from weakening the faith, discouraging the hearts, or relaxing the exertions of the friends of revelation, christianity and Universalism, [Brownson's actions] will serve as a beacon to all to be on their guard against such fatal delusion ... After all, however, we cannot – charity will not allow us to – look upon the course taken by Mr. Brownson in any other light than of its being the result of mental alienation.[50]

Doubleday agreed, "We do not think Mr. Brownson is entirely sane." Anticipating the later characterization of Brownson as a "religious weathervane," he suggested that before long "by another somerset ... you will find in the Orthodox ranks the very person, who has attempted to sell you to the Free Enquirer."[51]

Doubleday, however, was more inclined to censure Brownson for dishonesty than to exculpate him on grounds of insanity. As in the case of Fisk and the *Gospel Herald*, he accused Brownson of misusing privileged information. Brownson had promised that, if the *Advocate* were sold, he would not "be concerned in publishing a similar work" for a period of two years. "He now says that he considers the Free Enquirer a publication entirely different from the Advocate"– which of course it was – and therefore not covered by his promise. "But if the Enquirer is not calculated to interfere with the interests of the Advocate," Doubleday demanded, "why does he call by publick advertisement, on the readers of the latter to patronize the former? Why has he attempted to sell, to Miss Frances Wright, for a stipulated price the patrons of the Advocate? Is it honest to sell the same property of different persons?" In fact, Doubleday said, it was because he himself was "bound by honourable pledge, to do nothing to injure the purchase of brother Skinner" that he had been forced to dismiss Brownson when he discovered his connection with the *Free Enquirer*.[52]

The larger Universalist community agreed that Brownson must be either insane or dishonest. Otherwise, how could he have gone, in the course of a single day, from begging Skinner for a job, to accepting one from Frances Wright? As Skinner put it, "*If he is not insane*, he must be, in our estimation, one of the most mercenary, hypocritical, villainous, and hollow-hearted wretches in the world."[53] Doubleday, ascribing to Brownson all of the beliefs popularly associated with Frances Wright, asked, "If [Brownson] intended … to renounce all connection with Universalism and Christianity, and to deny that we have any evidence of the existence of God or any superiour intelligent Power, was it honest to go into Universalist meeting Houses, and accept of contributions, and lift up his hands and his voice in solemn prayer *to God*, and preach from the language of Jesus?"[54] Whittemore agreed that Brownson must secretly have been an infidel, even when he was trying to obtain a Universalist post in New England.[55]

The Universalists painted Brownson's apostasy in lurid colors because they were unwilling to admit that there were points of similarity between their beliefs and those espoused in the *Free Enquirer*. Brownson, however, had said months earlier that, while he did not accept Frances Wright's arguments against religion, he agreed with some of her philosophical ideas. "Indeed we have advanced the same principles both in our sermons and in our essays."[56] Since he did not see Universalism and Free Enquiry as entirely incompatible, he saw no contradiction in using his journalistic talents on behalf of both. He would have preferred to continue working for the Universalist press, but when that door was closed to him, he was able to find enough common ground with the *Free Enquirer* to justify accepting the position in order to keep his wife and sons from destitution.

As soon as the immediate furor had died down, the Universalists began to write Brownson out of their history. Skinner's introductory article in the first issue of the combined *Evangelical Magazine and Gospel Advocate* included a brief history of the new paper's two predecessors. He wrote that the *Gospel Advocate* had been founded by "Mr. Gross, a worthy and venerable father in our Israel" and carried on by "our worthy and esteemed brother, L. S. Everett." He said not a word of the turbulent year that had just passed under Brownson's editorship.[57]

Brownson's separation from the Universalist denomination was made formal in September 1830, when the Universalist General Convention voted "that there is full proof that said Kneeland and Brownson have renounced their faith in the Christian Religion, which renunciation is a dissolution of fellowship with this body."[58] Thus ended the on-and-off relationship with Universalism that had, in one way or another, defined Brownson's religious identity since early childhood.

AFTERWORD

Brownson's Infidelity

I was and am, in my natural disposition, frank, truthful, straightforward, and earnest ... So, wise and prudent men shake their heads when my name is mentioned, and disclaim all solidarity with me.

– Orestes Brownson, *The Convert*

Brownson's life has sometimes been seen as a search for a satisfactory balance between the principles of individualism and communalism.[1] In general terms it can be said that for the first half of his life, up to approximately 1842, individualism was in the ascendant. Although he understood in theory that human beings exist within a web of social relationships, he was deeply mistrustful of sects, denominations, parties, and groups of all kinds. "I am, and always have been, opposed to the associations which are so characteristic a feature of our times," he wrote to abolitionist William Lloyd Garrison in 1838. "I have regarded them as unfriendly to freedom, as striking at individual liberty, and merging the individual in the mass."[2] In *The Convert*, he explained, "The truth is, I never was and never could be a party man, or work in the traces of a party. I abandoned, indeed, after a year's devotion to it, the Working Men's Party, but not the working-men's cause, and to that cause I have ever been faithful according to my light and ability."[3] Similarly, in 1829 he abandoned the Universalist denomination without abandoning his belief in the Universalist message.

Brownson was not an "infidel" in the sense in which his fellow Universalists understood the term; that is, he was not an atheist, deist, or skeptic. His religious identity as a liberal Christian remained stable from the time he left the Presbyterian church until he converted to Catholicism some twenty years later. He believed in the existence of an all-powerful, benevolent Deity. His views on the Bible, the nature and mission of Christ, and the fate of the soul in the afterlife were within the range of beliefs held by Universalists at the time. Nevertheless, Brownson had good reasons for feeling uneasy in his role as a Universalist minister, and the Universalists had some justification for perceiving him as an alien in their midst.

In his discussion of Brownson's self-identification as an infidel, Patrick Carey suggested that Brownson "used the term 'infidelity' very broadly," to mean anyone who "protested against religious establishments because they were untrue to the religious spirit, or ... had serious doubts about specific religious doctrines held by the churches."[4] Adopting an even broader definition, we might understand Brownson's relationship with Universalism in terms of infidelity, not in the specifically religious sense, but in the larger sense of unfaithfulness or disloyalty.

At the time he left the Universalists, Brownson understood his relationship with them in terms not of infidelity, but of injury. In January 1830, he wrote, "What the Universalists have said respecting me may easily be accounted for. They have had a hard struggle for existence ... They supposed I had revolted from them and would join the ranks of their opponents. It was their policy to destroy my reputation, that I might not injure them."[5] In *The Convert* he used the same word to describe himself as he believed others saw him: as "a well-meaning man, perhaps an able man, but so fond of paradoxes and extremes, that he cannot be relied on, and more likely to injure than serve the cause he espouses."[6]

Brownson was not an unbeliever, but neither was he a loyal Universalist. He did not reject the basic tenets of Universalist belief, but he did not labor very assiduously to promote them. From the viewpoint of Dolphus Skinner and other devoted protectors and promoters of institutional Universalism, Brownson had been a troublemaker ever since he arrived in New York. He had never been properly deferential or respectful to his elders in the ministry. He had opposed the state convention and refused to place himself under its authority. Installed as editor of the *Gospel Advocate* through the patronage of the anti-Convention leader Linus Everett, he had used the paper to explore subjects that interested him, such as social reform and the philosophical basis of belief, without making much effort to relate them to the needs and concerns of the larger Universalist community. He was indifferent to the primary concern of American Universalists in the 1820s: the need to protect the constitutional rights of religious minorities. Instead of presenting a united front in the face of the evangelical threat, he ridiculed the threat and, by implication, the Universalists who took it seriously. While his fellow Universalists were struggling to establish their credentials as devout and respectable members of the Protestant mainstream, he was promoting the radical ideas of Robert Owen and Frances Wright. His commitment to free speech and free inquiry was admirable, but he did not do his cause any good by publicly accusing his fellow Universalists of cowardice and hypocrisy. If, as Brownson wrote, the Universalists cast him out because they feared he would injure them, it must be admitted that they had good reason to do so.

Brownson's difficulties with the Universalists must be understood in the context of his attitude toward organizations in general. At the heart of the matter were competing views of honor, honesty, loyalty and fidelity. Brownson defined "fidelity" in terms of truth, honesty, sincerity, and candor. Since he conceived of the good life as a pilgrimage in search of truth and knowledge, he could not tolerate any restrictions on his freedom to seek the truth "under whatever guise it may come." He could not commit himself wholly to any party, for "to join any [party] you must support its falsehoods as well as its truths."[7] Even while serving as editor of a Universalist newspaper, he wanted to be free to accept or reject all ideas as seemed good to him, regardless of whether they came from Universalists or from professed enemies of Universalism.

Brownson saw those Universalists who opposed him as putting worldly considerations above devotion to "the right." He could not understand that their "prudence" might be an expression of their fidelity to the cause of institutional Universalism. After more than a quarter century, he was still bursting with indignation at having "suffered so much from the *prudence* of associates." In *The Convert* he reflected on his Universalist experience:

> A man's life-blood is frozen in its current, his intellect deadened, and his very soul annihilated by the everlasting dinging into his ears by the wise and prudent, more properly the timid and selfish, of the admonition to be politic, to take care not to compromise one's cause or one's friends. My soul revolted, and revolts even to-day at this admonition ...
>
> If what a man says is true, and is evidently said with an honest intention, do not decry him, do not disown him, do not beat the life out of him with lectures on prudence; stand by him, and bear with him the odium he may incur by telling the truth, encourage him by your respect for his honesty and candor, and shelter him, as far as in your power, from the reproaches of weak and timid brethren.[8]

Since he refused to allow his affiliations to define his identity or dictate his beliefs, Brownson found it easy to move from one set of associates to another. There was probably not another Universalist who could have accepted an offer to write for the *Free Enquirer* as casually as he did. He did not see changes of affiliation as significant changes, and he was surprised when other people did. Of the years between 1828 and 1842 – during which he was successively a Universalist, a Free Enquirer, an independent preacher, a Unitarian, and a Transcendentalist – he wrote, "During the period of fourteen years, the greater part of which I was accused of changing at least once every three months, I never changed once in my principles or my purposes, and all I did change were my tools, my instruments, or my modes of operation."[9]

If Brownson saw his fellow workers as "tools," "instruments," "modes of operation," it is not surprising that they distrusted him and feared injury at his hands. He was a dangerous associate because he did not seem to understand that human relationships entail obligations. He saw fidelity to ideas and principles as moral imperatives, but fidelity to other people as weakness, cowardice, and selfishness. He would not intentionally injure anyone, but he would not go out of his way to avoid doing so.

Brownson's early life had afforded him few opportunities for learning to function as part of a group. In early childhood he had been separated from his mother and his siblings. His foster parents provided for his physical needs, but offered him neither companionship nor guidance. He did not attend either school or church regularly, and made no friends of his own age. As a teenager he was reunited with his family, but failed to develop close ties with them. He used his mentors as he used his books – as means of self-education – and parted from them without regret when they had served their purpose. His one experience of a really close-knit group, the Presbyterians of Ballston, had confused and frightened him; it was their group solidarity and their intrusive gaze, as much as their Calvinist theology, that filled him with dread. He suffered from loneliness, but, with the possible exception of Sally Healy and her sisters, he never felt at ease among his fellows. He came to the ministry with impressive intellectual attainments, a well-developed logical facility, and a lively religious imagination, but his social skills were ominously undeveloped and weak.

In his autobiographical novel *Charles Elwood*, Brownson mused on the ways in which character may be molded, or perhaps distorted, by early experience of "hardship, privation, and suffering":

> [The world] has supposed me incapable of generous sympathies and firm attachments. But the world has not known me: at least as I should have been, had it not been for the unfriendly circumstances of my earlier life

... My hand has been against every man, and every man's hand has been against me. Yet have I ever yearned toward my race, and separated from them only with the keenest regret.

Perhaps, like his alter-ego Charles Elwood, Brownson "concealed wells of deep feeling, and holy sentiment, and gushing sympathy" beneath his "careless, cold, and superficial" exterior.[10] We know from his diaries that he secretly yearned for attachment and companionship. At this stage of his life, however, he was unwilling or unable to embrace any allegiance that threatened to compromise his autonomy. The world – specifically, his brethren in the Universalist ministry – had good reason to suppose him "incapable of generous sympathies and firm attachments." This was the tragedy of Brownson's life, and the true nature of his infidelity.

Notes

Notes

Abbreviations Used in the Notes

Works by Orestes A. Brownson

Brownson papers, UND	Orestes Augustus Brownson papers, University of Notre Dame Archives (microfilm).
Brownson to Turner, 17 July 1834	Orestes Brownson to Edward Turner, 17 July 1834, Edward Turner papers, bMS 513, Andover-Harvard Theological Library.
Convert	*The Convert* (1857; vol. 5 of *Works of Orestes A. Brownson,* ed. Henry F. Brownson, Detroit, 1884).
Diary #2	*Orestes A. Brownson's: Notebook of Boston Reformer Clippings (Clippings Removed)*; in Orestes Augustus Brownson papers, University of Notre Dame Archives, Box 29½, 76. Unedited transcript by Patrick W. Carey, University of Notre Dame Archives.
Early Works 1	*The Early Works of Orestes A. Brownson vol. 1: The Universalist Years, 1826-29*, ed. Patrick W. Carey (Milwaukee: Marquette University Press, 2000).
Early Works 2	*The Early Works of Orestes A. Brownson vol. 2: The Free Thought and Unitarian Years, 1830-35*, ed. Patrick W. Carey (Milwaukee: Marquette University Press, 2001).
Notebook of Reflections	*A Notebook of Reflections, 1822-1825*; in Orestes Augustus Brownson papers, University of Notre Dame Archives.

Biographies

Brownson's Early Life	Henry F. Brownson, *Orestes A. Brownson's Early Life: from 1803 to 1844* (Detroit, 1898).
Carey, *Weathervane*	Patrick W. Carey, *Orestes A. Brownson: American Religious Weathervane* (Grand Rapids: Eerdmans, 2004).
Gilmore, *Orestes Brownson*	William James Gilmore, *Orestes Brownson and New England Religious Culture, 1803-1827* (Ph.D. diss., University of Virginia, 1971).

Maynard, *Yankee, Radical, Catholic*	*Orestes Brownson, Yankee, Radical, Catholic* (New York: Macmillan, 1943).
Ryan, *Definitive Biography*	Thomas R. Ryan, *Orestes A. Brownson: A Definitive Biography* (Huntington, IN: Our Sunday Visitor, Inc., 1976).
Schlesinger, *Pilgrim's Progress*	Arthur Schlesinger Jr., *A Pilgrim's Progress* (1939; reprint, Boston: Little, Brown and Company, 1966).

Related Topics

A. Ballou, *Autobiography*	*Autobiography of Adin Ballou* (1896; reprint, Providence: Blackstone Editions, 2016).
Hatch, *Democratization*	Nathan O. Hatch, *The Democratization of American Christianity* (New Haven: Yale University Press, 1989).
Miller, *Larger Hope*	Russell E. Miller, *The Larger Hope: The First Century of the Universalist Church in America 1770-1870* (Boston: Unitarian Universalist Association, 1979).
NYSCU Minute Book	New York State Convention of Universalists, Minute book, 1825-1866, bMS 390/1, Andover-Harvard Theological Library.
Stacy, *Memoirs*	*Memoirs of the Life of Nathaniel Stacy* (Columbus, PA, 1850).
Whittemore, *Hosea Ballou*	Thomas Whittemore, *Life of Rev. Hosea Ballou* (Boston, 1854-1855).

✦

Introduction

[1] "Introduction," *Brownson's Quarterly Review* 6, January 1844, 10.

[2] *Convert*, 3.

[3] *Convert*, 19.

[4] *The Convert* is the primary source for the discussion of Brownson's Universalism in the three major twentieth-century biographies – Arthur Schlesinger Jr.'s *A Pilgrim's Progress* (1939), Theodore Maynard's *Orestes Brownson, Yankee, Radical, Catholic* (1943), and Thomas R. Ryan's *Orestes A. Brownson: A Definitive Biography* (1976). Maynard dismissed this period of Brownson's life in two sentences, assuring his readers that "the details of Brownson's Universalist ministry are of slight importance." Patrick W. Carey, in *Orestes A. Brownson: American Religious Weathervane* (2004), pays more attention to the Universalist years and uses Brownson's articles and sermons from the 1820s to build up a picture of the young Brownson that contradicts *The Convert* at many points. However, Carey's work, like *The Convert*, is an intellectual and spiritual biography; the actions of other people and the larger religious and political context are for the most part outside its scope.

5   *Convert*, 36.

6   General Convention Proceedings, *Trumpet and Universalist Magazine*, 2 Oct. 1830.

7   The standard history of American Universalism tells Brownson's story in a chapter on "Universalism and Infidelity" during the second quarter of the nineteenth century. Miller, *Larger Hope*, 181-185.

8   *Convert*, 39. General Convention Proceedings, *Trumpet and Universalist Magazine*, 2 Oct. 1830. Carey, *Weathervane*, 20.

9   "Forgiveness of Sins," *Gospel Advocate*, 30 May 1829.

10 "Reasons for Loving God," *Gospel Advocate*, 3 Oct. 1829.

11 *Convert*, 39.

12 James Freeman Clarke, "Orestes A. Brownson's Argument for the Roman Church," *Christian Examiner*, March 1850, 227-229.

13 James Russell Lowell, "A Fable for Critics," *The Complete Writings of James Russell Lowell* (Boston: Houghton Mifflin and Company, 1904), 42.

14 Clarke, "Brownson's Argument," 231.

15 *Convert*, 46-47.

16 Maynard, *Yankee, Radical, Catholic*, xii.

17 Ryan, *Definitive Biography*, 726.

18 Schlesinger, *Pilgrim's Progress*, 292.

19 Analyzing the parental images in Brownson's writings on religion, Donald Capps argued in 1968 that "the death of Brownson's father and his separation from his mother at an early age were especially decisive experiences for his affiliations with religious groups in general and his conversion to the Catholic church in particular." Per Sveino identified Brownson's overriding concerns as "a never failing quest for unity or synthesis" and "his fervent search for a FATHER." Donald Capps, "Orestes Brownson: The Psychology of Religious Affiliation," *Journal for the Scientific Study of Religion* 7 (1968), 198; Per Sveino, *Orestes A. Brownson's Road to Catholicism* (New York: Humanities Press, 1970), 306-307.

20 Patrick W. Carey, introduction to *Early Works 1*, 3.

21 Carey, *Weathervane*, xvii.

22 Gilmore, *Orestes Brownson*, 1-2, 14-16, 19-20.

23 Carey, *Weathervane*, xii.

24 Carey, *Weathervane*, xv.

25 Clarke, "Brownson's Argument," 231.

26 Carey, *Weathervane*, 29.

Chapter 1

1. *Brownson's Early Life*, 3. Carey, *Weathervane*, 1-5. Gilmore, *Orestes Brownson*, 22-24.

2. Randolph A. Roth, *The Democratic Dilemma: Religion, Reform, and the Social Order in the Connecticut River Valley of Vermont, 1791-1850* (Cambridge University Press, 1987), 26-29.

3. Roth, *Democratic Dilemma*, 55-68.

4. Edward Turner, "Universalism," undated typescript in Edward Turner papers, bMS 513, Andover-Harvard Theological Library, 1-2.

5. Roth, *Democratic Dilemma*, 62.

6. Roth, *Democratic Dilemma*, 2. Whitney R. Cross, *The Burned-Over District: The Social and Intellectual History of Enthusiastic Religion in Western New York, 1800-1850* (Ithaca: Cornell University Press, 1950), 17-18, 43-45.

7. Caleb Rich, "A Narrative of Elder Caleb Rich," *Candid Examiner* (Montrose, PA), 30 April and 14 May 1827. Elmo Robinson has collected a number of similar stories in *American Universalism: Its Origins, Organization and Heritage* (New York: Exposition Press, 1970), 1-11.

8. John Calvin, *Institutes of the Christian Religion* (1559), 3:25.12.

9. Winchester's preaching tour in 1794 included various towns in the Boston area, eastern Connecticut, and central Massachusetts. Keene, New Hampshire, is not mentioned in the list of places he preached, but Keene is only about 20 miles from Warwick, Massachusetts, which is. Richard Eddy, *Universalism in America: A History* (Boston, 1884-86), 1:429-30.

10. Miller, *Larger Hope*, 36-38.

11. George Parsons Lathrop, "Orestes Brownson," *Atlantic Monthly* (June 1896), 770.

12. Alden M. Rollins, *Vermont Warnings Out, vol. 2: Southern Vermont* (Camden, ME: Picton Press, 1997), 398. The transcription of the "warning out" notice refers to "Release Brownson" and is dated 1803, which is incorrect. The correct year is probably 1805, but may be later.

13. Gilmore, *Orestes Brownson*, 24-30. Some of Brownson's biographers have stated that only the twins were sent away, but this is incorrect. The error seems to have originated with Henry F. Brownson. See *Brownson's Early Life*, 4.

14. Gilmore, *Orestes Brownson*, 72-74.

15. Orestes Brownson ["Xenophon"] to Elisha G. Calkins, 30 March 1823. Brownson papers, UND.

16. *Convert*, 30. Genealogical information on the Deans and Wights is from Lucius Paige, *History of Hardwick, Massachusetts* (Boston, 1883), 360; and

from http://www.ancestry.com. For Thorina's name, see for example Thorina (Brownson) Dean to Orestes Brownson, 1 Jan 1871. Brownson papers, UND.

17   Gilmore, *Orestes Brownson*, 27.

18   Brownson himself never referred to his foster family by name, saying only that from the age of six he was brought up by "an aged couple." *Convert*, 4. The Huntings are identified as his foster parents in Evelyn M. Wood Lovejoy, *History of Royalton, Vermont* (Burlington, VT, 1911), 635; and also in Mary Grace Canfield, "Early Universalism in Vermont and the Connecticut Valley," unpublished manuscript, 1941, bMS 165, Andover-Harvard Theological Library. Gilmore tentatively identified Brownson's foster parents as a different couple, Mr. and Mrs. James Huntington. Gilmore, *Orestes Brownson*, 26-27. I believe the *History of Royalton* and other Vermont sources are more likely correct, as drawing on actual local tradition, as opposed to Gilmore's deductions from census and similar data.

19   *Convert*, 24.

20   *Brownson's Early Life*, 4.

21   Daphne (Brownson) Ludington to Orestes Brownson, 16 September 1844, Brownson papers, UND.

22   Brownson to Turner, 17 July 1834.

23   Lovejoy, *History of Royalton*, 219-220.

24   *Convert*, 4.

25   Gilmore, *Orestes Brownson*, 75, 84-85.

26   "Patrick O'Hara: Chapter VI," *Philanthropist* 2, 23 July 1831; in *Early Works 2*, 60-65. It is unlikely that this is actually the sixth chapter of a larger work; the conceit that it is excerpted from an autobiography is part of the fiction.

27   *Convert*, 4, 6.

28   Brownson to Turner, 17 July 1834.

29   *Convert*, 7. A town historian has called Universalism "the most mythological of all Royalton religious organizations" though the doctrine was "a source of much anxiety" to the Baptist and Congregational churches. Lovejoy, *History of Royalton*, 496.

30   *Convert*, 7-8.

31   *Convert*, 5.

32   "Essay on Reform," part 3, *Philanthropist* 2, 14 Feb. 1832; in *Early Works 2*, 129-132.

33   *Convert*, 4-6.

34   *Convert*, 8.

35   Brownson to Turner, 17 July 1834.

36   For a short history of the "restoration movement" (not to be confused with the Restorationist wing of Universalism), of which the Christian Connection is a part, see Paul K. Conkin, *American Originals: Homemade Varieties of Christianity* (Chapel Hill: University of North Carolina Press, 1997), 1-56. The movement is also discussed in Hatch, *Democratization*, 68-81.

37   Warren Hathaway, *A Discourse on Abner Jones and the Christian Denomination* (Newburyport, MA, 1861), 23.

38   A. Ballou, *Autobiography*, 35-36. Ballou summed up the "Christian" creed as follows:

1. The plenary inspiration of the Bible;
2. The pre-existent divine sonship of Christ;
3. The personal unity of God, the Father;
4. The impersonal agency of the Holy Spirit in working out the divine designs;
5. The fall of man in Adam and consequent universal but not total depravity;
6. The indispensable necessity of the new birth;
7. Man's free moral agency;
8. This life the only probationary state for eternity;
9. The resurrection of the body;
10. The final general day of judgment;
11. The special immortalization of the righteous, both body and soul, at the Judgment Seat;
12. The just punishment of the wicked, terminating in their utter destruction – absolute non-existence.

39   On the relations between Elias Smith, the Christian Connection, and Universalism, see Michael G. Kenny, *The Perfect Law of Liberty: Elias Smith and the Providential History of America* (Washington: Smithsonian Institution Press, 1994), 221-256.

40   "Mr. Rains' Communication," *Gospel Advocate* 7, 24 Jan. 1829.

41   Carey, *Weathervane*, 6-7. Gilmore, *Orestes Brownson*, 103-104.

42   "Patrick O'Hara," in *Early Works 2*, 63-65.

43   *Convert*, 8. The "founder of the *Christian* sect" referred to here is probably Abner Jones, who organized the first "Christian" congregation in Lyndon, Vermont, in 1801, but it could be Elias Smith, who convened a Christian Conference in Sanbornton, New Hampshire, and drew up "Articles of Faith and Church Building" for the movement in 1802. Either Smith or Jones might have been known to the "Christians" of Royalton in 1816.

44   Similar reinterpretations of Brownson's Presbyterian and Universalist experiences will be discussed in later chapters.

45   *Brownson's Early Life*, 6.

46   Lovejoy, *History of Royalton*, 285, 635. Gilmore, *Orestes Brownson*, 54-57.

47 *Notebook of Reflections*, 14 January 1823. Unless otherwise specified, the dating of the entries in the *Notebook* follows the reconstruction in Gilmore, *Orestes Brownson*, Appendix B.

48 "The Times," part 2, *Gospel Advocate* 7, 2 May 1829; in *Early Works 1*, 283-286.

49 *Brownson's Early Life*, 6-8.

50 Roth, *Democratic Dilemma*, 55-68. Conkin, *American Originals*, 101.

51 "Thompson's *History of Vermont*," *Brownson's Quarterly Review* 1, April 1844, 278.

52 *Brownson's Early Life*, 6.

53 "Cooper's *Sea-Lions*," *Brownson's Quarterly Review* 6, July 1849, 404.

54 *Convert*, 6.

55 *Brownson's Early Life*, 8.

56 "The Yankee in Ireland," *Brownson's Quarterly Review* 17, Jan. 1860, 125.

57 "Thompson's *History of Vermont*," 278.

58 *Brownson's Early Life*, 8.

59 "History of Waterbury, Connecticut," *Brownson's Quarterly Review* 17, Oct. 1860.

Chapter 2

1 *Convert*, 6.

2 Brownson to Turner, 17 July 1834.

3 *Convert*, 9.

4 Edward F. Grose, *Centennial History of the Village of Ballston Spa 1763-1907* (Ballston Spa, 1907), 54-68. Nathaniel Bartlett Sylvester, *History of Saratoga County, New York* (Philadelphia, 1878), 228-230. William L. Stone, *Reminiscences of Saratoga and Ballston* (New York, 1875), 406-407.

5 Relief Brownson to Orestes Brownson, 18 Nov 1845, Orestes Augustus Brownson papers, UND.

6 *Brownson's Early Life*, 10.

7 Grose, *Centennial History*, 120, 131-135, 252. *Independent American*, 1816. On the relationship between James Comstock and Reuben Sears see Sylvester, *History of Saratoga County*, 249.

8 Milton W. Hamilton, *The Country Printer: New York State 1785-1830* (New York: Columbia University Press, 1936), 28-30.

9 Comstock advertised for an apprentice in the summer of 1819, and again in the fall of 1821. *People's Watch-Tower*, 16 June 1819; *Ballston Spa Gazette*, 24 October 1821.

10 There is much confusion about the dates of Brownson's employment at the printing office vis-à-vis his studies at Ballston Academy. Henry Brownson thought that his father attended school before beginning his apprenticeship. Theodore Maynard even asserted that "the reason for the move [to Ballston] was probably that there was an academy there which Orestes could attend." Although the Brownsons may have been in Ballston for a year or more before Orestes began his apprenticeship, it is unlikely that they could have afforded to send him to the academy at that time. He probably spent the time working on the family's farm and hiring out to neighbors, as he had done in Royalton. Brownson's own writings indicate that he did not attend the academy until he was in his late teens. Describing his conversion to Presbyterianism in October 1822, Brownson wrote, "I told my experience to the Presbyterian minister of the town where I was pursuing my academic studies." That is, he was living in Ballston Centre as a student when he was nineteen. *Convert*, 10. *Brownson's Early Life*, 10. Maynard, *Yankee, Radical, Catholic*, 6.

11 Gilmore, *Orestes Brownson*, 128-130.

12 On the relatively equal distribution of property in the New England hill country, see Stephen A. Marini, *Radical Sects of Revolutionary New England* (Cambridge: Harvard University Press, 1982), 30.

13 *Brownson's Early Life*, 5.

14 Theodore Corbett, *The Making of American Resorts: Saratoga Springs, Ballston Spa, Lake George* (New Brunswick: Rutgers University Press, 2001), 8-9, 30-39. Grose, *Centennial History*, 115.

15 Corbett, *Resorts*, 35-36, 127-128. Grose, *Centennial History*, 120-121. Thomas A. Chambers, *Drinking the Waters: Creating an American Leisure Class at Nineteenth-Century Mineral Springs* (Washington: Smithsonian Institution Press, 2002), 93-94.

16 On Brownson's racial attitudes, see Vincent A. Lapomarda, "Orestes Augustus Brownson: A 19th Century View of the Blacks in American Society," *Mid-America* 53 (1971), 160-169.

17 Orestes A. Brownson, *The Laboring Classes* (1840; reprint, ed. Martin K. Doudna, Delmar, NY: Scholars' Facsimiles & Reprints, 1978), 12.

18 *Brownson's Early Life*, 17-19.

19 *Convert*, 116.

20 *Brownson's Early Life*, 7-8.

21 Thomas A. Chambers, "Seduction and Sensibility: The Refined Society of Ballston, New York, 1800," *New York History* (July 1997), 248.

22 Edward K. Spann, *John W. Taylor: The Reluctant Partisan, 1784-1854* (Ph.D. diss., New York University, 1957), 156-161. Grose, *Centennial History*, 135. *Independent American*, 1 April 1818.

23   Spann, *John W. Taylor*, 161, 166. *Independent American*, 29 April 1818.

24   *People's Watch-Tower*, 7 April 1819.

25   Richard P. McCormick, *The Second American Party System: Party Formation in the Jacksonian Era* (Chapel Hill, University of North Carolina Press, 1966), 115-166.

26   *Independent American*, 1 April and 8 April 1818.

27   *Independent American*, 22 April 1818.

28   *Independent American*, 8 April 1818.

29   *People's Watch-Tower*, 13 May 1818.

30   "Address, To the Electors of the County of Saratoga," *Independent American*, 29 April 1818.

31   "The Rhode Island Question," *United States Democratic Review*, July 1842, 70-83. In this article Brownson questioned the exclusion of women and slaves from the body politic but, characteristically, dismissed these questions as distractions from the main argument.

32   "Reforms and Reformers," *Brownson's Quarterly Review*, April 1875, 181-183.

33   The historian George Waller has argued that Ballston was a more popular resort than Saratoga in the early years of the nineteenth century because it permitted dancing, drinking, gambling, and unchaperoned intimacy between male and female guests, while Saratoga languished in the grip of puritanical village elders and the nation's first temperance society. More recently, Theodore Corbett countered that the appeal of "wickedness" at early resorts has been exaggerated, and suggested that ample provision for guests' religious needs was one of the reasons Saratoga ultimately proved more successful than Ballston. Both agreed, however, that religion never flourished at Ballston Spa. George Waller, *Saratoga: Saga of an Impious Era* (Englewood Cliffs, NJ: Prentice-Hall, Inc., 1966), 62-66. Corbett, *Resorts*, 37.

34   The "Christian" evangelists Elias Smith and Nancy Cram had led a revival in Ballston in 1814, but had not established an ongoing organization. Michael G. Kenny, *The Perfect Law of Liberty: Elias Smith and the Providential History of America* (Washington: Smithsonian Institution Press, 1994), 169-171.

35   Grose, *Centennial History*, 75-81.

36   Orestes Brownson ["Xenophon"] to Elisha G. Calkins, 30 March 1823, Brownson papers, UND.

37   *Convert*, 9.

38   The history of Ballston Spa's first newspaper, which preserved its identity despite frequent changes of name and a brief change in ownership, is given incorrectly in both published accounts of the Ballston press. According to Nathaniel Bartlett Sylvester, Comstock took over the *Independent American* and changed the name to the *People's Watch-Tower* in 1815. Edward F. Grose, citing an unpub-

lished article by his father, Henry L. Grose, as the source of both his account and Sylvester's, stated that Spafford took over the *Independent American* and changed the name to the *Saratoga Farmer* in 1816, while Comstock simultaneously published the *People's Watch-Tower* from 1818 to 1822. Grose, *Centennial History*, 133-135. Sylvester, *History of Saratoga County*, 100-103.

The actual dates of publication may be established by examination of the newspapers themselves, which are available on microfilm as part of the Readex Early American Newspapers collection. Comstock took over as proprietor of the *Independent American* and moved it to Ballston Spa (from Ballston Centre) in 1811. The paper was variously known as the *Independent American* (1811-1818), *People's Watch-Tower* (1818-1820), *Saratoga Farmer* (1820-1821), *Ballston Spa Gazette and Saratoga Farmer* (1821-1822), and *Ballston Spa Gazette* (1822-1847). Spafford's tenure as proprietor of the *Saratoga Farmer* lasted from October 1820 to October 1821.

[39] Julian P. Boyd, "Horatio Gates Spafford: Inventor, Author, Promoter of Democracy," *Proceedings of the American Antiquarian Society* 51:2 (October 1941), 279-350.

[40] A story on an attempt by some Presbyterian clergy in Pennsylvania to exclude Freemasons from their communion appeared in the *Saratoga Farmer* under the headline "A New Inquisition!" *Saratoga Farmer*, 7 February 1821.

[41] Horatio Gates Spafford, *A Gazetteer of the State of New-York* (Albany, 1813), 33-34. Boyd, "Horatio Gates Spafford," 314.

[42] Thomas Jefferson to Horatio G. Spafford, 17 March 1814, *The Writings of Thomas Jefferson* (Washington: Thomas Jefferson Memorial Association of the United States, 1903), 14:119.

[43] *Laboring Classes*, 20.

[44] "A Sermon. On the Moral Condition of Mankind," *Gospel Advocate*, 13 Sept. 1828; in *Early Works vol. 1*, 170.

[45] *Laboring Classes*, 21.

[46] "On the Moral Condition of Mankind," *Early Works 1*, 171.

[47] *Laboring Classes*, 20.

Chapter 3

[1] Brownson to Turner, 17 July 1834.

[2] Whittemore, *Hosea Ballou*, 1:79.

[3] Alan Seaburg and Elmo Arnold Robinson, "The Universalist General Convention: An Historical Table," *Journal of the Universalist Historical Society* 8 (1969-70), 96.

[4] Stephen R. Smith, *Historical Sketches and Incidents, Illustrative of the Establishment and Progress of Universalism in the State of New York* (Buffalo, 1848), 1:22.

5   Joel Andrew Delano, *The Genealogy, History, and Alliances of the American House of Delano 1621 to 1899* (New York, 1899), 523.
6   *Convert*, 21-22.
7   Peter Hughes, "Early New England Universalism: A Family Religion," *Journal of Unitarian Universalist History* 26 (1999), 93-113.
8   Smith, *Historical Sketches,* 1:22. On the convention at Saratoga Springs see *Universalist Magazine*, 3 Nov. 1827.
9   *Convert*, 21-23.
10 *Convert*, 21.
11 Brownson to Turner, 17 July 1834.
12 Elhanan Winchester, *The Universal Restoration: Exhibited in Four Dialogues between a Minister and his Friend* (1788; reprint, Boston: 1831), iv.
13 Miller, *Larger Hope*, 98-100, 103-105.
14 *Convert*, 26.
15 Hosea Ballou, *A Treatise on Atonement* (3rd ed., Hallowell, ME, 1828), 34-41.
16 Ballou, *Treatise on Atonement*, 74, 108-120.
17 *Convert*, 23-24.
18 Brownson to Turner, 17 July 1834.
19 "A Sermon. On the Moral Condition of Mankind," *Gospel Advocate*, 13 Sept. 1828; in *Early Works 1*, 162-163.
20 "A Sermon. On Endless Punishment," *Gospel Advocate*, 22 Nov. 1828; in *Early Works 1*, 193. Cf. Ballou, *Treatise on Atonement*, 20-24.
21 "Reply to 'L. C.'" [sic], *Gospel Advocate*, 25 Oct. 1828; in *Early Works 1*, 182. The title should be "Reply to J. C." It was a response to a correspondent who objected to a passage in Brownson's series "The Essayist," in which he asserted that human beings bring suffering upon themselves by their ignorance of natural laws. Cf. Ballou, *Treatise on Atonement*, 49-53.
22 "Justification," *Philanthropist*, 3 Dec. 1831; in *Early Works 2*, 121.
23 *Convert*, 26.
24 Ballou, *Treatise on Atonement*, vi, 28-24, 77-79, 103, 137.
25 A. Ballou, *Autobiography*, 65.
26 *Brownson's Early Life*, 19.
27 Ballou, *Treatise on Atonement*, 27, 65-66.
28 Ballou, *Treatise on Atonement*, 66, 68-69.
29 "Reply to 'L. C.'," *Early Works 1*, 185-186.
30 "The Essayist," part 7, *Gospel Advocate*, 19 July 1828; in *Early Works 1*, 112.

[31] "An Essay on Divine Goodness," parts 4 and 5, *Gospel Advocate*, 2 May and 19 Sept. 1829; in *Early Works 1*, 264-267. "On the Moral Condition of Mankind," *Early Works 1*, 164. "Reply to 'L. C.,'" *Early Works 1*, 183.

[32] "Essay on Reform," part 3, *Philanthropist*, 14 Feb. 1832; in *Early Works 2*, 130.

[33] Thomas Whittemore, *The Early Days of Thomas Whittemore* (Boston, 1859), 173-174.

[34] *Brownson's Early Life*, 19.

[35] "Essay on Reform," part 3, *Early Works 2*, 129-131.

[36] *Convert*, 124.

[37] "Essay on Reform," part 3, *Early Works 2*, 131.

[38] *Convert*, 9.

Chapter 4

[1] Gilmore, *Orestes Brownson*, 130.

[2] *Brownson's Early Life*, 9. Notebook of Reflections, 12 Aug. 1825.

[3] *Notebook of Reflections*, 29 May 1823.

[4] *Notebook of Reflections*, 16 May 1823.

[5] Gilmore believed that Brownson had found such a mentor in a minister serving the Universalist society in Ballston, and that Brownson's decline into melancholy was precipitated by the death of this minister. As a source, Gilmore cited a story, "Priest and Infidel," in which Brownson described the effect on a community of the loss of a beloved minister. Gilmore believed the story to be autobiographical and to refer to the circumstances of the Universalist society in Ballston. However, there is nothing in the story to support such an interpretation. It is an example of Brownson's didactic fiction from his Unitarian period, contrasting the ideal minister, who "discouraged contentions about words, and strife about unintelligible dogmas," with his opposite, a doctrinaire Calvinist. Gilmore, *Orestes Brownson*, 132-133. "Priest and Infidel," *Philanthropist*, 29 May 1832; in *Early Works 2*, 191-202.

[6] *Convert*, 10.

[7] *People's Watch-Tower*, 5 April 1820.

[8] *Convert*, 9-10.

[9] *Convert*, 10-11.

[10] *Convert*, 11.

[11] Reuben Smith, "Orestes A. Brownson's Development of Himself," *Princeton Review* (April 1858), 390.

[12] Brownson to Turner, 17 July 1834.

[13] *Convert*, 18.

14 Brownson to Turner, 17 July 1834.

15 *Convert*, 10.

16 Edward K. Spann, *John W. Taylor: The Reluctant Partisan, 1784-1854* (Ph.D. diss., New York University, 1957), 15-16.

17 Spann, *John W. Taylor*, 13-14, 18-19.

18 Edward F. Grose, *Centennial History of the Village of Ballston Spa 1763-1907* (Ballston Spa, 1907), 241-242.

19 Alexander S. Hoyt, *An Historical Sketch of the Presbyterian Church of Ballston Centre, N. Y.* (Ballston, 1876), 46, 52.

20 Reuben Sears, *A Poem on the Mineral Waters of Ballston and Saratoga: with notes illustrating the history of the springs and adjacent country* (Ballston Spa, 1819).

21 Grose, *Centennial History*, 241-242.

22 *Independent American*, 10 April 1816 and other dates.

23 Information on works published by Comstock collected from the WorldCat database, on-line catalogs of antiquarian book dealers, and the Brookside Museum, Ballston Spa, New York.

24 Patrick W. Carey, introduction to *Early Works 1*, 5.

25 *Notebook of Reflections*, 13 Jan. 1823.

26 Reuben Smith, *Truth without Controversy: A Series of Doctrinal Lectures, intended principally for young professors of religion* (Saratoga Springs, 1824), ix.

27 Smith, *Truth without Controversy*, 163, 176-180.

28 Gilmore, *Orestes Brownson*, 151-152.

29 Smith, *Truth without Controversy*, 187.

30 Smith, *Truth without Controversy*, 182-183.

31 *Notebook of Reflections*, 23 Feb. 1823.

32 *Notebook of Reflections*, 31 Dec. 1822.

33 Loring Delano to Orestes Brownson, 23 March 1823. Moreau Delano to Orestes Brownson, 11 Jan. 1823. Brownson papers, UND.

34 Smith, *Truth without Controversy*, x.

35 Brownson to Turner, 17 July 1834; *Brownson's Early Life*, 19.

36 *Notebook of Reflections*, 17 Jan. 1823, 12 Feb. 1823, 3 Feb. 1823.

37 *Notebook of Reflections*, 19 Jan. 1823.

38 "Spiritual Diary," in Patrick W. Carey, ed., *Orestes A. Brownson: Selected Writings* (New York: Paulist Press, 1991), 91 n.25.

39 Gilmore, *Orestes Brownson*, 147-166.

40 *Notebook of Reflections*, 31 Dec. 1822.
41 *Notebook of Reflections*, 10 Feb. 1823, 15 May 1823.
42 *Notebook of Reflections*, 13 Jan. 1823.
43 Carey, introduction to *Early Works 1*, 6. *Convert*, 13.
44 Maynard, *Yankee, Radical, Catholic*, 8.
45 Ryan, *Definitive Biography*, 27-28.
46 *Convert*, 11-12.
47 Smith, "Brownson's Development," 391.
48 *Convert*, 13.
49 *Convert*, 16.
50 *Convert*, 13.
51 *Convert*, 13.
52 *Convert*, 14-15.
53 *Convert*, 17, 19.
54 Maynard, *Yankee, Radical, Catholic*, 8.
55 "The Princeton Review and Ourselves," *Brownson's Quarterly Review* 15, April 1858, 253.
56 Smith, "Brownson's Development," 392.
57 Smith, "Brownson's Development," 391.
58 *Convert*, 18.
59 *Convert*, 17-18.
60 "Strike, but hear," *Philanthropist* 5 Nov. 1831.
61 *Notebook of Reflections*, 30 July, 19 Aug. 1823.
62 *Convert*, 13.
63 *Notebook of Reflections*, 10 Feb. 1823.
64 See, for example, Relief Brownson to Orestes Brownson, 18 Nov. 1845, 19 March 1849, 17 Jan. 1856. Brownson papers, UND.

Chapter 5

1 The town of Camillus is sometimes called Elbridge (and sometimes treated as two separate places) in Brownson biographies. It was one town, called Camillus, when Brownson was there. It was split into Camillus, Elbridge, and Van Buren in 1829. Dwight H. Bruce, *Onondaga's Centennial: Gleanings of a Century* (Boston 1896), 1:659-682. Horatio Gates Spafford, *A Gazetteer of the State of New-York* (Albany, 1824), 76-77.

²   Carl F. Kaestle, *Pillars of the Republic: Common Schools and American Society, 1780-1860* (New York: Hill and Wang, 1983), 14-17.

³   Samuel Sidwell Randall, *History of the Common School System of the State of New York* (New York, 1871), 38-41, 53. Charles E. Fitch, *The Public School: History of Common School Education in New York from 1622 to 1904* (Albany, 1904), 19-21.

⁴   Kaestle, *Pillars of the Republic*, 20-22.

⁵   *Diary #2*. Since no definitive dating scheme has been established for the entries in this book, they are identified by the page number in the transcription by Patrick W. Carey.

⁶   Patrick W. Carey, introduction to *Early Works 1*, 8-10. This chronology is often badly garbled in biographies of Brownson; Carey's reconstruction, based on unpublished sources, is the most accurate.

⁷   *Notebook of Reflections*, 29 May 1823.

⁸   *Notebook of Reflections*, undated, probably August 1823.

⁹   *Brownson's Early Life*, 481, 485.

¹⁰   Gilmore, *Orestes Brownson*, 270-273.

¹¹   Whitney R. Cross, *The Burned-Over District: The Social and Intellectual History of Enthusiastic Religion in Western New York, 1800-1850* (Ithaca: Cornell University Press, 1950), 17-18, 43-45.

¹²   Stacy, *Memoirs*, 329, 348.

¹³   Bruce, *Onondaga's Centennial*, 666-668. New England General Convention minutes, 1821, in *Universalist Magazine* 3, 27 Oct. 1821.

¹⁴   *Convert*, 26.

¹⁵   *Diary #2*, 16-17, 47.

¹⁶   *Diary #2*, 54-55.

¹⁷   *Diary #2*, 54.

¹⁸   *Brownson's Early Life*, 20.

¹⁹   Malaria and its impact on the settlement of Michigan is discussed in Kenneth E. Lewis, *West to Far Michigan: Settling the Lower Peninsula, 1815-1860* (East Lansing: Michigan State University Press, 2001), 66-67.

²⁰   *Brownson's Early Life*, 20.

²¹   Orestes Brownson to Henry F. Brownson, 1 Jan 1867. Brownson papers, UND.

²²   Floyd R. Dain, *Education in the Wilderness* (Lansing: Michigan Historical Commission, 1968), 22-23, 126.

23   Sister Mary Rosalita, *Education in Detroit Prior to 1850* (Lansing: Michigan Historical Commission, 1928) contains information about subscription schools in the Detroit area, compiled from the ledgers and account books of the parents. A few agreements between teacher and parents have survived, and some information about curriculum, costs, and classrooms can be gleaned from the account books. In other cases, nothing is known but the name of the teacher. Brownson is mentioned (p. 54) as having taught in Springwells for "a few months in 1821 and 1822," but this must be a misreading for 1824 and 1825.

24   For example, Gilmore wrote that at Springwells Brownson "was actually quite at home, participating in the spreading of the culture of New England." Gilmore, *Orestes Brownson*, 268.

25   Silas Farmer, *History of Detroit and Wayne County and Early Michigan* (1890; 3rd ed. Detroit: Gale Research Co., 1969), 336.

26   Dain, *Education in the Wilderness*, 57-60, 115-118, 123-124.

27   The northernmost part of the original township of Springwells became the township of Greenfield in 1833. The eastern part of Springwells was annexed by Detroit in several stages between 1849 and 1916. In 1925 the remaining part was renamed Fordson in honor of Henry Ford, who was born in Springwells. Fordson was consolidated with Dearborn in 1929. Clarence M. Burton and M. Agnes Burton, *History of Wayne County and the City of Detroit, Michigan* (Chicago, 1930), 1:430. See also "Dearborn: the city Henry Ford made," *Detroit News*, 9 June 2003.

28   Orestes Brownson to Henry F. Brownson, 1 Jan 1867.

29   Burton, *History of Wayne County*, 1:430.

30   Orestes Brownson to Henry F. Brownson, 1 Jan 1867.

31   Farmer, *History of Detroit and Wayne County*, 533-534. Burton, *History of Wayne County*, 1:621. On the history of the Spring Hill School, see Dain, *Education in the Wilderness*, 43-56.

32   Farmer, *History of Detroit and Wayne County*, 554-557, 581, 594.

33   Burton, *History of Wayne County*, 1:693.

34   *Diary #2*, 57, 70-71. "When Thou My Righteous Judge Shall Come" is attributed to the British Methodist leader Selina Hastings, Countess of Huntingdon (1707-1791).

35   "Literary Notes and Criticisms," *Brownson's Quarterly Review*, July 1875, 432.

36   There was no Presbyterian minister in Michigan from 1821 until after Brownson had left the area in 1825. There was an Episcopal priest in Detroit from June 1824, but it hardly seems likely that he would have taken time out from organizing the territory's first Episcopal church to harangue a sick schoolteacher in Springwells. Other than that, the only Protestant clergy in the area were the

37 Farmer, *History of Detroit and Wayne County*, 555.
Methodists of the Rouge River mission. Burton, *History of Wayne County*, 1:696, 707-708. Farmer, *History of Detroit and Wayne County*, 581.

37 Farmer, *History of Detroit and Wayne County*, 555.
38 *Diary #2*, 12-13, 44-45, 50.
39 *Diary #2*, 85-94.
40 Orestes Brownson to Henry F. Brownson, 1 Jan 1867.
41 "A Letter, To the Rev. William Wisner, of the First Presbyterian Church in Ithaca, N.Y." *Gospel Advocate*, 1 March 1828.
42 "An Essay on the Progress of Truth," part 9, *Gospel Advocate*, 15 March 1828; in *Early Works 1*, 71.
43 *Convert*, 132.

Chapter 6

1 *Convert*, 29.
2 Ryan, *Definitive Biography*, 35. Maynard, *Yankee, Radical, Catholic*, 15. Maynard has Brownson studying Winchester and Ballou in Michigan: "We must suppose he had borrowed his aunt's library when he left Ballston."
3 Hatch, *Democratization*, 125-126.
4 Miller, *Larger Hope*, 285.
5 Quoted in Miller, *Larger Hope*, 289.
6 Miller, *Larger Hope*, 287-289.
7 Miller, *Larger Hope*, 291-295.
8 Brownson to Turner, 17 July 1834.
9 Alexander Pope, Essay on Man 1.291-292. See, for example, "Divine Benevolence," *Rochester Magazine and Theological Review*, July 1824.
10 *Rochester Magazine and Theological Review*, Jan. 1824, i.i-v.
11 *Diary #2*, 15, 20.
12 *Diary #2*, 6.
13 *Convert*, 28.
14 *Gospel Advocate*, 28 March 1823. "Hellology," *Rochester Magazine and Theological Review*, Sept. 1824.
15 "Demonology," *Rochester Magazine and Theological Review*, Aug. 1824.
16 *Convert*, 28.
17 A. Ballou, *Autobiography*, 59-61.
18 *Diary #2*, 56.

[19] *Convert*, 20. This was not strictly true, as the Universalist press was assiduous in reporting the spread of Unitarianism and the growing numbers of Unitarian churches in Britain and America. However, at this stage Brownson knew of unitarianism mostly as a doctrine held by Universalists. Although various Congregational churches in eastern Massachusetts had adopted a unitarian theology by this time, there was as yet no Unitarian denomination; the American Unitarian Association was not organized until 1825.

[20] Jacob Wood, *Brief Essay on the Doctrine of Future Retribution* (Worcester, MA, 1817).

[21] Peter Hughes, "The Origins and First Stage of the Restorationist Controversy," *Journal of Unitarian Universalist History* 27 (2000), 18-19.

[22] Hughes, "Origins and First Stage," 19-23.

[23] Letters (often pseudonymous) on future punishment and related issues appeared in the *Universalist Magazine* from mid-1821 onward, particularly during June-Aug. 1821 and Dec 1821-Feb 1822. See also Hughes, "Origins and First Stage," 29-34.

[24] Hughes, "Origins and First Stage," 37-39. The "Appeal" and "Declaration" were printed in the *Christian Repository*, Dec. 1822, 159-168.

[25] Richard Eddy, *Universalism in America: A History* (Boston, 1884-86), 1:535-536, 2:48-50, 60-61. Miller, *Larger Hope*, 84-86. Hughes, "Origins and First Stage," 6-7.

[26] New England General Convention minutes, 1823, in *Christian Repository*, Oct. 1823, 184. Whittemore, *Hosea Ballou*, 2:235-236.

[27] Hughes, "Origins and First Stage," 49-50.

[28] Hughes, "Origins and First Stage," 50-52.

[29] *Evangelical Repertory*, May 1824, 167.

[30] *Christian Repository*, Dec. 1823, 149.

[31] *Christian Repository*, Aug. 1824, 78 ff.

[32] *Christian Repository*, July 1820, 21.

[33] *Evangelical Repertory*, Jan.-Apr. 1824, 103-104, 116-121, 138-141, 149-151.

[34] *Evangelical Repertory*, Feb. 1824, 119-121.

[35] Brownson to Turner, 17 July 1834.

[36] *Diary #2*, 80, 99-100, 110.

[37] *Diary #2*, 130-135.

[38] Hughes, "Origins and First Stage," 50-51.

[39] *Evangelical Repertory*, April 1824, 151.

40   Brownson to Turner, 17 July 1834.
41   *Notebook of Reflections*, undated, summer 1825.
42   *Notebook of Reflections*, 12 Aug. 1825.
43   A. Ballou, *Autobiography*, 62.
44   *Notebook of Reflections*, 12 July 1825.
45   *Convert*, 29.
46   *Convert*, 6.
47   *Diary #2*, 111.
48   *Notebook of Reflections*, 1 and 23 January 1823.
49   *Diary #2*, 58 (quoting Joseph Addison).
50   *Notebook of Reflections*, 27 February, 30 July 1823.
51   New England General Convention minutes, 1825, in *Christian Repository*, Dec. 1825, 170.
52   A. Ballou, *Autobiography*, 152.
53   Hatch, *Democratization*, 45.
54   Miller, *Larger Hope*, 659. John G. Adams, *Fifty Notable Years: Views of the Ministry of Christian Universalism during the Last Half Century* (Boston, 1883), 199-200. Edith Fox Macdonald, *Rebellion in the Mountains: The Story of Universalism and Unitarianism in Vermont* (Concord, NH: New Hampshire Vermont District of the Unitarian Universalist Association, 1976), 155.
55   Gilmore, *Orestes Brownson*, 299, 319-337. Macdonald, *Rebellion*, 154-155. Holmes Slade, *The Life and Labors of the late William Stevens Balch* (Chicago, 1888), 54-56.
56   Gilmore, *Orestes Brownson*, 331.
57   *Christian Repository*, Aug. 1826, 65-67. *Convert*, 29-30. The account of the event in *The Convert* is inaccurate in a number of respects.
58   *Christian Repository*, Aug. 1826, 65-67.
59   *Christian Repository,* Dec. 1822, Aug. 1824, Aug. 1825. Miller, *Larger Hope*, 673. Whittemore, *Hosea Ballou*, 2:205, 2:267, 2:303, 2:356. *Autobiography of the First Forty-One Years of the Life of Sylvanus Cobb, D.D.* (Boston, 1867), 216.
60   "The Influence of Religion on Prosperity," *Christian Repository*, Aug. 1826, 49-58; in *Early Works 1*, 38.
61   Oren Brownson to Orestes Brownson, 28 September [year unknown]. Brownson papers, UND.
62   Daphne (Brownson) Ludington to Orestes Brownson, 16 Sept 1857. Brownson papers, UND.

Chapter 7

[1] *Convert*, 31. Patrick W. Carey, introduction to *Early Works 1*, 16-17. On Fort Ann and Whitehall, see William L. Stone, *Washington County, New York: Its History to the Close of the Nineteenth Century* (New York, 1901), 462.

There is some confusion about the identity of the towns where Brownson's congregations were located. Carey has Geneva instead of Genoa. Both are towns in the Finger Lakes region of New York: Geneva is near Seneca Lake in Ontario County, while Genoa is south of Auburn in Cayuga County. *The Convert* clearly specifies Genoa, Cayuga County. There were two communities called Litchfield in New York. Brownson lived in the town of Litchfield, in Herkimer County near Utica, not the hamlet of Litchfield (now part of the town of Nichols) in Tioga County near Binghamton.

[2] On Brownson's marriage see Carey, *Weathervane*, 16-18.

[3] The *Universalist Register and Almanac* for 1836 lists societies in Fort Ann (75 members), Genoa (75 members and a meetinghouse), and Auburn (100 members and a meetinghouse). It gives the founding date for the Fort Ann society as 1831, five years after Brownson preached there. The Auburn society is listed as having been founded in 1833; it had dissolved and been re-formed since Brownson's time.

[4] Mable Crosby, "The History of Universalism in Cayuga County, New York," unpublished typescript, 1966, Andover-Harvard Theological Library. Joel H. Monroe, *Historical Records of a Hundred and Twenty Years: Auburn, N.Y.* (Auburn, 1913), 101, says that Brownson (whom it calls Augustus Bronson) "did effective work for some time," but that the society dwindled after his departure.

[5] Paul K. Conkin, *The Uneasy Center: Reformed Christianity in Antebellum America* (Chapel Hill: University of North Carolina Press, 1995), 114-115, 295.

[6] Joseph Story, *Commentaries on the Constitution of the United States* (1833); in John F. Wilson and Donald L. Drakeman, eds., *Church and State in American History* (Cambridge, MA: Westview Press, 2003), 85-86.

[7] Ezra Stiles Ely, *The Duty of Christian Freemen to Elect Christian Rulers: A Discourse Delivered on the Fourth of July, 1827...* (1828); in Wilson and Drakeman, *Church and State*, 96, 99.

[8] Story, *Commentaries on the Constitution*, 85.

[9] An account of the controversy, and Hosea Ballou's remarks on the subject, is in Whittemore, *Hosea Ballou*, 3:31-37.

[10] *Christian Intelligencer*, 9 Feb., 9 March, and 1 June 1827.

[11] Ely, *The Duty of Christian Freemen to Elect Christian Rulers*.

[12] *Christian Intelligencer*, 21 Dec. 1827, 18 July 1828, 1 Aug. 1828.

[13] Constantin François Chasseboeuf, comte de Volney (1757-1820) was a French philosopher and historian who championed the cause of deism and free inquiry.

His most influential work was *Les Ruines, ou méditations sur les révolutions des empires* (1791). The English translation commonly known as *Volney's Ruins*, published anonymously in Paris in 1802, is now known to be largely the work of Thomas Jefferson.

Brownson read *Volney's Ruins* as part of his program of self-education in 1823. His diary contains a long summary of the book's main arguments, including the idea that God rules through immutable natural laws rather than by direct intervention in human history. "God rules by ordinary means. He gave to nature birth – he established her laws. Man ~~violated these and by these~~ Deviated from them and fell he became morally depraved." *Notebook of Reflections*, 6 April 1823.

[14] Stacy, *Memoirs*, 326-327.

[15] NYSCU minute book, first entry, undated.

[16] NYSCU minute book, first entry, undated.

[17] Stacy, *Memoirs*, 328-332.

[18] Proceedings of 1827, NYSCU minute book. Minutes of Conventional Association, *Utica Evangelical Magazine*, 12 July 1828.

[19] Minutes of the Universalist Convention, May 1826, NYSCU minute book.

[20] "I [had] always been an advocate for societies, and also for a Convention." O. A. Brownson to L. S. Everett, *Gospel Advocate*, 24 Nov. 1827.

[21] Peter Hughes, "The Restorationist Controversy: The Disciplinary Crisis and the Restorationist Schism, 1824-1831," *Journal of Unitarian Universalist History* (2001), 47-48.

[22] Proceedings of 1827, NYSCU minute book.

[23] Proceedings of 1827, NYSCU minute book.

[24] Proceedings of 1827, NYSCU minute book.

[25] Proceedings of 1827, NYSCU minute book.

[26] Proceedings of 1827, NYSCU minute book.

[27] Proceedings of 1827, NYSCU minute book.

[28] Proceedings of 1827, NYSCU minute book.

[29] In October 1827, Everett had been one of three anti-Convention clergy who, taking advantage of inclement weather that kept most of the delegates from attending the Convention's constitutional conference, pushed through a resolution "that a convention of any kind, is not called for by the present circumstance of the order of Universalists in the state." Conference at Auburn, Oct. 1827, NYSCU minute book.

[30] L. S. Everett, "Universalist Convention of the State of New-York," *Gospel Advocate*, 4 Aug. 1827.

31 For some responses to Everett's column on the Convention's treatment of Brownson, see *Gospel Advocate*, 27 Oct.1827. Everett's letter to Brownson was dated 16 Nov. 1827, and printed in the *Gospel Advocate*, 24 Nov. 1827.

32 *Gospel Advocate*, 24 Nov. 1827.

33 Brownson to Everett, *Gospel Advocate*, 24 Nov. 1827.

34 *Utica Magazine*, 10 Nov. 1827.

35 Brownson to Everett, *Gospel Advocate*, 24 Nov. 1827.

36 *Gospel Advocate*, 13 Oct. 1827.

37 See, for example, L.S. Everett, "Extract from a Sermon," *Gospel Advocate*, 24 March 1827.

38 Whittemore, *Hosea Ballou*, 3:40-42. Ernest Cassara, *Hosea Ballou: The Challenge To Orthodoxy* (1961; reprint, Washington, University Press of America, 1982), 131. Miller, *Larger Hope*, 338.

39 "The Essayist," parts 2, 6, and 7, *Gospel Advocate*, 10 May, 5 July, and 19 July 1828; in *Early Works 1*, 99-101, 108-111, 112-114.

Chapter 8

1 *Convert*, 32-59.

2 *Convert*, 36.

3 *Convert*, 36, 38.

4 "The Essayist," part 10, *Gospel Advocate*, 30 Aug. 1828; in *Early Works 1*, 119-122. "An Essay on Christianity," part 3, *Gospel Advocate*, 7 Feb. 1829; in *Early Works 1*, 211. "The Mission of Christ," *Gospel Advocate*, 19 Sept. 1829; in *Early Works 1*, 378.

5 *Convert*, 38-39.

6 *Convert*, 39.

7 "A Question Proposed," *Gospel Advocate*, 2 May 1829.

8 "The Essayist," part 6, *Early Works 1*, 109.

9 "A Question Proposed," *Gospel Advocate*, 2 May 1829.

10 "A Sermon. On the Salvation of All Men," *Gospel Advocate*, 30 Aug. 1828; in *Early Works 1*, 156.

11 "The Essayist," part 11, *Gospel Advocate*, 13 Sept. 1828; in *Early Works 1*, 123.

12 *Convert*, 38, 40.

13 *Convert*, 40.

14 "An Essay on the Progress of Truth," part 1, *Gospel Advocate*, 17 Nov. 1827; in *Early Works 1*, 44.

15 "Universalism – An Extract," *Gospel Advocate*, 30 Aug. 1828.

16 "A Sermon. On the New Birth," *Gospel Advocate*, 16 Aug. 1828; in *Early Works 1*, 148.

17 "Reply to 'L. C.'" [sic], *Gospel Advocate*, 25 Oct. 1828; in *Early Works 1*, 185.

18 "An Essay on Divine Goodness," part 5, *Gospel Advocate*, 19 Sept. 1829; in *Early Works 1*, 266.

19 "Essay on Divine Goodness," part 4, *Gospel Advocate*, 2 May 1829; in *Early Works 1*, 262.

20 "A Sermon. On the Moral Condition of Mankind," *Gospel Advocate*, 13 Sept. 1828; in *Early Works 1*, 164.

21 "Essay on Christianity," part 3, *Early Works 1*, 213-214.

22 "Essay on Christianity," part 5, *Gospel Advocate*, 7 March 1829; in *Early Works 1*, 219. "Essay on the Progress of Truth," part 8, *Gospel Advocate*, 1 March 1828; in *Early Works 1*, 68.

23 "Essay on Christianity," part 4, *Gospel Advocate*, 21 Feb 1829; in *Early Works 1*, 216-217. "The Essayist," part 9, *Gospel Advocate*, 9 Aug. 1828; in *Early Works 1*, 119.

24 *Convert*, 34.

25 "On the New Birth," *Early Works 1*, 148.

26 "Free Inquiry," *Gospel Advocate*, 16 Aug. 1828. Brownson chose to write this particular communication as a letter to the editor, even though by this time he was responsible for a large proportion of the content of the *Gospel Advocate*, and could have expressed his ideas in a signed column, article, or editorial if he had wished.

27 "Essay on Christianity," part 3, *Early Works 1*, 214.

28 "Essay on Divine Goodness," part 1, *Gospel Advocate*, 7 Feb. 1829; in *Early Works 1*, 253-254.

29 Theophilus Fisk quoted Brownson's "I see nothing in nature..." out of context in order to show that Brownson was not a Christian (*Gospel Herald*, 28 March 1829). Fisk's attack on Brownson is discussed in more detail in chapter 9.

30 For example, Brownson's essay on "The Mission of Christ" begins, "The following article is occasioned by some remarks of a correspondent. The editor has said less on the doctrinal parts of the gospel than his readers might desire." "Mission of Christ," *Early Works 1*, 376.

31 "Weakness," *Gospel Advocate*, 19 Sept. 1829.

32 "Essay on Christianity," part 2, *Gospel Advocate*, 24 Jan. 1829; in *Early Works 1*, 209. "Mission of Christ," *Early Works 1*, 377.

33 "Mission of Christ," *Early Works 1*, 376-379.

34   *Convert*, 36.

35   "Mission of Christ," *Early Works 1*, 377-380.

36   "Mission of Christ," *Early Works 1*, 378, 380.

37   *Convert*, 38.

38   "Essay on Divine Goodness," part 2, *Gospel Advocate*, 21 March 1829; in *Early Works 1*, 256.

39   "Essay on Divine Goodness," parts 1-2, *Early Works 1*, 254-256.

40   "Essay on Divine Goodness," part 3, *Gospel Advocate*, 18 April 1829; in *Early Works 1*, 259-260.

41   "Essay on Divine Goodness," part 4, *Early Works 1*, 264. See "On the Moral Condition of Mankind," *Early Works 1*, 161-172; and "Essay on Christianity," part 1, *Gospel Advocate*, 10 Jan. 1829; in *Early Works 1*, 205.

42   "Essay on Christianity," parts 3-5, *Early Works 1*, 260-265.

43   *Convert*, 48.

44   *Convert*, 40.

45   "Essay on Christianity," part 1, *Early Works 1*, 205.

46   "The Essayist," part 10, *Early Works 1*, 122.

47   "Essay on Christianity," part 3, *Early Works 1*, 216.

48   "A Sermon," *Gospel Advocate*, 7 June 1828. "Universalism – An Extract," *Gospel Advocate*, 30 Aug. 1828.

49   See, for example, "Essay on the Progress of Truth," part 1, *Early Works 1*, 47, in which Brownson looks forward to a time "when men shall have recovered mental independence, and shall dare reason on the nature and propriety of existing institutions."

Chapter 9

1   Paul Dean to Edward Turner, 29 Sept. 1824, 20 Nov. 1827. Edward Turner papers, bMS 513, Andover-Harvard Theological Library. Whittemore, *Hosea Ballou*, 3:41-42.

2   "To Our Readers," *Gospel Advocate*, 10 Jan. 1829.

3   "To Our Readers," *Gospel Advocate*, 10 Jan. 1829.

4   "An Essay on Christianity," part 1, *Gospel Advocate*, 10 Jan. 1829; in *Early Works 1*, 203.

5   "Essay on Christianity," part 1, *Early Works 1*, 205.

6   The constitution is found in the NYSCU minute book, and in the *Utica Evangelical Magazine*, 31 May 1828. Though the Cayuga Association did not join the Convention, at its meeting in October 1828, it appointed Brownson and

Everett a committee to visit the General Convention at its meeting the following May. By that time, however, Everett had moved out of state, and Brownson did not attend. "Minutes of the Annual Meeting of the Cayuga Association of Universalists for 1828," *Gospel Advocate*, 25 Oct. 1828.

7   Patrick W. Carey, introduction to *Early Works 1*, 16-17. Elliot G. Storke, *History of Cayuga County, New York* (Syracuse, 1879), 206. Mable Crosby, "The History of Universalism in Cayuga County, New York," unpublished typescript, 1966, Andover-Harvard Theological Library.

8   Miller, *Larger Hope*, 288-289.

9   Nathaniel Bartlett Sylvester, *History of Saratoga County, New York* (Philadelphia, 1878), 102.

10   When he printed the letter in the *Gospel Advocate*, Brownson identified the writer only as "an esteemed brother in the ministry" living in York, Livingston County, New York. Internal evidence makes it clear that the writer was an agent for the *Gospel Advocate*. "New-York Gospel Herald," *Gospel Advocate*, 21 Feb. 1829. Flagler is identified as the agent for the *Gospel Advocate* in York in *Gospel Advocate*, 22 Nov. 1828.

11   *Gospel Advocate*, 21 Feb. 1829.

12   Stacy, *Memoirs*, 332.

13   "New-York Gospel Herald," *Gospel Advocate*, 21 Feb. 1829. "Remarks by the Publisher," *Gospel Advocate*, 18 April 1829.

14   "New-York Gospel Herald," *Gospel Advocate*, 21 Feb. 1829. "Remarks by the Publisher," *Gospel Advocate*, 18 April 1829.

15   *Gospel Advocate*, 22 Nov. 1828.

16   "New-York Gospel Herald," *Gospel Advocate*, 21 Feb. 1829.

17   *Gospel Advocate*, 7 March 1829.

18   "Remarks by the Publisher," *Gospel Advocate*, 18 April 1829. "Letter: To the readers of the Gospel Advocate," *Gospel Herald*, 28 March 1829.

19   "New-York Gospel Herald," *Gospel Advocate*, 21 Feb. 1829. "Letter: To the readers of the Gospel Advocate," *Gospel Herald*, 28 March 1829.

20   "New-York Gospel Herald," *Gospel Advocate*, 21 Feb. 1829.

21   "Letter: To the readers of the Gospel Advocate," *Gospel Herald*, 28 March 1829.

22   "Letter: To the readers of the Gospel Advocate" and "Gospel Advocate," *Gospel Herald*, 28 March 1829.

23   *Gospel Herald*, 28 March 1829.

24   *Gospel Herald*, 28 March 1829.

25   "Sermon IV," *Gospel Herald*, 17 Jan. 1829.

26 "Sermon VI," *Gospel Herald*, 14 Feb. 1829.

27 *Autobiography of Rev. Abel C. Thomas* (Boston, 1852), 73-74. Abel C. Thomas, *A Century of Universalism in Philadelphia and New-York* (Philadelphia, 1872), 82, 85.

28 Miller, *Larger Hope*, 185-187.

29 Thomas, *Century of Universalism*, 276.

30 On Kneeland's support for the Owenite community at Haverstraw, NY, see *New-Harmony Gazette*, 31 May 1826. On his reading of Owen's address, see *Christian Telescope*, 8 Sept. 1827, and Kneeland's letter to Turner, 18 Sept. 1827, Turner papers, Andover-Harvard. The text of Owen's speech is from *New-Harmony Gazette*, 12 July 1826.

31 Thomas, *Century of Universalism*, 275. Miller, *Larger Hope*, 187.

32 For example, see David Pickering's writings against Kneeland in *Christian Telescope*, 8 and 29 Sept. 1827.

33 "Minutes of the Hudson River Association," *Christian Telescope*, 29 Sept. 1827.

34 "Minutes of the proceedings of the Hudson River Association ... September 10th & 11th, 1828 ...," *Utica Evangelical Magazine*, 18 Oct. 1828.

35 *Gospel Herald*, 3 Jan. 1829.

36 *Utica Evangelical Magazine*, 24 Jan. 1829.

37 "Gospel Herald and Universalist Review," *Christian Intelligencer*, 22 Jan. 1829.

38 Thomas, *Century of Universalism*, 277-278.

39 "To the Second Universalist Society in the City of New-York," *Gospel Herald*, 17 Jan. 1829.

40 Abner Kneeland, *Appeal to Universalists, on the Subject of Excommunication, or the Withdrawing of Fellowship, on Account of Diversity of Opinion* (New York, 1829), 14-15.

41 "Our cause in this City," *Gospel Herald*, 14 Feb. 1829.

42 "False Theism," *Christian Intelligencer*, 30 Jan. 1829.

43 "Minutes of the Proceedings of the Kennebec Association of Universalists," *Christian Intelligencer*, 6 Feb. 1829. George W. Tinker (1798-1882) was a member of the class of 1822 at the Medical School of Maine.

44 "Rev. Abner Kneeland," *Utica Evangelical Magazine*, 7 March 1829.

45 Letter from "R. S.," *Christian Intelligencer*, 27 Feb. 1829.

46 Abner Kneeland to Stephen R. Smith, 30 March 1829, in *Utica Evangelical Magazine*, 23 May 1829.

47 "Rev. Abner Kneeland," *Christian Intelligencer*, 5 June 1829.

48 "Essay on Christianity," part 5, *Gospel Advocate*, 7 March 1829; in *Early Works 1*, 218.

49   Quoted in Stephan Papa, *The Last Man Jailed for Blasphemy* (Franklin, NC: Trillium Books, 1998), 15.
50   "Essay on Christianity," part 5, *Early Works 1*, 222.
51   Papa, *Last Man Jailed*, 15.
52   *Gospel Advocate*, 21 Feb. 1829.
53   "Free Enquirers," *Gospel Advocate*, 21 March 1829; in *Early Works 1*, 279.
54   "Rev. Abner Kneeland," *Gospel Advocate*, 4 April 1829; in *Early Works 1*, 290-291.
55   "Excommunication," *Gospel Advocate*, 16 May 1829.
56   "Rev. Abner Kneeland," *Early Works 1*, 291.
57   "Mr. Reese's Letter," *Gospel Advocate*, 25 July 1829; in *Early Works 1*, 371.
58   "A Solemn Appeal to All Liberal Christians," *Utica Evangelical Magazine*, 4 Oct. 1828.
59   An account of the campaign against Sunday mail, including tables breaking down the petitions by year and state, is found in John G. West, Jr., *The Politics of Revelation and Reason: Religion and Civic Life in the New Nation* (Lawrence, KS: University Press of Kansas, 1996), 137-170, 260-262.
60   "Circular Letter," *Utica Evangelical Magazine*, 18 Oct. 1828.
61   "Circular to Post-Masters," *Gospel Advocate*, 10 Jan. 1829.
62   "More Petitions," *Gospel Advocate*, 24 Jan. 1829.
63   *Gospel Advocate*, 7 Feb. 1829.
64   "Sunday Affairs," *Gospel Advocate*, 7 Feb. 1829.
65   "Union of Papers – New Arrangement," *Evangelical Magazine*, 31 Oct. 1829.
66   "Church and State," *Gospel Advocate*, 2 May 1829; in *Early Works 1*, 307.
67   "Horrid Impiety," *Gospel Advocate*, 30 May 1829.
68   "Solemn Appeal to All Liberal Christians," *Utica Evangelical Magazine*, 29 Nov. 1828.
69   "Controversy," *Gospel Advocate*, 25 July 1829.
70   "Rev. Abner Kneeland," *Gospel Advocate*, 27 June 1829. "Miss Frances Wright," *Gospel Advocate*, 8 Aug. 1829. "Weakness," *Gospel Advocate*, 19 Sept. 1829. Brownson printed an address by Robert Dale Owen, on the tyranny of public opinion as a threat to American liberty, in the *Gospel Advocate*, 22 Aug. 1829.

Chapter 10

1   "Remarks by the Publisher," *Gospel Advocate*, 18 April 1829.
2   "Infidelity," *Gospel Advocate*, 18 April 1829.

3   "Infidelity," *Gospel Advocate*, 18 April 1829.
4   "Infidelity," *Gospel Advocate*, 18 April 1829.
5   *Gospel Advocate*, 18 April 1829.
6   "Vindication of Universalism," *Gospel Advocate*, 2 May 1829. "Forgiveness of Sins," *Gospel Advocate*, 30 May 1829. *Gospel Advocate*, 13 June 1829.
7   *Gospel Advocate*, 13 June 1829.
8   W. I. Reese, "Letter to the Editor," *Gospel Advocate*, 25 July 1829.
9   *Gospel Advocate*, 16 May 1829.
10 "Gospel Advocate," *Gospel Herald*, 1 Aug. 1829.
11 *Christian Intelligencer*, 29 May 1829.
12 *Gospel Advocate*, 13 June 1829.
13 "Black River Association," *Gospel Advocate*, 11 July 1829.
14 *Brownson's Early Life*, 34. See also Schlesinger, *Pilgrim's Progress*, 15-16; Carey, *Weathervane*, 28-29.
15 "My Creed," *Gospel Advocate*, 27 June 1829; in *Early Works 1*, 352.
16 "My Creed," *Gospel Advocate*, 27 June 1829; in *Early Works 1*, 350-351.
17 *Gospel Advocate*, 27 June 1829.
18 W. I. Reese, "Letter to the Editor," *Gospel Advocate*, 25 July 1829. "Mr. Reese's Letter," *Gospel Advocate*, 25 July 1829; in *Early Works 1*, 365-367.
19 W. I. Reese, "Letter to the Editor," *Gospel Advocate*, 22 Aug. 1829.
20 W. I. Reese, "Letter to the Editor," *Gospel Advocate*, 25 July 1829. "W. I. Reese," *Gospel Advocate*, 22 Aug. 1829. *Christian Intelligencer*, 4 Sept. 1829.
21 "Extract of a letter dated Ohio, July 30, 1829," *Gospel Advocate*, 22 Aug. 1829.
22 As a case in point, the letter from the Ohio correspondent is immediately preceded by a letter from New York City, containing a minute description of Fisk's refusal to print a pamphlet because it contained some material by Kneeland. A reader not intimately acquainted with the circumstances could hardly be expected to follow the intricacies of the doings of Messrs. Bates, Thomas, Canfield, Bussing, and Fisk, the committee of twenty-one members and the committee of nine, and the superiority of the 32-page over the 20-page version of the pamphlet. "Extract of a letter dated New-York, August 1st, 1829," *Gospel Advocate*, 22 Aug. 1829.
23 *Gospel Advocate*, 12 Dec. 1829.
24 Lemuel Willis, "Dolphus Skinner" (No. 7 of "Recollections Pertaining to the Universalist Church during the first Half of this Century"), *The Universalist*, 19 Sept. 1874.
25 "Orestes A. Brownson," *Trumpet and Universalist Magazine*, 11 November 1829; reprinted in *Gospel Advocate*, 12 Dec. 1829.

26 "Letter from the Editor," *Gospel Advocate*, 17 Oct. 1829.
27 "Union of Papers – New Arrangement," *Evangelical Magazine*, 26 Sept. 1829.
28 *Gospel Advocate*, 12 Dec. 1829.
29 Willis, "Dolphus Skinner."
30 "Letter from the Editor, No. 2," *Gospel Advocate*, 31 Oct. 1829.
31 "Universalism in Albany," *Gospel Advocate*, 14 Nov. 1829.
32 "O. A. Brownson," *Evangelical Magazine*, 19 Dec. 1929.
33 Willis, "Dolphus Skinner."
34 D. Skinner, "A Sermon: Atonement – Punishment – Forgiveness," *Gospel Advocate*, 17 Oct. 1829.
35 "A Gospel Creed," *Gospel Advocate*, 3 Oct. 1829; in *Early Works 1*, 390.
36 W. I. Reese, "Letter to the Editor," *Gospel Advocate*, 25 July 1829.
37 "Weakness," *Gospel Advocate*, 19 Sept. 1829.
38 "O. A. Brownson," *Evangelical Magazine*, 19 Dec. 1929.
39 "Union of Papers," *Gospel Advocate*, 14 Nov. 1829.
40 *Gospel Advocate*, 14 Nov. 1829.
41 "Miss Wright," *Gospel Advocate*, 14 Nov. 1829.
42 *Free Enquirer*, 7 Nov. 1829; reprinted in *Brownson's Early Life*, 41-42.
43 *Gospel Advocate*, Nov. 1829.
44 "Universalist Hymn Book," *Gospel Advocate*, 28 Nov. 1829.
45 "From the Cayuga Patriot," *Gospel Advocate*, 28 Nov. 1829.
46 Elliot G. Storke, *History of Cayuga County, New York* (Syracuse, 1879), 206.
47 "To the Universalists," *Free Enquirer*, 28 Nov. 1829; in *Early Works 1*, 393-394.
48 "To the Editors of the Free Enquirer," *Free Enquirer*, 2 Jan. 1830; in *Early Works 1*, 395-396.
49 Dolphus Skinner, *A series of letters on important doctrinal and practical subjects...* (Utica, 1833), 169-171.
50 "Illustration of 1 John, ii; 18, 19," *Evangelical Magazine*, 21 Nov. 1829.
51 *Gospel Advocate*, 12 Dec. 1829.
52 *Gospel Advocate*, 12 Dec. 1829.
53 *Evangelical Magazine*, 19 Dec. 1829.
54 *Gospel Advocate*, 12 Dec. 1829.
55 "Orestes A. Brownson," *Trumpet and Universalist Magazine*, 11 November 1829.

56 "Free Enquirers," *Early Works 1*, 277.

57 "To the Public," *Evangelical Magazine and Gospel Advocate*, 2 Jan. 1830.

58 General Convention Proceedings, *Trumpet and Universalist Magazine*, 2 Oct. 1830.

Afterword

1 Carey, *Weathervane*, xii.

2 Daniel R. Barnes, *An Edition of the Early Letters of Orestes Brownson* (Ph.D. diss., University of Kentucky, 1970), 29.

3 *Convert*, 63.

4 Patrick W. Carey, introduction to *Early Works 2*, 2.

5 *Free Enquirer*, 23 Jan. 1830.

6 *Convert*, 46.

7 *Brownson's Early Life*, 52.

8 *Convert*, 45-46.

9 *Convert*, 48.

10 *Charles Elwood, or The Infidel Converted* (1840; vol. 4 of *Works of Orestes A. Brownson*, ed. Henry F. Brownson, Detroit, 1883), 196-197.

Index

Albany, NY, 154
Alcott, Amos Bronson, 1
atheists, atheism. *See* doubt and disbelief
Auburn, NY, 145; map, 96
    Universalist society, 95, 97, 107, 127, 128, 159, 190n n.3-4
Ballou, Adin, 19-20, 44, 79-80, 88, 90-91, 176n.38
Ballou, Hosea, 13, 42; illustration, 41
    theology, *Treatise on Atonement*, 40-45, 85; influence on OAB, 42-43, 110-111, 153
    as Universalist leader: friends and disciples, 46, 110, 135, 140; Universalist journalism, 76, 110; Restorationist controversy, 80-83, 86, 92, 102
Ballou, Hosea 2d, 76, 83, 86, 110
Ballston / Ballston Spa, NY, 25-26, 27-31, 33-34, 179n.33; illustrations, 26, 28
    Presbyterian church, 50-53; *see also* Brownson > LIFE > Presbyterianism
    Universalist society, 38-39
Baptists: in Royalton, VT, 17; in Ballston, NY, 33-34, 52; in Fort Ann, NY, 95
Barnard, VT, map, 14
    Universalist society, 13
Bartlett, Robert, 91, 92
Boston, 2, 91; visit to, 111, 153-154, 156, 159
Briggs, Levi, 82, 84
Brown, Thomas, *Philosophy of the Human Mind*, 47
Brownson family, 10, 12-15, 25, 26, 93-94
    Universalism, 12, 13, 38-40, 42, 55
Brownson, Daniel (brother), 13, 42
Brownson, Daphne (twin sister). *See* Ludington, Daphne Brownson

Brownson, Henry F. (son). *See under* Brownson > INTERPRETERS AND INTERPRETATIONS > biographers
Brownson, Oren (brother), 13, 93
Brownson, Orestes Augustus
LIFE
    summary of his life, 2-3
    death of father, breakup of family, 12-15
    religion in childhood: instructed by his mother, 13; instructed by foster parents, 15-17; childhood religious experiences, 17-19, 21
    childhood in Royalton, VT, 21-24
    adolescence in Ballston, NY: reunited with family, 25-26, 61-62; apprenticeship, 26-27, 178n.10; impressions of Ballston Spa, 27-31; education at Ballston Academy, 48, 178n.10
    skepticism, doubt, disbelief: worldliness of Ballston Spa, 34; anticlericalism, 35-37; shaken by ultra Universalism, 40-44; unconvinced by natural theology, 46-47
    Universalism: introduced to Universalist classics by his aunt, 38-40; encounters ultra Universalism, 40-44; considers joining Universalists, 66-67, 75-80, 85, 86; decides in favor, 86-88; *see also* Brownson > IDEAS AND OPINIONS > Universalism
    Presbyterianism: as father's religion, 12, 55, 62; visits Presbyterian church, 49; joins church in Ballston, 49-53; experiences in church, 53-56; reasons for leaving, 57-61
    teaching: in New York state, 63, 64-65, 72; in Michigan, 67-68, 186 n.23

Brownson, Orestes Augustus, *cont'd.*
  courtship and marriage, 65, 72, 95
  sojourn in Michigan, 67-75; malaria, 67, 71; first encounter with Catholicism, 69-70, 72-74; self-education, 72
  Universalist ministry
    education for ministry, 90-91
  Universalist ministry, *cont'd.*
    ordination, 91-92
    early career: ministry, 95-97; journalism, 93, 97, 109
    incident at meeting of NY Convention of Universalists, 103-108
    re-examines beliefs, 113-118; *see also* Brownson > IDEAS AND OPINIONS > theology
    minister in Auburn, NY, and editor of *Gospel Advocate*, 127-129, 149; controversy with T. Fisk and *Gospel Herald*, 129-135, 147-149
    accused of infidelity, 133-135, 140-143, 148-149; denies that he is an infidel, 147-152
    accepts position with *Free Enquirer*, 156-157
    dismissed from *Gospel Advocate* and Auburn society, 157-159; farewell message, 160-161
    removed from fellowship by Universalist General Convention, 163
  later career, 2-3
  IDEAS AND OPINIONS
    anticlericalism, 34, 35-37, 89
    Bible, 79-80, 84-85, 113, 114, 119-120, 125, 140-141, 151
    Calvinism: dislike of; 15-16, 21, 59-61; attempts to adopt, 49-50, 54-57
    Catholicism: encounter with Catholicism in Michigan, 69-70; praise of Catholicism, 71, 72-74; 101
    education, 21-23, 89-90
    hell, dislike of hellfire preaching, 21, 71
    politics, economics, social justice, 8-9, 29-30, 33, 124-125; *see also* Brownson > IDEAS AND OPINIONS > theology > Christianity and reform
    Protestantism: questions legitimacy of Protestant churches, 18-19, 58-59; alienated from Protestant mainstream, 9, 18-19, 59-61, 101, 144-146

Brownson, Orestes Augustus, *cont'd.*
    race and slavery, 29
    reason, revelation, intuition, 9, 61, 77, 79, 113, 114, 119-120
    theology
      Christianity and reform, 36, 114, 121-122
      divine rewards and punishments, 42-43, 84, 110, 115
      focus on this world, 116-118, 125
      God and nature, 46-47, 120-121
      good and evil, 44-46, 110, 117-118, 122-125
      human nature, 60-61, 118, 123-125
    tolerance, freedom of speech, 141, 145-146
    Universalism: praise of Universalism, 86-88, 116-117, 125-126; criticism of Universalists and Universalism, 108, 112-116, 142-143, 145-146, 160-161
  INTERPRETERS AND INTERPRETATIONS
    biographers
      Brownson, Henry F., 21, 23, 48, 56, 65, 67, 150, 174n.13
      Capps, Donald, 173n.19
      Carey, Patrick W., ix, 4, 7-8, 56, 165, 172n.4, 185nn.5-6
      Gilmore, William, 7, 15, 27, 91, 175n.18, 182n.5
      Maynard, Theodore, 7, 57, 59, 172n.4, 178n.10, 187n.2
      Ryan, Thomas R., 7, 57, 172n.4
      Schlesinger, Arthur M. Jr., 7, 172n.4
      Sveino, Per, 173n.19
    character
      balance of opposing forces, 7-8, 164
      childhood experiences, effect on character, 7, 167-168, 170n.19
      consistency of ideas throughout life, 8-9
      loneliness, longing for human connection, 7, 18, 48-49, 72, 167-168
      loyal to ideas rather than to people or institutions, 111, 164-167
      "religious weathervane", 5-6, 8, 161
      seeker of truth, 6-7, 108-109, 110-111, 118, 145-146, 156, 166-167
    Universalist history, place of OAB in, 4, 162-163, 173n.7

INDEX 203

Brownson, Relief Metcalf (mother), 10, 12-13, 14, 25, 26, 38, 42, 55, 62, 93
Brownson, Sally Healy (wife), 65, 72, 95
Brownson, Sylvester A. (father), 10, 12
Brownson, Thorina (sister), 13, 93
Burder, George, *Closet Companion*, 54
Calvinism
    liberal, 16, 51-52
    New Light/evangelical, 10-12, 17, 49
    Old Light/traditional, 12, 15
    theology, 15, 16, 53-54, 59-60
    Universalist response to, 11-12, 43-44, 65-66, 77, 161
    See also evangelical Protestantism; Presbyterians
Camillus, NY, 63, 64-66, 72, 184n.1; map, 96
Canfield, Russell, 132
Carrique, Richard, 104-105
Catholics, Catholicism: in Michigan, 68-70; *see also* Brownson > IDEAS AND OPINIONS > Catholicism
Channing, William Ellery, 27
Charlestown, MA, 110, 127, 153-154; *see also* Turner, Edward
Chauncy, Charles, *The Mystery Hidden from Ages and Generations*, 39
Christian Connection, 17, 19-21, 49, 176n.38, 176n. 43, 179n.34
church and state, 97-101, 127, 143-145
Clarke, James Freeman, 5, 6, 8
Clarke, Samuel, *Demonstration of the Being and Attributes of God*, 47
Clinton, NY, meeting of Universalist General Convention, 83, 102
Coffin, Michael, 38
"common sense" philosophers, 47
Comstock, James, 27, 31-32, 34, 35, 50-51, 52-53
Congregationalists, Congregationalism, 15-16, 18, 70
Corbett, Theodore, 28, 179n.33
Dean, Paul, 13, 82-84, 91, 110-111
Dean, Seth, 13
deists, deism. *See* doubt and disbelief
Delano, Asenath Metcalf (aunt), 12, 25, 38-39, 42
Delano, Moreau and Loring (cousins), 55
Detroit, MI, 67-71, 73; illustration, 68, 69
Doubleday, Ulysses F., 129, 131-133, 147, 148, 152-153, 156, 157-159, 161-162

doubt and disbelief (atheism, deism, infidelity skepticism, etc.), 11, 100, 190n.13
    disbelief as a reaction to Calvinism, 77, 123, 161
    Universalists accused of atheism, infidelity, etc., 81, 112, 134-135, 137-138, 143
    OAB as infidel, unbeliever, etc. *See* Brownson > LIFE > skepticism, doubt, disbelief; Brownson > LIFE > Universalist ministry > accused of infidelity
    See also Kneeland, Abner; Owen, Robert; Wright, Frances
Drew, William, 99-101, 137, 138-139, 149, 152
education: in New York State, 64-65; in Michigan, 68. *See also* Brownson > IDEAS AND OPINIONS > education
Ely, Ezra Stiles, 98, 100
Emerson, Ralph Waldo, 1
evangelical Protestantism
    as dominant religion in US, 97-98; Universalist anxiety about, 98-101, 143-146
    See also Calvinism; Christian Connection; church and state; Methodists; Presbyterians
Everett, Linus Smith, 27, 97, 107-110, 127, 128-129, 152, 153, 163, 191n.29
Fisk, Theophilus, 129-135, 137-138, 140-141, 142, 147-148, 159
Fitzpatrick, John Bernard, 27
Flagler, John S., 130-131
Fort Ann, NY, Universalist society, 95, 190n.3
Free Enquirer. *See under* newspapers (secular)
freethinkers, freethought. *See* doubt and disbelief
Freewill Baptists, 11
Garrison, William Lloyd, 164
Genoa, NY, 190n.1; map, 96
    Universalist society, 95, 97, 109, 190n.3
Gospel Advocate. *See under* newspapers (Universalist)
Gross, Thomas, 76, 129, 162
Hartford, CT, 14, 132, 152, 153
Healy, Sally. *See* Brownson, Sally Healy
Hudson, Charles, 82-84, 86, 91, 110
Hunting, William and Lydia (foster parents), 13, 15-17, 18, 175n.18
Huntington, Joseph, *Calvinism Improved*, 39

infidelity. *See* doubt and disbelief
Ithaca, NY, map, 96
    Universalist society, 95, 109
Jefferson, Thomas, 35, 190n.13
Keene, NH, 12, 14, 174n.9
King, Thomas F., 103, 106
Kneeland, Abner, 103, 104, 135-140, 140-141, 142-144, 146, 148, 151, 153, 156, 161, 163; illustration, 136
Leroux, Pierre, 2
liberal Christianity, 2, 16, 80, 93, 99-100, 143, 149, 164
Litchfield, NY, 95, 103, 108, 190n.1
Locke, John, *Essay Concerning Human Understanding* and *Reasonableness of Christianity*, 23, 47, 119
Loveland, Samuel, 92, 95; as journalist, 76-77, 84-85, 87; as educator, 90-91, 110
Low, Nicholas, 28-29, 34
Lowell, James Russell, 6
Ludington, Daphne Brownson (sister), 13-14, 93-94
Mead, Matthew, *The Almost Christian Discovered*, 54, 57, 61
Methodists: in Vermont, 11, 17, 18-19, 21; in New York, 52, 66, 95; in Michigan, 70-71, 186n.36
Michigan, 68-70; *see also* Detroit, Springwells
Morse, Pitt, 76
natural theology, 47
New York City
    First Universalist Society (Prince St.), 136-137
    Second Universalist Society, 135-138
New York (state)
    education, 64-65
    Universalism, *see* Universalism > New York State; Universalist associations > New York State Convention of Universalists
    See also Auburn; Ballston; Camillus; Clinton; Fort Ann; Genoa; Ithaca; Litchfield; New York City; Stillwater; Whitehall
newspapers (secular)
    Boston Quarterly Review, 1
    Cayuga Patriot, 129, 159
    Free Enquirer, 120, 156-157, 160-162
    Independent American (a.k.a. *People's Watch-Tower*, *Saratoga Farmer*), 27, 32, 34-35, 179n.38

    Saratoga Courier, 129
newspapers (Universalist), 75-77, 130
    Christian Inquirer, 152
    Christian Intelligencer, 99-101, 137, 138-139, 142
    Christian Repository, 76-77, 82, 84-85, 91, 93
    Evangelical Magazine (a.k.a *Evangelical Magazine and Gospel Advocate*), 139-140
    Evangelical Repertory, 77, 84-85; illustration, 78
    Gospel Advocate: edited by T. Gross, 76, 77, 79; edited by L. S. Everett, 97, 107-108, 109-110, 129; edited by OAB, 95, 121, 127-135, 147-148, 149, 151-152, 156-157; union with *Evangelical Magazine*, 152-156, 159, 162-163; illustration, 158
    Gospel Herald, 129-135, 137-138, 147
    Gospel Visitant, 81-82
    Herald of Salvation, 76-77
    Olive Branch, 137, 153
    Religious Inquirer, 132-133, 156
    Rochester Magazine and Theological Review, 76-77, 79
    Utica Magazine, 103, 105, 108
    Universalist Expositor, 110
    Universalist Magazine (a.k.a. *Trumpet and Universalist Magazine*), 76, 82, 132, 152
Owen, Robert, 120, 126, 135-136, 166
Owen, Robert Dale, 120, 151, 197n.70
Paley, William, *Evidences of Christianity* and *Natural Theology*, 46
Parker, Theodore, 1
Philadelphia, PA, 12, 129, 135
political parties
    Democrats, 33
    People's Party (Saratoga County, NY), 31-33
    Republicans, 31-32
    Workingmen's Party, 2, 33, 164
Presbyterians, Presbyterianism
    in Ballston, NY, 50-53; *see also* Smith, Reuben
    in Camillus, NY, 66
    in Detroit, 70
    See also Brownson > LIFE > Presbyterianism
Reese, William I., 103, 105-106, 148, 151, 152, 156

INDEX

Reid, Thomas, *Inquiry into the Human Mind* and *On the Intellectual Powers of Man*, 47
Restorationist Controversy. *See under* Universalism
Rich, Caleb, 11
Richard, Gabriel, 70
Ripley, George, 2
Royalton, VT, 13, 15, 17, 21-24; map, 14
Saratoga County, NY, Court Party vs. People's Party, 31-32
Saratoga Springs, NY, 25, 28, 179n.33
    Universalist society, 39, 90
Sawyer, Thomas J., 76
Sears, Reuben, 27, 51, 52-53
skeptics, skepticism. *See* doubt and disbelief
Skinner, Dolphus: friend and mentor to OAB, 90-92; Universalist leader in New York State, 103, 137, 155-156; opposes OAB, 106-109, 149, 157, 161-162; theology and opinions, 143, 145, 154-155, 161; purchase of *Gospel Advocate*, 152-154, 159; illustration, 155
Skinner, Warren, 91
Smith, Elias, 20
Smith, Reuben, 27, 49-50, 53-55, 58-60
Smith, Stephen R., 39
Spafford, Horatio Gates, 34-35
Springwells, MI, 67, 69-70, 186n.23, 186n.27
Stacy, Nathaniel, 66, 101-103, 106, 130
Stewart, Dugald, *Philosophy of the Human Mind*, 47
Stillwater, NY, 63, 65
Stockbridge, VT, 10, 12-13
Story, Joseph, 98
Streeter, Barzillai, 82, 84
Streeter, Russell, 139
Taylor, John W., 31-32, 35, 51-53; illustration, 51
Thomas, Abel C., 135, 136, 137
Thompson, John S., 76-77
Tillotson, John, *Natural Religion*, 47
Tinker, George, 139, 196n.43
Transcendentalists, 1, 2
Turner, Edward, 11, 27, 77-78, 81-87, 91, 92, 110
    1834 letter from OAB, 15, 19, 38, 40, 42, 50, 56, 85, 87
Underwood, William, 103, 105-109
Unitarians, Unitarianism, 2, 16, 35, 188n.19

Universalism
    and the Bible, 77, 79, 84-85, 119-120
    in Brownson family, 12, 13, 38-40, 42, 55
    discipline of clergy, 102, 104-108, 142
    and evangelicalism: Universalism as shadow of evangelical Calvinism, 11-12, 65; Universalists' anxiety about evangelical dominance, 98-101, 143-146
    journalism. *See* newspapers (Universalist).
    in New York State
        in Auburn, 95, 97, 107, 127, 128, 159, 190nn.3-4
        in Ballston, 38-39
        in Camillus, 66;
        in Fort Ann, 95, 190n.3
        in Genoa, 95, 97, 109, 190n.3
        in Ithaca, 95, 109
        in New York City, 135-138
        in Whitehall, 38, 95
        See also Universalist associations > New York State Convention of Universalists
    Restorationist Controversy, 80-84, 86, 91-92
    theology: "Calvinism Improved," 39-40; restorationist, 84-85; ultra Universalist, 40-43, 77, 110. *See also* Ballou, Hosea; Brownson > IDEAS AND OPINIONS > theology
    tolerance, as a Universalist value, 82-83, 86, 125-126; limits of, 140-142
    in Vermont, 11, 13, 17
Universalist associations, 92
    Black River Association, 149
    Cayuga Association, 109, 128, 194n.6
    Conventional Association, 102-104, 108
    Franklin Association, 92
    Hudson River Association, 104-105, 136-137, 140
    Kennebec Association (Maine), 139
    New Hampshire Association, 91-92
    New York State Convention of Universalists, 101-109, 128, 130, 137
    Rockingham Association, 92
    Southern Association, 83-84, 92, 104, 140
    Universalist General Convention, 4, 38, 81, 82-83, 86, 90, 92, 102, 163

Utica, NY, 152, 154, 156
Vermont, 10-11, 22, 23-24, 38
   Universalism, 11, 13, 17
   See also Barnard, Royalton, Stockbridge, Windsor County
Volney, comte de (Constantin François Chasseboeuf), 101, 190n.13
Whitehall, NY, Universalist society, 38, 95
Whitnall, Isaac, 66
Whittemore, Thomas, 46, 76, 132, 152, 162

Wight, Benoni and Bridget, 13
Willis, Lemuel, 91, 92, 110, 152, 153, 154
Winchester, Elhanan, 12, 39, 40, 52, 174n.9; illustration, 41
Winchester Profession, 82-83
Windsor County, VT, 10, 12, 13; map, 14
Wood, Jacob, 80-82, 84
Wright, Frances, 120, 137-138, 141, 146, 151, 156-157, 159, 162; illustration, 138

www.ingramcontent.com/pod-product-compliance
Lightning Source LLC
Chambersburg PA
CBHW050633300426
44112CB00012B/1786